A Veldt Official
A Novel of Circumstance

by

Bertram Mitford

Double9
BOOKS

A Veldt Official
A Novel of Circumstance
by Bertram Mitford

ISBN: 978-93-68094-63-0

Published by

DOUBLE 9 BOOKS
2/13-B, Ansari Road
Daryaganj, New Delhi – 110002
info@double9books.com
www.double9books.com
Tel. 011-40042856

ABOUT THE AUTHOR

Bertram Mitford was an English colonial writer, novelist, essayist, and cultural critic, born on June 13, 1855, in Bath, United Kingdom. He was the third son of Edward Ledwich Osbaldeston Mitford, a member of the prominent Mitford family. Mitford is best known for his novels set in South Africa, a country he came to know intimately and where much of his writing is based. His works often reflect the political, social, and environmental challenges of life in colonial Africa. Over the course of his career, Mitford wrote forty-four books, with many focusing on adventure, colonial conflicts, and the complexities of the British Empire in Africa. His vivid descriptions of the South African landscape and his nuanced portrayal of colonial life garnered him a lasting place in the genre of adventure fiction. Mitford's deep understanding of the region and its cultures also made him a respected cultural critic and essayist. Mitford passed away on October 4, 1914, in Cowfold, United Kingdom. His books continue to be valued for their insight into the colonial period and their exciting plots.

CONTENTS

Chapter One
"Where's doppersdorp?"

"Now where the very mischief *is* Doppersdorp?"

He who thus uttered his thoughts aloud looked up from the sheet of paper in his hand, and gazed forth over the blue waters of Algoa Bay. Over the vessels riding at their anchorage his gaze wandered, over the stately hulls of two or three large mail steamships similar to that upon whose deck he then stood; over the tall, tapering masts and web-like rigging of numerous sailing craft; over the flotilla of cargo-boats and lighters; over the low, sandy shores and sunbaked buildings of busy, dusty Port Elizabeth, right away to the bold ridges of the Winterhoek range looming black and hazy to the blue heavens; then returned to re-peruse the large official communication. Thus it began:—

Sir,—I have the honour to inform you that His Excellency the Governor, with the advice of the Executive Council, has been pleased to appoint you to be—provisionally—clerk to the Resident Magistrate of Doppersdorp, and distributer of stamps... Then followed particulars as to salary, and, with the request that the recipient would be good enough to proceed to that place as soon as possible, somebody whose name he could not quite decipher, but whose style was "Acting Under Colonial Secretary," had the honour to be his obedient servant.

The letter was dated from the Colonial Secretary's Office, and was directed to "Roden Musgrave, Esq."

"The pay is not profuse," soliloquised the fortunate recipient of this missive, "especially to make a fresh start upon at my time of life. Well, the old saw about beggars and choosers holds good, but—where the very deuce *is* Doppersdorp?"

"Hallo, Musgrave! Had ten thousand a year left you?" cried a jolly, hail-the-maintop sort of voice behind him.

Its owner was a powerfully built man of middle age, whose handsome face, bronzed and bearded, was lit up by a pair of keen brown eyes with a merry twinkle in them which was more than half satirical. He was clad in a dark blue, gold-laced, quasi-naval uniform.

"You know something about this country, eh, skipper?" said the other, turning away from the taffrail, over which he had been leaning.

"I ought to by now, considering the number of years I've had to do with it," was the confident reply.

"So? Well, I'll bet you a bottle of Heidsieck you don't answer the first question I put to you concerning it. But whether I win or lose it'll be our parting drink together."

"Our parting drink? Man alive, what sort of humbug are you talking? Aren't we going on as far as Natal together, and haven't we only just begun our unlading? That means two days more here, if not three. Then we are sure to be kept a couple of days at East London. So this day week we can talk about our parting drink, not to-day."

"Never mind that for a moment. Is that bet on?"

"All right—yes. Now then, what's the question?"

"Where is Doppersdorp?"

"Eh?"

"To be more explicit—what section of this flourishing colony is distinguished by the proud possession of the town or village of Doppersdorp?"

"I'll be hanged if I know."

"I thought not. Skipper, you've lost; so order up the Monopole, while I dive down and roll up my traps, for to that unpromising township, of so far nebulous locality, I am officially directed to proceed without loss of time."

"The dickens you are! That's a nuisance, Musgrave; especially as all the other fellows are leaving us here. I thought you were going on to Natal with us."

"So did I. But nothing is certain in this world, let alone the plans of such a knock-about as yours truly. Well, we've done more than our share of lie-splitting during the last three weeks, Cheyne, and it'll be for your moral good now to absorb some of the improving conversation of that elderly party who is dying to come down to your end of the table; also of Larkins, who can succeed to my chair."

"Oh, Larkins!" grunted the other contemptuously. "Every voyage the saloon has its percentage of fools, but Larkins undoubtedly is the prize fool of the lot. Now, if there's one thing more than another I cannot stand, it's a fool."

The commander of the *Siberian* was not exactly a popular captain, a fact perhaps readily accounted for by the prejudice we have just heard him enunciate; yet he was more feared than disliked, for he was possessed of a shrewd insight into character, and a keen and biting wit, and those who came under its lash were not moved thereby precisely to love its owner. But, withal, he was a genial and sociable man, ever willing to promote and assist in the diversions of his passengers, as to sports, theatricals, concerts, and the like; so, although a trifle merciless towards those, and they were not few, whose ambition in life seemed to consist in asking questions and making remarks of a stark idiotic nature, he got on very well with his passengers on the whole. Moreover, he was an excellent sailor, and, without being a martinet, was a strict disciplinarian; consequently, in consideration of the comfort, and shipshape readiness of the ordering of things on board the *Siberian*, passengers who were capable of appreciation could forgive a little sarcasm at the hands of her commander.

Those whom Captain Cheyne liked invariably returned the predilection, those whom he disliked were sure not to remain unaware of the fact. And out of a full complement of first-class passengers this voyage, the one to whom he had taken most was Roden Musgrave; perhaps because of the quality they held in common, a chronic cynicism and a rooted contempt for the weaker-minded of their fellows—i.e., the bulk of human kind. Anyhow, they would sit and exchange aphorisms and anecdotes illustrative of this, until one of the other two or three passengers who almost nightly participated in that snug and convivial gathering, was wont to declare that it was like the sharpening of saws steeped in vinegar, to sit and listen to Musgrave and the skipper in the latter's cabin an hour or so before turning in.

"But if you don't know where this place is, how the deuce do you know you've got to go ashore here, eh?" pursued the captain.

"Ha, ha! Because I don't want to, of course. Fancy you asking such a question!"

"It may be nearer to go on to East London and land there. Here, I say, Walker," he broke off, hailing an individual who, laden with bags and bundles, was superintending the heaving of his heavier luggage into a boat alongside; "where on earth is Doppersdorp?"

"Ha! There you are, are you captain? I was hunting for you everywhere to say good-bye. Doppersdorp? Doppersdorp? No, hang me if I do know!

Sounds like some good old Dutch place, buried away up in the Karroo most likely. Well, ta-ta. Excuse my hurry, but I shall barely catch the Uitenhage train." And he made for the gangway again.

"That looks bad," said Musgrave. "A place nobody seems so much as to have heard of is likely to be a hole indeed."

"What are you going there for, if it's not an impertinent question?" said the captain.

"Got a Government billet."

"Well, come along to my crib and we'll settle that bet. I've got a map or two that may give the place."

Not without a qualm did Musgrave find himself for the last time within that snug berth where he had spent so many festive evenings, whether it was when the rain and spray was lashing the closed scuttles while the vessel was rolling under half steam against the tempestuous Biscayan surges, or with door and windows alike thrown wide open as she glided through the oily stillness and moist heat of tropical waters. In his heart of hearts he was perhaps a little sorry that the voyage was over. Most of the passengers had left the ship at Capetown, and the remainder on dropping anchor in Algoa Bay early that morning, with the exception of half a dozen or so, bound for the other coast ports, among whom until a few minutes ago he had reckoned himself.

"Here's the place," said the captain after a brief scrutiny of the map he had just unrolled; "I thought as much. Stuck away in the middle of the Karroo. Yes, you'd better land here after all. You can get at it easier from here, but it will mean about two days or more of post-cart travelling after you leave the train. Well, I wonder when we shall meet again! Perhaps we'll take the run home together one of these days."

The other shrugged his shoulders.

"Probably that event will never come off," he said. "The magnificent start I'm making doesn't seem to hold out large margin for saving up a fortune against ripe old age. So here goes for assisting to represent the Colonial Government among the Boers and the boundless Karroo."

"Hold on, though. You needn't be in such an all-fired hurry to start off there," said the captain. "I'm going ashore myself this afternoon, and there's plenty of room for your luggage in my gig. Then we might dine at the Phoenix, and start you off all snug and comfortable by the night train. There's the second lunch bell going now. Come along down, and we'll get outside that bottle of Heidsieck, for I own I fairly lost the bet."

Roden Musgrave was neither young nor old, but just touching middle age; a vague term, however, and variable, according to the inclination of whoever may define it. He was a clean-built, well-set-up man, whose dark hair was just beginning to be tipped here and there with frost. His face was clean shaven, save for the moustache which helped to hide a firm, though somewhat melancholy, mouth. He had good, clear-cut features and rather deep-set grey eyes, in which there was something which seemed to tell that he had known strange experiences; an impression which was heightened by a curious, indented double scar on the left side of the chin, and which, standing out livid from a complexion sun-tanned almost to swarthiness, gave an expression at times bordering on the sinister. Somehow, too, the face was not that of a man whose record is open to all comers. There was a schooled and guarded look upon it, which seemed to show plainly enough to the close observer that it was not the face its owner had started with in life. But what such record might be the curious could only guess, for this man was the closest of mortals. On the topic dearest to the heart of most of us—self to wit—he never talked, and after weeks of the unguarded companionship of life at sea, during which people are apt to wax confidential—a great deal too much so—not one of his fellow-passengers knew a jot more about him than when he first stepped on board; that is to say nothing.

"Who the devil is that fellow Musgrave?" queried the smoke-room.

"Oh, some card-sharper, most likely," would reply a Kimberley-bound Jew, disgusted in that he had met with more than his match. But this of course was no more than conjecture, and a satisfactory answer was not to be had.

"Now who can that Mr Musgrave be?" was the more soft-toned interrogative of the saloon. "Surely you must know, Captain Cheyne. What is he going out for?"

To which the captain would reply, with a laugh of cynical delight, that he knew no more than they did, but that the readiest way of solving the difficulty would be to apply to Musgrave himself, drawing down from the discomfited fair ones the oft-repeated verdict that he was so horridly sarcastic.

But whoever Musgrave was or was not, the fact remained that he went down the side of the *Siberian* that afternoon, glad to take up the subordinate post in the Cape Government service, which a bit of lucky interest had procured for him; content to start afresh at his time of life in a far-away, up-country township, upon a not extravagant salary.

Chapter Two
The Post-Cart Travellers

Drip, drip, drip, in one unbroken downpour falls the rain. Scuds of floating wrack are wreathing the tree-tops and boulders higher up the bush-grown slopes, and the grey, opaque, lowering sky renders the desolate waste yet more gloomy and forbidding. Floundering, splashing, stumbling, even the team of four serviceable nags appears to experience some difficulty in drawing its load, a two-wheeled Cape cart to wit, crammed pretty nearly to the full measure of its carrying capacity; for the whole well of the cart is filled up. Even the seats cannot be turned to their original purpose, for they too are loaded up with sacks; and upon this irregular pile are three human beings, who are under the necessity of holding on as best they may, insecurely perched upon a sort of dome of rough and uneven surface. Some *reims*, or rawhide thongs, have been lashed across the top of this perch for them to hold on to, a concession to human weakness for which they are expected to feel jubilantly grateful; for they are only passengers, and—as those who have gone through the experience can certify, to their cost—the comfort, well-being, and safety of mere passengers are held by every self-respecting colonial post contractor in the profoundest contempt. For the vehicle is a post-cart, and the sacks upon which a limited number of Her Majesty's lieges are graciously permitted to travel—if haply they can hold on—contain Her Majesty's mails.

Some of the oft-detailed horrors of post-cart travelling seem to have fallen to the lot of the occupants of this one. Apart from the insecurity of their perch already mentioned, they are shelterless, and it has been raining hard and unintermittently for about seven hours. Swathed in theoretical waterproofs—for no waterproof displays a practical side when put to such a test—they grovel upon the lumpy and uneven surface of the sacks, jolted, shaken, bruised, the beat of the rain in their faces, varied from time to time by a copious splash of rich, red liquid mud—lately dust—thrown up from the road. All are wet, cramped and uncomfortable; sore and aching from the jolting and constrained position.

Of this luckless trio, one is a female. Another is a small wiry-looking, stolid-faced man, who might be a farmer or a transport rider, and is very likely both. The third is our newly formed acquaintance, Roden Musgrave.

We have referred to three occupants of this luxurious vehicle. It boasted a fourth. He, however, was not in like pitiable case. He was the proud occupier of a seat—a tolerably secure one. Likewise was he able to indulge in the use of his limbs, and occasional strong language—this, however, in subdued tone, in deference to the presence of the lady passenger— untrammelled by the dire necessity of clinging on for dear life. He was, in fact, the driver. To him the colonial-born passenger:

"How are our chances of getting through the drift to-night, Henry? The river must be rolling yards high."

"Chances!" echoed the man—a stalwart fellow whose yellowish skin betrayed just a strain of native blood, notwithstanding his ruddy and slightly grizzled beard. "Chances? Ha-ha! No chance at all—no damn chance. There's nothing to keep you from going *over* it though."

"How are we going to poll that off?" struck in Roden.

"There's a very good box. Swing you across in no time," replied the driver, with a grin, and a wink at the colonial man.

"Mercy on us!" exclaimed the lady passenger, showing a very white face beneath the hood of her mackintosh. "I'll never be able to do it. Those horrible boxes! I know them."

"You've got to do it, Missis, or stay this side!" returned the driver, with a fiendish grin.

And now as the cart crests another rise, a dull rumbling sound is audible through splash of hoof and wheel, which, as they draw nearer, breaks into a booming roar. It is the voice of the swollen river. The clouds hang low above the scrub, lying, an opaque veil, against the slopes of the opposite heights; and ever, without a break, the rain falls steadily down. The colonial man has managed to light a pipe, and, with characteristic philosophy, smokes steadily and uncomplainingly; an example Roden Musgrave would fain follow, but that he finds his fair companion in adversity literally such a handful, that he cannot even get at his pipe, let alone fill and light it: the fact being that he is obliged to devote all his energies to holding the latter on her perch, for so exhausted is the poor thing with fatigue and discomfort that, were it not for his support, her insecure place would promptly know her no more.

Another rise is topped, and now the river-bed lies before and beneath them; and in truth the spectacle is enough to make the heart of the timid or inexperienced traveller feel somewhat small. The stream is indeed rolling yards high—a red, turbid flood coursing along some fifty feet below, in the bottom of its bed—rearing its mighty masses up in great hissing, crashing waves, rolling over tree-trunks and all kinds of driftwood, with here and there a drowned bullock, whose branching horns and ghastly staring eyes leap weirdly into view, immediately to be drawn in and sucked under by the flood. And this wild, roaring, seething horror—this crashing resistless current whose thunderous voice alone is deafening, appalling—has to be crossed somehow.

"Nay, what! Can't even swim the horses through that!" says the driver, Henry, as he descends from his seat, while a couple of Hottentot boys, who have emerged from a squalid shanty by the roadside, are busy outspanning. "We shall have to send over passengers and mails in the box."

"Oh heavens!" faintly ejaculates the distressed fair one; "I can never do it!"

"Oh yes you can!" says Roden, who has assisted her to alight. "It's perfectly safe if you sit still and keep your head. Don't be in the least afraid; I'll see you across all right."

She gives him a grateful glance, and answers that she will try. Seen as she stands up she is a good-looking woman of about thirty, with light brown hair and blue eyes. She is rather above the middle height, and there is a piteous look in her white and travel-worn face, half expressive of a consciousness of looking her worst, half of the mingled apprehension and discomfort born of the situation.

"Go on up to the box, lady and gentlemen," says Henry, the post driver. "I'll bring along your traps, and send 'em over with the mail-bags."

Roden recognises that if he is to get his charge, for such she has now become, to cross at all, the less time she has to think about it the better; wherefore he seconds this proposition, and accordingly they get under way.

The bed of the river is some sixty feet deep by nearly twice that distance in width, and, like that of most South African streams, in ordinary weather is threaded by a comparative trickle. Such rivers, however, after a few hours of heavy rain, or even one of those deluging thunder showers which are at certain times of the year of frequent and momentous occurrence, are wont to roll down in a furious, raging flood, and that with scant warning, if any;

and now the bottom of this one is covered with at least ten feet of foaming, swirling water, coming down with a velocity and power against which the strongest of swimmers would stand not the ghost of a chance.

High in mid-air, looking like the mere gossamer thread of a spider's web spanning the abyss, is a rope of galvanised iron, and swung on this, dependent on a couple of pulleys, is the "box." It is literally a box, a low-sided, flat concern, seven feet long, and just wide enough for a human being to sit in, and when it is remembered that occupants of this, for it will carry two at a time, are under the strictest necessity of keeping carefully in the centre, under pain of capsizal, and must also lower their heads to avoid the rope, it follows that, to a nervous person, the process of being swung out over a very abyss of boiling, seething waters, and gradually hauled across to the other side, is an ordeal which verges upon the terrific. And, as if to enhance the effect, the spot chosen for this particular apparatus to be hung is the highest point of the steep, well-nigh precipitous bank; the real reason being, of course, that such point is the clearest from which to work it.

"I had better take the lady across first," suggests Roden to his other travelling companion. The latter nods, and proceeds to fill a fresh pipe with the utmost unconcern, an example followed by a brace of stolid-faced Boer transport-riders, who stand watching the proceeding with characteristic phlegm. Two grinning Kaffirs stand prepared to work the rope.

But at sight of the rolling flood, whirling its load of tree-trunks and driftwood right beneath her feet, the frightened woman utters a piteous cry and draws back. She would rather wait for days, she protests, than be swung in mid-air over that horrible river. What if anything were to give way; what if the box or even the iron rope were to break, for instance! "There isn't a chance of anything of the sort," urges her self-constituted protector; "I've been over far shakier concerns than this. Come now, jump in. We have only to sit opposite each other, and talk, and they'll have us over in a twinkling. Only be careful and sit well in the middle, and keep perfectly still."

He makes as though he would help her in, but she shrinks back in terror, then turns a wild stare upon him and upon the river, then sways, staggers, and would fall but that he has caught her. She has swooned.

"Now, mister, now's your time," says the other man. "If you feel equal to taking her across, now's the time to do it. Don't try to bring her round. She'll go easier that way."

The idea is a good one. Roden, prompt to act, takes his seat in the "box," which is drawn up upon the bank, and the post driver having now come up, the two men raise the limp form of the unconscious woman, and place it so that she lies, her head and back resting against him as though they were tobogganing. In this attitude he has her under perfect control, even should she regain consciousness during the transit.

"Ready!" he says. "Lower away now!"

Their shout having met with a response on the other side, the two Kaffirs carefully launch the box, and, with a whirring, creaking accompaniment of the pulleys, down it goes, to stop suddenly as it reaches the utmost droop of the iron cord on which it runs. Then those on the other side start hauling, and slowly and laboriously it ascends. Still Roden's charge remains blissfully unconscious. Ten yards—five—the bank is nearly reached—when—there is a snap, a jerk; and with a suddenness and velocity which nearly overbalances it, away goes the thing back again over the centre of the stream. The hauling line has given way. The box with its human freight hangs helplessly over the seething, roaring abyss.

The volley of curses attendant upon this mishap having subsided, those on the further bank are heard in loud discussion as to what shall be done next. The simplest plan will be to haul the box back again, but Roden does not want this. Having embarked on the enterprise, he feels an obligation to carry it through; and then as the situation strikes him, he laughs queerly over the absurdity and unexpectedness of the same. Here he is, swung in mid-air like a bale of goods in a crate, hanging above a furious torrent, supporting the unconscious form of a fair stranger, who leans against him as heavily as if she belonged to him. Yes, the situation is ridiculous, and supremely uncomfortable; for he is cramped and dead tired, and it is beginning to get dark.

"Heave a fresh line!" he shouts. "I'll catch it if you throw straight."

"All right, mister," answers the voice from the bank. "But you be darn careful not to move from the middle. Now—*Pas op!*"

The line whistles out into the air. Roden, keeping a careful watch upon his balance, catches it deftly, for it has been noosed. Then, planting his feet firmly against the end plank, to do which necessitates that he shall lie almost flat and still preserve the balance both of himself and his charge, he shouts to them to haul away.

In vain. In his constrained position he cannot support the tension. It is a case of letting go or being dragged bodily from the receptacle. So he sings out to them to slacken out again, and the box drops back to the centre of the iron rope. The only thing to be done now is to be hauled back, where those on the bank he has just left can fasten the line securely to its bolt.

No sooner is this done than his charge shows signs of returning consciousness.

"Where am I?" she ejaculates, wildly striving to sit up, an effort which, did he not forcibly repress, would result in their prompt capsizal.

"Sit still! sit still! We shall be across directly!" he says.

But as the box shoots down and dangles motionless for a moment above the centre of the flood, then moves forward in jerky tugs as it is hauled to the opposite side, the terrified woman gives vent to a series of hysterical shrieks, struggling wildly to tear herself from his grasp, so utterly lost are all her capabilities of reason in the mad frenzy of her terror. It is a perilous moment, for now darkness has set in, and the bellowing, seething rush of the great flood adds an indescribable element of horror to the situation.

"Sit still, and don't be so idiotically foolish. Do you hear?" he shouts angrily into her ear as he realises that her frantic struggles almost succeed. "You are perfectly safe; but if you go on at this rate you will upset us both."

The loud, almost brutal tone is entirely successful. It turns her thoughts into a new channel, and seems to quiet her. Then, before she has time to relapse, the bank is reached, and the box, grasped by half-a-dozen pairs of hands, is dragged up into safety.

"Better take her up to the hotel, mister," says one of the men who is working the box apparatus.

The whitewashed walls of a house standing back from the river bank some two hundred yards are just visible above the low mimosa bushes. It is a roadside inn, and thither Roden half leads, half carries, his fainting charge. She, it turns out, is known to the landlady, to whom, nothing loth, Roden now consigns her, and hurries back to witness the crossing of the others. The colonial man is the first to arrive, half-buried in mail-bags, and smoking his pipe as philosophically as ever. Then the inanimate contents of the cart being sent over, Henry, the driver, follows.

"Well, gentlemen," is the first thing he says. "Better get dinner as soon as possible. We must start soon as the new cart's inspanned."

"The devil!" says Roden. "Why, it's going to be the beastliest night on record."

"Can't help that; I've got to get on, or get the sack. So on it is."

"But the lady! She won't be fit to travel as soon as that."

"Can't help that either, mister. If she can't travel she must stay here. I can't wait for nobody."

And so eventually it turns out. On reaching the hotel they find that their fellow-traveller is unable to proceed. They find, too, that she is known to the people who run the place, and will be well cared for. So Roden and the colonial man, having got outside a good dinner and a few glasses of grog, take their places in the new cart which has been inspanned—now more comfortable, for some of the mail-bags have been got rid of here, and with a crack of the driver's whip, away they go careering into the night, under the pitiless pelting rain—to meet with more adventures and mishaps or not, according as luck befriends them. For luck has a great deal to say to the safety, or otherwise, of post-cart travellers in South Africa.

Chapter Three
Peter Van Stolz, R.M.

"Before Peter Van Stolz, Esq., R.M., Gonjana, a Tambookie Kaffir, charged with stealing one sheep, the property of his master, Charles Suffield, farmer," scribbles the reporter of the *Doppersdorp Flag*, who indeed is proprietor, editor, reporter, and comp., all rolled into one.

The Doppersdorp Court-house is a large and spacious room. The "bench" is represented by a green baize-covered table upon a raised daïs, a similar table beneath providing accommodation for the clerk. In front of this again, and facing the bench, a couple of rows of desks accommodate the men of law and their clients, and a few forms, the usual contingent of loungers behind. The witness-box stands on the left of the Bench, and on the right the dock. This latter is now occupied by a thick-set, forbidding-looking Kaffir, clad in a pair of ragged moleskins and a very dirty shirt.

Roden Musgrave, who occupies the clerk's table, is reading out the legal rigmarole which constitutes the indictment. This is interpreted in few words to the prisoner by a native constable standing beside the dock. Asked to plead Guilty or Not Guilty, he merely shrugs his shoulders, and says he doesn't know anything about the matter.

"Enter it as a plea of Not Guilty, Mr Musgrave," says the magistrate, in an undertone. Then aloud, "Does any one appear for him? Has he got a lawyer, Jan?"

Jan Kat, the native constable aforesaid, puts the question. The prisoner answers voluminously, and gazes towards the door.

"He says he has, sir. Mr Darrell appears for him."

"Then why isn't Mr Darrell here?" says the Bench shortly. "Call the prosecutor."

The latter steps into the witness-box—a tall, fair-bearded man with a pleasant face. He deposes that his name is Charles Suffield, that he is a farmer residing at Quaggasfontein in that district—all of which every one there present knows as well as he does—that the prisoner is in his service as herd—which they do not know—and then there is an interruption, as a black-coated individual with a bundle of blue papers and a portentous-looking law book or two, bustles into the front row of desks and announces that he is instructed to appear for the accused.

Mr Van Stolz, the Resident Magistrate, is the most genial and kind-hearted of men, but he is touchy on one point—a sense of the respect due to the dignity of his court. And rightly so, bearing in mind the casual, happy-go-lucky, let-things-slide tendency of the dwellers in Doppersdorp, and like places.

"The case has already begun, Mr Darrell," he says shortly. "Did you instruct the prisoner to plead guilty?"

The attorney starts, then asks rather anxiously—

"Has he pleaded guilty, your worship?"

"No, he hasn't; but he was left, in the lurch as far as his legal adviser was concerned," retorts the Bench, with rather a cruel emphasis on the word "legal," for the practitioners at Doppersdorp are not precisely shining lights in their profession.

An appreciative chuckle from the audience, started by a professional rival, greets this sally, and the Bench, mollified, accepts graciously the defaulting attorney's excuses.

Then the prosecutor goes on to describe how he had been riding round his farm on such and such a day, and had come upon the prisoner's flock left to itself. Instead of shouting for the missing herd he had searched cautiously for him, suspecting he was up to mischief of some sort. Then he had lit upon traces of blood, and following them he came to a spot where a sheep had recently been killed, amid a clump of mimosa. There were footmarks around, which he traced to some rocks hard by, and there he found the meat, roughly quartered, hidden in a cleft. It was quite fresh, and must have been deposited there that day. As he left the place he saw somebody lying behind a low bush watching him, but pretended not to notice. Shortly afterwards, as he returned to where the flock was left, the accused came hurrying up. He accounted for his absence by a cock-and-bull story, that he had seen a jackal skulking near the sheep, and bad gone after it to drive it away. Witness pretended to believe this tale, but as he was listening he noticed two splashes of blood on the prisoner's leg. He evinced no suspicion whatever, but on reaching home sent off at once for the District Police. When the sheep were counted in that night one was missing. The prisoner's hut was searched that night, and the skin was found, hidden among a lot of blankets. It was quite fresh, and must have been flayed off that day. He could swear that, and could swear to the skin. He produced it in court. It bore his mark—an "S" reversed. On the discovery of the skin Gonjana was arrested. The value of the sheep was about 1 pound.

The prisoner's attorney, who all this time has been taking copious notes or pretending to, jumps up to cross-examine. But little enough change can he get out of the witness, whose statement is clear enough, nor does anybody expect he will, least of all himself. As for the man he saw lying behind the bush watching him, the prosecutor cannot absolutely swear it was Gonjana, but he is certain of it short of that. The spoor was the spoor of one man. He is accustomed to follow spoor—has been all his life; he is certain, too, that no other people were in the neighbourhood. He did not analyse the blood spots on the prisoner's leg—they *might* have been pig's blood, as Mr Darrell so sagely suggests, there being hardly such a thing as a pig in the whole district of Doppersdorp—but they were blood spots anyhow; that he can swear. Why should the skin found in the prisoner's hut have been brought home and not the meat? Well, skins were negotiable at some canteens, and natives were fond of grog. He made no allegations against any canteen keeper in the district, he merely answered the question. Gonjana had been with him about a year, and twice he had suspected him of killing sheep before. In other respects his behaviour was far from satisfactory. Why did he keep him in his service? Well, servants were scarce just then, and good ones scarcer still. He employed a bad one, as some people employ an attorney—as a necessary evil.

Amid a great splutter of mirth Mr Darrell appeals vehemently to the Bench to protect him against the insults of the witness, but there is a twinkle in his eye and a half-suppressed grin on his face as he does so.

"Any more questions?"

"No."

So the prosecutor steps down, and is replaced by the police sergeant, who deposes to the finding of the skin and the arrest of the prisoner. The latter made no remark except that he supposed some one must have put it there, as he knew nothing about it. This witness is not cross-examined.

No evidence has Mr Darrell to call. But he draws a pathetic picture of his unfortunate client, wrongfully accused—mistakenly rather, for nobody who knows Mr Suffield would suspect him of wilfully making a false accusation. This unfortunate man then—the very nature of whose work obliges him to be alone in the lonely veldt, cannot of course call any rebutting evidence, cannot prove an *alibi*—is being victimised by the real culprit, but would rather take the punishment upon himself than inform against the real culprit; and so on, and so on. The while Gonjana, standing nonchalantly in the dock, is marvelling at the stupendous idiocy of the white man, who can take up all that time determining the plainest and clearest proofs of his guilt. And the Bench shares in substance his opinion.

"This case," says the Bench, "is as plain as the nose on one's face. Mr Darrell has made the best of a bad job on behalf of his client, but even he could hardly be sanguine enough to expect to succeed. Tell him I find him guilty," concludes the magistrate. And the constable interprets accordingly.

"What is he saying?" as the man is vehemently muttering something.

"He say, sir, nobody see him kill dat sheep."

"Of course not. If every crime had to be seen by an eye-witness, how many criminals would be convicted at all? Has he the means of paying a fine? It will make a difference in his sentence."

"Yes, sir. He say he has one cow and fifteen sheep and goats."

This statement having been corroborated by the prosecutor, the Bench goes on:—

"If he had possessed no means I had intended giving him the heaviest sentence in my power, namely, a year's imprisonment with hard-labour. Stock-stealing has assumed alarming proportions of late, and I am determined to check it in this district, by making an example of every offender. As it is, I sentence Gonjana to pay a fine of 4 pounds, to pay Mr Suffield 1 pound, the value of the sheep, and to receive twenty-five lashes with the 'cat.' Call on the next case."

Kaffirs are stoical folk. This one's expression of countenance undergoes no change, nor does he make any remark as, his sentence having been interpreted to him, he shambles down from the dock to take his seat on the prisoners' bench until the rising of the court. His place is taken by a fellow-countryman, who is charged with contravening the Masters and Servants Act by refusing to obey the lawful commands of his master, Petrus Jacobus Botha.

The latter, an unkempt, corduroy-clad Dutchman, ascends the witness-box, and, placing his greasy slouch hat on the rail, spits on the floor two or three times, Sartly from nervousness, partly from sheer force of habit; then he takes the oath, unctuously and with right hand uplifted, as the manner of his countrymen is. He, too, is a farmer, and the accused native is a herd. The facts of the case are soon got at, and resolve themselves into a matter of "six of one, and half a dozen of the other." The accused has no legal representative, but Mr Van Stolz holds the scale of justice with rigid evenness. He listens to the statements of all parties with infinite patience, and, having given the prosecutor a little of his mind, he summarily dismisses the case, with the metaphor that "people should come into court with clean hands, which is just what the prosecutor has not done"; a remark which evolves a laugh from two or three who grasp the humour underlying it.

Two Hottentot women, old offenders, are sent to gaol for a week for lying drunk about the streets, and then the civil business begins. This consists of a series of unimportant cases, mostly recovery suits, which are soon disposed of; and by one o'clock the court work is over for the day.

"Well, Musgrave," says the little magistrate, as he and his new clerk stroll down the street together towards their respective dinners. "You are getting quite into the swim of things, considering you have only been at it ten days."

"If I am, Mr Van Stolz, it's thanks to the kindness and patience you have shown to an utterly inexperienced hand, in teaching him what to do, and how to do it."

"Oh, no one can be expected to know all about a thing by instinct. Some men expect absurdities. A new clerk is appointed to them who knows nothing whatever of his work, naturally, and they don't give him a chance to learn. They expect him to have everything at his fingers' ends the day he joins the Service, as much as if he had twenty years of it at his back. It isn't fair on a young fellow; though by the way, you're not a young fellow either, Musgrave. Some men at your age are already Civil Commissioners."

The remark, though made in perfect innocence, and with no ulterior thought whatever, was one of those which caused the hearer to shrink imperceptibly into his shell. Though he had been ten days in the place, not a soul in Doppersdorp knew a thing about him, beyond that he was entirely new to the Service. It was a rare thing for a man of his age to start in this, and at the salary of a youngster. It was a rare thing, too, in a place like Doppersdorp, for a man's private affairs to be so thoroughly a sealed book; there where everybody knew as much about his neighbour's concerns as he did about his own, ofttimes a great deal more.

"I've always got on well with my clerks," pursues Mr Van Stolz, "except one, and I worked the oracle so as to get him changed; but, with that exception, they have always been sorry to leave me, even when it meant promotion."

The boast is a very pardonable one because true. The man who could not get on well with Peter Van Stolz could get on with nobody. An excellent official, he was the most genial and unassuming of men, and with such of his subordinates as were gentlemen he was more like a comrade than an official chief. They were all fellow Civil Servants, and he held that there should be a strong *esprit de corps* among such. Himself of Dutch extraction, he was the right man in the right place, in charge of a district ninety per cent, of whose population consisted of Boers. He was deservedly popular, for he held the scale evenly between all parties and all nationalities, whether Boers, natives, or British, and in his judicial capacities, wherever it was possible with due regard to strict justice to err on the side of indulgence, he was sure to do so. In outward aspect he was a little man, sturdy and well knit withal, extremely brisk in his movements, yet not in the least fussy; indeed, such briskness seemed to express in itself his expansive and fun-loving nature, and when a joke or a good story was to the fore, no laugh was more spontaneous or heartier than his.

Their ways part here, and they separate. Roden, as he strolls down towards the hotel where he has for the present taken up his quarters, recalls the verdict which had irresistibly been forced upon his mind, as he had been rattled into the place in the ramshackle post-cart one hot and dusty afternoon ten days ago.

"Heavens! what a God-forsaken looking hole!" had been his unspoken utterance as he viewed for the first time the ugly, mean-looking town, and realised that this was to be his home for an indefinite period.

To say truth the aspect of Doppersdorp was calculated to impress nobody in its favour. It lay upon an open plain, shut in on three sides by bare and craggy mountains, and consisted at first sight mainly of a couple of hundred mud-coloured tenements looking like lumps of clay dropped upon the veldt and left to dry in the sun. It improved, however, on closer inspection. The streets were broad and well laid out, and bordered by willows—and on the lower side of the town were gardens, which made a pleasant oasis of green against the prevailing aridity. Some of the houses were double-storeyed, but the most prominent building of all was the Dutch Reformed Church, an appalling specimen of architecture, staringly new, and surmounted by a badly proportioned steeple. The inhabitants of this place were firmly under the impression that Doppersdorp was the most attractive, and nearly the most important, town in the world; which was a comfortable form of belief for themselves, if a bore to the new arrival, who was expected to acquiesce.

"What d'you think of Doppersdorp?" was fired into the said new arrival by every one with whom he was brought into contact, socially or officially, unawares or with premeditation. And each individual querist would be sure to continue in a tone of complacency, which might convey the idea that it owed its attractiveness, if not its very existence, mainly to himself:

"Ah, it's not half a bad little place, Doppersdorp; not half a bad little place."

To which Roden Musgrave would agree, from the double-barrelled motive of expediency, and the needless exertion entailed by maintaining the contrary. His real opinion, like everything else, he held prudently in reserve.

Chapter Four
Carte and Tierce!

"I wonder what the new magistrate's clerk is like!"

And the speaker who had been staring meditatively skyward, her hands locked together behind the coiled masses of her brown hair, raises her magnificent form from the hammock in which it has been luxuriously resting, and, sitting upright, stretches her arms and yawns. The hammock is slung beneath a group of green willows whose drooping boughs afford a cool and pleasant shade. Beyond, bordered by a low sod wall and a ditch, is a large garden planted with fruit trees soon to be weighed down with golden apricots and ripening peaches, albeit these are at present green. Over the tree-tops shimmers the corrugated iron roof of a house.

"It's awfully hot still, but not so hot as it was," continues the speaker. "Why, Grace, I do believe you're asleep!"

The other occupant of this cool retreat starts violently, nearly falling from her chair with the awakening. She is a tall, slightly built woman, some years older than the first speaker; good-looking, albeit with rather a faded and 'washed-out' air.

"Yes, I was; nodding, at any rate. What were you trying to say, Mona?"

"I was saying, 'I wonder what the new magistrate's clerk is like!'"

"Why didn't you go into Doppersdorp with Charlie this morning? Then you could have seen for yourself."

"Charlie would insist on starting at each an unholy hour. Charlie delights in turning me out at four o'clock if he can, and I am constitutionally lazy. Charlie is a barbarian."

"I wonder what Gonjana will get? A year, I hope. Mr Van Stolz has been heavily down upon sheep-stealing of late."

"Grace Suffield, I'm surprised at you! That's a most unchristian sentiment. You ought to be more merciful to the poor benighted heathen, who doesn't know any better."

"He's the worst 'boy' we have ever had on the place, and I for one shall be heartily glad to get rid of him."

"Bother Gonjana! I was talking of the new magistrate's clerk, 'Roden Musgrave!' It has quite a romantic sound, hasn't it?"

"Romantic fiddlestick!" laughs Mrs Suffield. "You're not in luck's way this time, Mona. They say he isn't young, and is awfully reserved and stiff; quite a middle-aged fogey, in fact."

"Not young, eh! That makes him the more interesting, if only for a change. I believe I'm beginning to have enough of boys."

"Oh, poor Mr Watkins! Why, Mona, I believe you were more than half engaged to that poor boy, and now you are preparing to throw him over for his successor."

"Poor fellow, he was rather fond of me!" is the complacent rejoinder. "I don't know that I ever saw any of them so cut up as he was when he said good-bye. But, look here, Gracie. He is no older than am, and has only been a couple of years in the Service! What sort of aged and wrinkled hag shall I be by the time he gets even a third-class magistracy?"

"Quite so. And having broken his heart—done your best to I should say, for hearts don't break at young Watkins' age—you are going to set to work to subjugate his successor."

"What is life worth without its little excitements?" is the soft, purring reply; but no attempt does the speaker make to repudiate the imputation.

"Little excitements, indeed! Did you ever try and count the number of men you have made fools of? Let's begin. There was young Watkins here; the new doctor at Villiersdorp; then there was that man on board ship—two rather—for I hear you were playing off one against the other. And while you were in England—"

"Oh, that'll do, that'll do! I didn't make fools of them. They made fools of themselves."

"You'll do it once too often one of these days. You'll end by singeing your own wings, and that when you least expect it. And when you do it'll be a scorcher, my child—a scorcher, mark my words."

"I don't know that I'd mind that. I believe I should positively enjoy it. Such an experience would be delicious."

"Wait until it comes, Mona, and then tell me how 'enjoyable,' how 'delicious' you find it," is the reply, given rather shortly, and, it might be thought, with a dash of bitterness.

But Mona Ridsdale says nothing as she slides from her hammock, and, standing upright, stretches her magnificent limbs and again yawns. Looked at now she is seen to be a splendidly developed, and perfectly proportioned specimen of womanhood: whose lines the fall throat and bust, the symmetrical curves of the waist, and the swelling, rounded hips, show faultless in the lithe, natural grace of her attitude. The face, however, is a puzzling one, for its upper and lower parts are contradictory. The higher aspirations, a great capacity for tenderness, and the better and nobler qualities suggested in the broad, smooth brow and melting hazel eyes, are negatived by the setting of the lower jaw and the straight compression of the lips, which convey the idea of a hardness of purpose—when purpose runs on the same lines as inclination—a recklessness of consequence, self-will, ruthlessness. The effect of these contradictions is not a little curious, and is calculated to draw from the observer of character a mingled verdict, to convey an uncomfortable impression of unreliability. It is a face which has just missed being beautiful, and, as it is, can become wondrously attractive; as, judging from the foregoing conversation, some must already have discovered, to their cost.

"Why, I believe Charlie has come back!" cries Mrs Suffield, rising to her feet. "What a noise the dogs are making. Yes, it is him," as a male voice is heard, pacifying those faithful, if uproarious, guardians. Then its tones are mingled with those of another; and they are approaching. "Who on earth has he got with him?" she continues.

Two men appear among the fruit trees, and, getting over the low sod wall, now come up.

"Hallo, Grace!" cries the foremost. "Thought we'd find you and Mona lazing somewhere, so instinctively made for the coolest spot. I've brought you a visitor. This is Mr Musgrave, Watkins' successor."

The effect upon Grace Suffield of this introduction is strange—to the two witnesses thereof inexplicable. Quite a rush of colour comes into her ordinarily pale face, and there is the trepidation of suppressed eagerness in her manner.

"Well, this is an unexpected pleasure! I *am* glad to see you, Mr Musgrave." Then, turning to her mystified husband, "Charlie, this is the gentleman who was so kind to me during that awful post-cart journey. That horrible river—ugh!" with a shudder.

"The deuce it is! Then, Musgrave, you must accept my best thanks, and a thousand per cent, more of hearty welcome," says Suffield. "My wife swears her days would have been numbered but for you. She has done nothing but talk of your kindness to her ever since."

"That's a pity, because it's making a great deal out of very little," is Roden's reply. "But I am very glad we have met again, Mrs Suffield. I often wondered how you had got on after your scare and hardships in general."

"And you neither of you knew each other's names!" says Suffield. "That reminds me, I haven't completed the introduction. My cousin, Miss Ridsdale."

And then these two stand mentally appraising each other in one quick, searching glance, while their hands meet, and, as though conveyed in the magnetism of the touch, very much the same idea runs through the mind of each,—namely, that between this their first meeting, and the eventual and final parting, lie grave and boundless potentialities.

A little more desultory talk, and a move is made towards the house, and Suffield, owning to a magnificent drought after their eight-mile ride in the sun, produces a bottle of grog; then presently, excusing a temporary absence on the ground of it being time to count in the stock, departs, for the sun is touching the craggy heights which bound the view on every side; and already, over the bare treeless plains stretching away for miles in front of the house, are moving white patches, the flocks returning to their nightly fold.

As he disappears so does his wife, for the uproar and occasional howl emanating from an adjacent nursery seem to require her presence. Mona Ridsdale thus left to entertain the stranger, fails to do so, unless as a dumb show, for she is standing at the open window in silence, gazing meditatively out over the veldt, her splendid figure outlined against the blushing glow of the sunset sky. A hostile witness might even have insinuated that she was "posing."

"Well, Mr Musgrave," she says at length, alive to the necessity of saying something, "how do you think you will like Doppersdorp?"

"Ah! Now that is something like a rational version of the question I am by this time prepared to answer, from sheer force of habit before it is asked, wherever I make a new acquaintance. The stereotyped form is, 'How do you like Doppersdorp?' not how do I think I will. Now, between ourselves, I *don't* like it at present, I don't say I never shall, but so far I don't. I don't say I dislike it, for both sentiments are too active to define my views towards it. I simply make the best of the place. And you, do you live here always?"

"Oh yes. This is my home. Charlie and Grace are the only relatives I can at all get on with, and we pull very well together."

"Well, and how do *you* like Doppersdorp? It is a refreshing novelty to be able to ask the question instead of answering it."

"My answer is the same as yours. I make the best of it."

"Ah! You are not very long back from England?"

"About a year. But—how on earth did you know that! Did Charlie tell you?"

"Not a word. I deduced it. There was a discontented ring about your tone, and colonial girls always take on discontent after a visit to England, whereas men are glad to get back."

"Now, what can you possibly know about colonial girls, Mr Musgrave, you, who are only just out from England yourself?"

He smiles slightly, and does not attempt to answer this question.

"How old are you?" he says at length.

Mona favours him with an astonished stare, and colours a little. She does not know whether to laugh or to be angry, to answer or to snub him; and in fact, such a question from a perfect stranger would amply justify the latter course. But she only says—

"Guess."

"Twenty-four."

"Oh, Charlie told you, or somebody did."

"Upon my honour they didn't. Am I right?"

"Yes."

"H'm! A discontented age. Everybody is discontented at twenty-four. But you—well, at whatever age, you always will be."

"You are not a flattering prophet, I doubt if you are a true one."

"Time will show."

"You seem great at drawing deductions and wonderfully confident in their accuracy."

"Perhaps. Human beings are like books; some are made to be read, while others are made apparently to serve no purpose whatever. But all *can* be read."

"And I?"

"A very open page. As, for instance, at this moment, the subject of your thoughts is my unworthy self. You are speculating how at my time of life I come to take up a berth usually occupied by raw youngsters, and mystifying yourself over my record in general; though, womanlike, you are going to deny it."

"No I am not. There! Womanlike, I am going to do the unexpected, and prove you no true prophet as to the latter statement. That is exactly what I was thinking."

"Hallo, Musgrave! Is Mona beginning to give you beans already?" says Suffield, who re-enters, having returned from his farm duties. "Grace, where are you?" he proceeds to shout. "Hurry up! It's feeding time." And then they all adjourn to another room, where the table is laid, and the party is augmented by a brace of tow-headed youngsters, of eleven and twelve respectively, who devote their energies to making themselves a nuisance all round, as is the manner of their kind if allowed to run wild, finishing up with a bear-fight among themselves on the floor, after which they are packed off to bed—a process effected, like the traditional Scotch editor's grasp of the joke, with difficulty.

"And now, Mr Musgrave," says the latter's hostess, when quiet is restored, "you haven't told me yet. How do you like—"

"Stop there, Grace," cries Mona. "Mr Musgrave has just been bewailing his fate, in that he is condemned to answer that question the same number of times there are inhabitants of Doppersdorp, that is to say, about four hundred. And now you are the four hundred and first. In fact, he now answers before the question is asked, from sheer force of habit."

"Ha, ha!" laughs Suffield. "Now you mention it, the thing must become a first-class bore, especially as you're expected to answer every time that you think it a paradise, on pain of making a lifelong enemy. Now, for my part, I'd rather hang myself than have to live in Doppersdorp. As a deadly lively, utterly insignificant hole, there can be few to beat it among our most one-horse townships. And the best of the joke is that its inhabitants think it about as important as London."

"Your verdict is refreshing, Suffield; nor does it inspire me with wild surprise, unless by reason of its complete novelty," rejoins Roden. "But, however true, I don't find its adoption for public use warranted upon any ground of expediency."

"Where are you staying, Mr Musgrave?" asks Mona.

"At the Barkly, for the present. I went to it because it was the first I came to, and I felt convinced there was no choice."

"Do they make you comfortable there?"

"H'm! Comfort, like most things in this world, is relative. Some people might discover a high degree of comfort in being stabled in a three-bedded room with a travelling showman, the proud proprietor of a snore which is a cross between a prolonged railway whistle and the discharge of a Gatling; and farther, who is given to anointing a profuse endowment of ruddy locks with cosmetics, nauseous in odour and of sticky consistency, and is not careful to distinguish between his own hair brash and that of his neighbours. Some people, I repeat, might find this state of things fairly comfortable. I can only say that my philosophy does not attain to such heights."

"Rather not," says Suffield. "Jones is a decent fellow in his way, but he's no more fit to run an hotel than I am to repair a church organ. How do you find his table, Musgrave?"

"I find it simply deplorable. A medley of ancient bones, painted yellow, and aqueous rice, may be *called* curry, but it constitutes too great an inroad upon one's stock of faith to accept it as such. Again, that delectable dish, termed at The Barkly 'head and feet,' seems to me to consist of the refuse portions of a goat slain the week before last, and when it appears through one door I have to battle with a powerful yearning to disappear through the other. No—I am not more particular than most people, nor do I bear any ill-will towards Jones, but really the catering in a *posada*, on the southern slope of the Pyrenees is sumptuous in comparison with his."

"Yes, it's beastly bad," assents Suffield. "Every one growls, but then there's no competition. The other shop's no better. Why don't you get some quarters of your own, Musgrave—even if you do go on feeding at Jones'? You'd be far more comfortable."

"I have that in contemplation. Is there a moon to-night, by the way, Suffield? I don't want to ride into any *sluits* or to get 'turned round' in the veldt."

"Moon! You've no use for any moon to-night. You've got to wait till to-morrow for that ride back. You'll be in ample time for court at ten, or earlier if you like. It's only eight miles."

A chorus of protest arising on all hands, Roden allows himself to be persuaded, and they promptly adjourn to pipes, and re-try the case of Gonjana, and agree that that bold robber obtained no more than his full deserts. Then the eventful post-cart journey is brought up, and Grace Suffield says—

"I should never have believed you were only a newly arrived Englishman, Mr Musgrave. Why, you seemed to know your way about on that awful night better than the other man who was with us, and he has never been outside the Colony."

"A 'raw' Englishman is the approved way of putting it, I believe," is the unconcerned reply. "Well, Mrs Suffield, you will hardly find such a thing now. Most of us have done some knocking about the world—I among others."

That is all. No explanation, no experiences volunteered. The natural curiosity of two at least among his hearers is doomed to disappointment. He does not even say in what part of the said world he has done the knocking about.

Two hours later Mrs Suffield goes to Mona's room for a final gossip.

"Well, dear. You were wondering what he was like! Now, what *is* he like?" she says.

"Tiresome! Unutterably tiresome!"

"Tiresome!" wonderingly. "Not a bore?"

"Oh no, not that. Only I can't make him out. But—I will. Oh yes, I will."

The speaker has her face half hidden in her splendid hair which she is brushing and otherwise arranging, and consequently does not see a queer look flit swiftly across the face of her friend.

"I told you he wasn't young, and was said to be very reserved," pursues the latter.

"Oh yes. A middle-aged fogey, you said."

Before she goes to sleep that night Mona Ridsdale lets her thoughts dwell to a very great extent upon the stranger guest; and for his part, the latter, but a few yards off, allows his thoughts to run very considerably upon her.

That he does so evolves a kind of feeling of self-pity pity not far removed from contempt, yet can he not help it. Beautiful, according to the accepted canons of beauty, she is not, he decides. But of far greater potency than the most faultlessly chiselled features, the classic profile, the ivory-and-roses complexion, which she does not possess, is a certain warm, irresistible power of attractiveness which she does possess, and that to a dangerous degree—the strong under-current of vitality pulsating beneath the dark-complexioned skin, the faultless grace of movement, the straight glance from beneath those clearly marked brows, the vast potentialities of passion that lurk within the swiftly playing eyes. None of this escaped him—all was summed up in the moment he stood face to face with her. In that moment he has read a faulty character, full of puzzling inconsistencies; one which attracts while it repels, yet attracts more than it repels, and it interests him. Nevertheless, the steel armoury of defence, forged by a life's strange experience, is around him. His mental attitude is that of one who is thoroughly "on guard."

Chapter Five
Concerning Small Things

In due course of time—that is to say, from two to three weeks—Gonjana's sentence was confirmed by the Eastern Districts Court—such confirmation being required before a judgment involving lashes could be carried out.

"It's hard lines on the poor devils, Musgrave," observed Mr Van Stolz, as he received the confirmation. "Instead of getting their warming at once, and have done with it, they're kept in gaol for about three weeks, expecting it every day. It may be a necessary precaution with some magistrates, but I have never had a conviction quashed or a judgment upset. I don't say it to brag, but it's a fact. But—it's nearly twelve o'clock now. We'll go down and see it done."

The gaol at Doppersdorp was an oblong brick building containing ten cells. These formed three sides of a central courtyard, the fourth constituting the gaoler's quarters and the kitchen where the prisoners' rations were prepared. A line of men in broad-arrow stamped suits, all natives, guarded by two armed constables, was filing in from the veldt. This was the hard-labour gang, returning to the most congenial task in the whole twenty-four hours, the consumption of dinner, to wit; to-day combined with a scarcely less attractive one, to those figuring in it only as spectators—punishment parade.

The convicts, after the regulation search, were drawn up in a line in the prison yard. A long ladder standing against the wall did duty as the triangles. There was another to suffer besides Gonjana, a yellow-skinned Hottentot named Bruintjes, and for a similar offence. Half beside himself with fear, this fellow stood, shivering and moaning, with quaking, disjointed appeals for mercy. The Kaffir, on the other hand, might have been one of the spectators, for all the sign he gave to the contrary; though now and again his tongue would go up to the roof of his month in a disdainful "click," as he watched the contortions of his fellow-sufferer.

"Which shall I take first, sir?" said the gaoler.

"Oh, the Hottentot," answered Mr Van Stolz. "The poor devil will be dead if he has to wait for the other chap. He isn't quite so cheeky now as he was in Court. Seems to be taken out of him. Ready, doctor?"

The district surgeon, whose presence on such occasions was required by law, replied in the affirmative, and the Hottentot, stripped to the waist, was triced to the ladder. With the first "swish" of the lash, which the gaoler, an old soldier, understood the use of, he set up a screech like a cat in a steel trap; and this he kept up throughout. At the end he was untied, whimpering and howling, and his back sponged.

"Pah! Twenty-five lashes!" growled the gaoler, running his fingers through the strings of his "cat." "A soldier would have taken it grinning, in my time."

Then Gonjana was triced up. But he was made of very different stuff. A slight involuntary quiver in the muscles of the brawny chocolate-coloured back as the lash cut its terrible criss-cross, but that was all. Not a sound escaped the throat of the sturdy barbarian, not even a wriggle ran through his finely-modelled limbs from first to last. It was like flogging a bronze statue.

"By Jove, he took that well!" exclaimed Roden, moved to admiration.

The Kaffir, who had undergone the sponging as though he were merely being washed, had now huddled his ragged shirt upon his raw and bleeding back.

"He's a plucky fellow!" said Mr Van Stolz, going up to him. "Tell him, Jan, that it will pay him best to be honest in future. But he took his licking well. He can go now."

This the constable duly interpreted. But Gonjana seemed in no hurry to enter upon the sweets of his newly restored liberty. He stood looking at the magistrate with a queer, sidelong expression, his broad nostrils snuffing the air. Then he said something in his own language. The constable sniggered.

"He say, sir," interpreted the latter, "he say de lash hurt, but he not afraid of being hurt. He say, sir—he very hungry. He hope sir will not send him away without his dinner."

From the open windows of the prison kitchen the strong fumes of a savoury stew were wafted into the yard, for it was the dinner-hour. The gaol ration of meat and mealies was a liberal one, and it was noteworthy that every convict who had completed his term of hard-labour came out of prison sleek and fat, whatever might have been his condition at the time of incarceration. Mr Van Stolz burst out laughing.

"Give the poor devil his dinner and let him go," he said. "He took his dose well. It's little enough dinner I'd want if I were in his shoes, eh, doctor?"

This to the district surgeon, who had joined them as they left the gaol. He was a young M.D. named Lambert, a new arrival, newer even than Roden, having been recently appointed. There was nothing specially remarkable about him, unless it were a species of brisk self-assertiveness which some might call bumptiousness, and which might not altogether be to his disadvantage in a place like Doppersdorp, where the District Surgeon was something of a personage, and apt to be toadied accordingly. But between him and Roden Musgrave there was an indefinable instinct of antipathy, which is perhaps best expressed in saying that they had not taken to each other.

This feeling being, for the present at any rate, merely a passive one, they found themselves strolling towards the Barkly Hotel together, Mr Van Stolz having left them. Two ladies were seated on the *stoep*, who as they drew near took the identity of Mrs Suffield and Mona Ridsdale.

"Well, Dr Lambert," said the latter, with a wicked look at Roden, when greetings had been exchanged; "and how do you like Doppersdorp? But there, I forgot, I must not ask you that. Well then, what was the meaning of that dreadful noise we heard going on at the gaol just now, for we could hear it all the way from here?"

"Only a fellow getting a licking in due course of law—a Hottentot, for sheep-stealing," answered the doctor. "The other nigger took it like a man."

"Oh, how dreadful! And do you mean to say you went to see that?"

"I had to. You see I am compelled to be present on such occasions," answered Lambert; with a stress on the pronoun, as if to convey the idea that the other was not, which, strictly speaking, was the case.

"What horrid creatures men are!"

"I agree; they are," said Roden. "The remark is made so often that it must be true."

Then he went indoors, and Mona, thus deprived of all opportunity of reply, did not know whether to feel angry or not. For these two had seen something of each other daring the three weeks which had elapsed since Roden's first visit to the Suffields. In fact, there were not lacking ill-natured people, who declared that Mona had got a new string to her bow, or rather, a new bow to a very well-worn string.

The young doctor, however, who had met her once before, had, for his part, been very much struck at first sight, as was the wont of Mona's admirers: they were apt to cool off later, but that was her fault.

Now being left with the coast clear, Lambert laid himself out to be excessively agreeable, and the bell having rung, hurried them in to dinner, in order to secure the seat next to Mona before the objectionable Musgrave should reappear. But the latter did not seem to care two straws, when he came in presently with Suffield, whom he had picked up in the bar.

"So he took it well, did he?" that worthy was saying as they sat down. "Gonjana is a good bit of a *schelm*, but Kaffirs are generally plucky. Talking of that, there's rumour of a scare in the Transkei."

"There always is a scare in the Transkei," struck in Jones, the landlord, who was carving.

"Well, scare or no scare, it wouldn't affect us much," said Suffield.

"Oh, wouldn't it? I don't know so much about that. There's them Tambookie locations out Wildschutsberg way; they're near enough to make it lively, I imagine."

"That's where you get your best custom from, eh, Jones? They'll come to you first, if only that they know the way to your grog. What's this, eh? Not mutton. Buck, isn't it?"

"Yes, rhybok. Mr Musgrave shot it yesterday morning."

"So! Where did you go, Musgrave?"

"As nearly as possible on your own place, Suffield," said Roden, starting, for he had been in something like a brown study. "You know that big double *krantz* you see from the road? Well, just under that."

"Why didn't you come and look us up, man?"

"Hadn't time. You see, I have to turn out almost in the middle of the night to get among the rocks by the time it's light enough to shoot; rhybok are precious leery. Then I've got to be back early, too, so as to be at the office by half-past nine."

"I didn't know you were such a Nimrod," said Mrs Suffield.

"He brings back a buck every time he goes out," said Jones. "Piet Van der Merwe was here the other day fuming because some one had been shooting on his farm; but when I told him who it was, he said he didn't mind, because no Englishman could hit a haystack if he were a yard away from it. He told Mr Musgrave he could go there whenever he liked, and I expect soon there won't be a buck left on the place."

"If I were Musgrave, I should make you take me at half-price, on the strength of keeping your larder supplied, Jones," laughed Suffield. "We must get up a day's shoot, though. Doctor, are you keen on shooting?"

The doctor replied that he was, and then followed much discussion as to when a good long day could be arranged.

"Why not come out with us this afternoon?" proposed Suffield. "We could get away upon the *berg* by sundown, and perhaps pick up a buck or two."

"Can't do it, unfortunately," said Roden. "Got to go back to office."

But the other accepted with alacrity, though it is I probable that the venatorial side of the programme is not, if the truth were known, constitute the most attractive part. All the time they were at table he had been making the most of his opportunities, apparently to some purpose, for when they got up, and Mona declared she had some shopping to do, with her went Lambert in close attendance.

Although continuing to dine at Jones' dubious board, Roden had so far carried out his project that he had secured for himself a tiny red brick cottage, which boasted two rooms and a kitchen, with a back yard and stable. It was large enough for him, however, and he promptly proceeded to make himself comfortable therein, in a modest sort of way. Hither, having bidden good-bye to the Suffields, without waiting to see them inspan, he adjourned, and, in company with a solitary pipe, fell into a train of thought.

The first thing was to stifle a strong inclination to reconsider Suffield's proposal. It was not too late now. His pony was only grazing on the town commonage hard by; he could have him brought in less than half an hour. And then came the thought that the motive of this was not the prospect of sport, and the conviction was an unwelcome one. As we have said, he had already seen a good deal of Mona Ridsdale. There was something about her that attracted him powerfully. What was it? He was not in love with her; the bare idea that he might ever become so stirred him uncomfortably. She was a splendid creature, a physical paragon, but love! ah, that was another thing. Besides, what had he to do with love, even were he capable of feeling it? That sort of blissful delusion, veiling Dead Sea ashes, was all very well when one was young; which he no longer was. His life was all behind him now, which made it perhaps the more easy to start again almost where others left off. The modest salary wherewith the Colonial Government saw fit for the present to requite his services, did not constitute his sole means of existence; he possessed something over and above it, though little, and all combined gave him just enough to get along with a moderate degree of comfort. And as his thoughts took this practical turn, the association of ideas caused him to rise suddenly in disgust. It was time to be doing something when his meditations landed him in such a slough of grotesque idiocy, and with that intent he went straight away to his office.

But times were easy just then. He wrote a couple of official letters, and took down the deposition of a lanky Boer with a tallow countenance, adorned by a wispy beard, who, amid much expectoration and nervous shifting of his battered and greasy wide-awake from one hand to another, delivered himself of a long and portentous complaint against a neighbour, for rescuing by force certain cattle, which his servants were driving to the nearest pound. Then, having satisfied this seeker of redress, with the assurance that justice would overtake the footsteps of the aggressor in the shape of a summons, and thus got rid of him, Roden took down two or three of the office volumes and set to work to study a little statute law, in which occupation he was presently disturbed by the cheery, bustling step of Mr Van Stolz.

"Well, Musgrave, not much doing!" cried the latter, perching himself on the side of the table and relighting his pipe. "What's this?" picking up the official letters. "'With reference to your circular—um—um—asking for a return of—um—um—' Those damn circulars! Every post we get about twenty of them. Return! They'll soon want a return of the number of buttons each official wears on his shirt," —signing the letters. "What's this? Another complaint? 'Pound rescue,—Willem Cornelia Gerhardus Van Wyk.' One of the biggest liars that ever trod God's earth. I've fined him over and over again for licking his niggers or trying to do them out of their pay or something; and you'll see him in church on Sunday with a face as long as a fiddle; he's one of the 'elders,' too. He'll have to come in and swear this, though."

"He said he couldn't wait, sir, but he'll be in the first thing to-morrow, before court time."

"Oh, that'll do just as well, as I wasn't here, I say, Musgrave, old boy, we'll shut up shop and go for a walk. Got your pipe with you? Try some of this tobacco. Yes, we may as well take it easy while we can; we shall have enough to do next week with the monthly returns."

So away they started, leaving the little baked-mud town behind them; away over the open veldt, with its carpet of wax blossoms, lying beneath the slopes of the great hills which stood forth all green and gold in the afternoon sun.

"What do you think of the new doctor, Musgrave?" said the magistrate at last, as they were discussing things and people in general.

"Lambert? H'm! Well, strictly between ourselves—not much."

"Not, eh? I thought he seemed a nice fellow."

"I don't want to prejudice anybody against him, far from it; but I've noticed that between two given people there often exists an antipathy at sight. Now, Lambert may be a decent fellow enough in the main; but between him and me that antipathy exists."

He did not add that from unerring signs he had taken the measure of the subject under discussion, and that that measure was as mean as mean could be.

"You don't take to Lambert, then?"

"No. But I know nothing against him, and so it wouldn't be fair to say anything against him on the score of a mere instinctive dislike."

"How is it you didn't go out to the Suffields this afternoon, Mr Musgrave?" said the magistrate's wife as, having returned from their walk, they were sitting on the *stoep* awaiting dinner—for with characteristic geniality his official superior had insisted upon Roden considering himself on a "run-of-the-house" footing.

"I don't know," was the reply. "There was something to be done at the office, I suppose, or perhaps I felt lazy."

Mrs Van Stolz laughed. She was a pretty, dark-eyed woman, also of Dutch extraction, as amiable and sunny-natured as her husband.

"Oh yes, of course," she retorted mischievously. "But Miss Ridsdale was consoling herself with the new doctor—at any rate, as they drove past here. He'll cut you out, Mr Musgrave, if you don't take care. But, seriously, how do you like her on further acquaintance?"

"Oh, we seem to get along fairly well. Fight without ceremony, and all that sort of thing."

"And make it up again. Take care, Mr Musgrave; she's dangerous. Poor Mr Watkins completely lost his heart."

"Well, I haven't got one to lose, Mrs Van Stolz; so I'm safe."

"I don't know. I've already heard in two quarters that you are engaged to her."

"Hardly surprising, is it? I believe we have been seen twice in the same street. That would be more than enough for Doppersdorp."

"Don't you let the new doctor cut you out," she rejoined merrily.

"He has the advantage of youth on his side, at any rate," responded Roden. And thus the conflict of chaff went on.

Chapter Six
The Verdict of Doppersdorp

Notwithstanding the exalted opinion of it professed by its inhabitants, the interests of Doppersdorp were from the very nature of things circumscribed. They embraced, for the most part, such entrancing topics as the price of wool, the last case of assault, ditto of water rights—for the burgesses of Doppersdorp were alike a pugnacious and litigious crowd—the last Good Templar meeting, and the number of liquors Tompkins, the waggon builder, could put away without impairing his centre of gravity; whether Macsquirt, the general dealer, would bring his threatened libel action against the *Doppersdorp Flag*—a turgid sheet of no apparent utility, save for enveloping a bar of yellow soap—that leader of public opinion having referred to him as "an insignificant 'winkler'" (i.e., small shopkeeper), instead of "that enterprising merchant," and whether he would succeed in obtaining a farthing of damages or costs from its out-at-elbows proprietor and editor, if he won—such, with slight variation, were the topics which exercised the minds and the tongues of this interesting community from year's end to year's end. Such a variation was afforded by the arrival of two new and important members in its midst. Upon these Doppersdorp was not slow to make up its mind, and whether foregathered in council and the bar of the Barkly Hotel, or secure in the privacy of home circle, hesitated not to express the same in no halting terms.

Now, the collective mind on the subject of Roden Musgrave was adverse. His demerits were of a negative order, which is to say that his sins had been those of omission rather than of commission, and, as was sure to be the case, had rendered him unpopular. Who was he, Doppersdorp would like to know, that he shut himself up like an oyster, as if nobody was worth speaking to? though the possibility that the motive attributed to the bivalve delicacy might be wide of the mark did not occur to the originator of this felicitous simile. His predecessor, young Watkins, had been hail-fellow-well-met with everybody; was, in fact, as nice a young fellow as they could wish—and here Doppersdorp unwittingly answered its own indignant query.

Roden Musgrave had no idea of being "young Anybody" to Dick, Tom, and Harry, or hail-fellow-well-met—i.e., on terms to be patronised by the various ornaments of Doppersdorp society, shading off in imperceptible gradations to the local tailor, whom he would be obliged to indict nearly every Monday morning for having overstepped the limits of public order during the Saturday night's "spree," and been run in by the police therefor. He had a wholesome belief in the old proverb regarding too much familiarity, seeing in it a happy application to a man holding the post he did in such a place as Doppersdorp. Wherein his reasoning was sound; but the collective sense of the community opined differently, and was wont to pronounce with graphic, if somewhat profane indignation, that the new magistrate's clerk mistook himself for his omnipotent Creator, and, in fact, wanted taking down a peg.

Not all, however, were of this opinion: his official chief, for instance, as we have seen, and perhaps two or three others, among them the retiring District Surgeon, Lambert's predecessor, a somewhat cynical, at bottom, though on the surface rollicking, kind of individual. He to Roden, while making his adieux: "We are sure to tumble up against each other again somewhere, Musgrave, but one consolation is that it couldn't be among a set of more infernal scoundrels than we shall leave behind us here, as you'll find out by the time you get a quarter of my experience of them." Which caustic delivery Roden was at no pains to controvert, feeling sure that it covered a large substratum of truth. Indeed, he was not long in suspecting that to the dictum of Lambert's predecessor there was every possibility Lambert might contribute, in his own person, his full share of confirmation.

But whatever Roden's opinion of the new doctor, it was not shared by the community at large. Lambert possessed all those qualities calculated to make him "go down" in a place like Doppersdorp. He was young and energetic—he had a certain breezy geniality of manner, and was very much hail-fellow well-met with all classes. Doppersdorp opened its arms and took him to its heart. He soon became as popular as the other was the reverse.

But, for his own unpopularity Roden Musgrave cared not a rush. He was not over eager to court the doubtful honour of being voted a "reel jolly good chep," by Dick, Tom, and Harry, as the price of his self-respect. His ambition did not lie that way. In private life he was not given to the exchange of shoulder slaps, or jocose digs in the ribs, or other genialities in the way of horseplay dear to the heart of that surprising trinity; nor in his official capacity was he inclined to wink at certain preposterous swindles, which the honest practitioners of Doppersdorp were wont to plant upon their clients in the form of "bills of costs," which latter it was his business to tax, nor would he connive at any undue laxity in the matter of taking out licences, or other omissions which might fall within his sphere. So, officially and socially, he found scant favour in Doppersdorp.

He was seated in his office one day, doing some routine work, when the door was flung open unceremoniously, and a voice demanded angrily in German English—

"What is dis—what is dis?"

Roden looked up. "Dis" consisted of a sheet of blue paper, partly printed, partly written upon, and held out between a finger and thumb of doubtful cleanliness. At the other end of the uncleanly finger and thumb was an ordinary-looking individual of Teutonic and generally unwholesome aspect, bearded, and his poll thatched with a profusion of dark bush. This worthy held the office of postmaster at Doppersdorp—an office whose emolument was not great. Still it was something. Anybody ambitious of incurring Sonnenberg's enmity for life had only to hint at his being of Hebraic extraction, and indeed, if only from the horror in which he affected to hold such suggestion, it is highly probable he was. For the rest he had all the self-conceit of the average Teuton, who has made, or is making, a fair success of life.

"What is dis—what is dis?" he repeated in a tone tremulous with rage, flinging the paper upon the table. Roden picked it up.

"A summons," he said, glancing down it. "A summons, citing one Adolphus Sonnenberg (that's yourself, isn't it?) to appear before the Resident Magistrate on Monday next, for neglecting to comply with the Revenue Acts, in keeping a retail shop without a licence. Perfectly correctly drawn, I think," looking up inquiringly. "Eh, what? 'Damned impudence' did you say? Well, yes. I'm inclined to agree with you. It is—on the part of a man who gets a civil reminder more than a week ago that he is liable to penalties, and treats it with contempt until he is summoned in due course, then comes bursting in here and kicks up a row, with no more regard for the laws of decent behaviour than for those of his adopted country. Yes. I quite agree with your definition of it. Anything more?"

This was said blandly—suavely. The other was bursting with rage.

"Anything more?" he bellowed. "Plenty more. Wait till I see Mr Van Stolz about it. We've known each other for years. See if he'll see me insulted by a twopenny-halfpenny magistrate's clerk."

"Quite so. He'll be here by-and-by. Meanwhile, kindly leave my office."

"I shall leave when I choose," was the defiant rejoinder.

"Ah, indeed!" Then, raising his voice, "Hey! Jan Kat! Come in here."

There was a shuffling of feet. The native constable, who had been roosting in the son on the court-house steps, appeared at the door.

"Turn Mr Sonnenberg out of my office."

Just those few words—quietly spoken—no further appeal to leave. Roden prepared to go on with his work again.

"Come, sir, you must go," said the constable.

Sonnenberg was speechless with rage. He glared first at Roden, then at the stalwart Fingo, as though he had some thoughts of assaulting one or both of them. To be turned out of the room ignominiously, and by a native! It was too much of an outrage.

"Come, sir, you must leave the office," repeated the constable more peremptorily.

Then Sonnenberg opened his mouth and there gurgled forth weird and sonorous German oaths mingled with full-flavoured English blasphemies, all rolling out so thick and fast as to tread upon each other's heels and well-nigh to choke the utterer. In the midst of a forced breathing space a voice—quick and stern—was heard to exclaim—

"What is all this about?"

Sonnenberg started. In the doorway stood the magistrate himself. But there was that in the latter's face which sadly disconcerted the frenzied Teuton. The ally he had reckoned on seemed to wear an uncommonly hostile look. However, he began volubly to explain how he had been insulted when he came in, and how the constable had been ordered to eject him. Mr Van Stolz heard him to the end, Roden putting in no word; then he looked at the summons, which still lay on the table, where it had been thrown.

"Mr Sonnenberg," he said, "I can see through a brick wall as far as most people and I don't want to be told the ins and outs of this. Whatever you have had to put up with you have brought upon yourself. You received a perfectly courteous letter reminding you that you had not yet taken out your licence. You chose to take no notice of that, so Mr Musgrave, by my instructions, drew up a summons. In coming here to talk about it you have committed an act of gross impertinence, bordering on a contempt of court, and if you think that you can come into these offices for the purpose of kicking up a row, we shall soon show you your mistake. Whatever day is set forth on the summons, that day you had better be in court—which is all I need say in the matter. Now, you may go."

Astounded, bewildered, snubbed down to the very dust, Sonnenberg slunk off. The silent, absolutely indifferent contempt of Roden, was more galling than any look of cheap triumph might have been, for the latter had not even thought it worth while to put in one word of his version of the story, wherein he was right. But the vindictive Jew vowed within his heart the direst of dire vengeance did the chance ever present itself.

"That damned Jew!" exclaimed Mr Van Stolz in his free and confidential way, when he and his subordinate were alone together again. "You were quite right, Musgrave. You must not stand any humbug from such fellows. Watkins was too much hand-in-glove with them all, and they thought they could do anything with him in the way of trying it on, but he was young. Still, of course, it doesn't do to be too sharp on fellows. I don't mean in this case, or any other. I'm speaking generally. That impudent dog, Sonnenberg, got only half what he deserved. When is the case to come on?"

"Next Monday, sir."

"So! Well, he'll be as mild as Moses then," chuckled the other.

On another occasion a worthy representative of Doppersdorp was destined to learn that the new magistrate's clerk was not altogether born yesterday. This was a law-agent, a bumptious, ill-conditioned fellow named Tasker, who owed Roden a grudge for having ruthlessly taxed down bill after bill of costs, of a glaringly extortionate nature. He, entering the office one day, asked for twopenny revenue stamps to the amount of two pounds sterling, which having received, he threw down a deed.

"Stamp that, please."

Roden cast his eye down the document, and satisfied himself that the stamp duty was precisely the amount just purchased.

"It wants a 2 pound stamp," he said.

"Just so," returned the other briskly. "Stick these on, please," handing him the two hundred and forty stamps, with a malicious grin.

"Stick them on yourself," was the answer.

Then Tasker began to rave. It was the duty of the Distributer of Stamps to stamp all documents brought to him, and so forth. What did he mean? To all of which Roden turned a deaf ear, and proceeded to occupy himself with other matters.

"So you refuse to stamp this document!" foamed the agent at length.

"Distinctly. Do it yourself."

"We'll soon see about that." And this fool started off to the magistrate's room to complain to that functionary that the Distributer of Stamps refused to perform the office for which he was paid. Mr Van Stolz, who knew his man, rose without a word and went into the clerk's office.

"What is the meaning of this, Mr Musgrave? Mr Tasker complains that you refuse to stamp his deed."

Roden saw the look on his chief's face that he knew so well. He anticipated some fun.

"I refused to do so on his terms, sir," he answered; "I asked him whether he wanted a 2 pound stamp, but he replied that I was to stick those two hundred and forty stamps on a bit of paper that won't hold the half of them. I ventured to think I was right in retorting that the Government time was not to be played the fool with in that fashion."

"You're bound to stamp all deeds," struck in the agent sullenly, realising that he was likely to undergo a severe snub for his ill-conditioned idiocy.

"We are bound to supply you with the stamps, Mr Tasker," returned Mr Van Stolz, "but we are not bound to lick them for you. Therefore, if you want it done, you must do it yourself."

The agent stared, then looked foolish.

"Can I change these for a 2 pound one, then?" he growled, but quite crestfallen.

"Well, you can this time; but we are not even bound to change them for you, once they have been delivered. You can oblige Mr Tasker in this way, Mr Musgrave."

"Certainly," said Roden blandly, and, the exchange being effected, the agent departed.

"It would have served him right to have made him pay for another stamp, Musgrave," chuckled the magistrate, when they were alone together. "But the poor devil is generally so hard up that it's doubtful if he could have mustered another 2 pounds."

Now the foregoing incidents were only two out of many; which went to show that, if a man was unpopular in Doppersdorp, it was not necessarily his own fault.

Still there were some, though few, by whom Roden was well liked. Among these was Father O'Driscoll, the priest who shepherded the scanty and scattered Catholic inhabitants of the town and district, a genial and kindly-natured old man, and by reason of those qualities widely popular, even with some of the surrounding Boers, whose traditional detestation of the creed he represented it would be impossible to exaggerate. A native of Cork, and in his younger days a keen sportsman, it was with unbounded delight he discovered that the new official was well acquainted with a considerable section of his own country and the fishing streams thereof— and frequent were the evenings which these two would spend together, over a steaming tumbler of punch, killing afresh many a big salmon in Shannon, or Blackwater, or Lee. And with sparkling eyes the old priest would disinter brown and weather-beaten fly-books, turning over, almost reverently, the soiled parchment leaves, where musty relics of the insidious gauds which had lured many a noble fish to its undoing still hung together to carry back his mind to the far, far past.

Chapter Seven
Lambert—Out of it

"...And I can really give you no other answer."

"Don't say that, Mona. We haven't known each other so very long, certainly, but still..."

"It isn't that, Dr Lambert. I like you very much, and all that sort of thing, but I can say no more than I have said."

The two were alone together under the shade of the trees behind the house: Mona, still furtively engaged in the favourite pastime Lambert had come upon her more actively pursuing—viz., lying in a hammock admiring her own magnificent proportions. The doctor's infatuation, fired to fever heat over the symmetrical and sensuous grace of this splendid creature, had taken words, and we have just come in for the end of his proposal and—rejection.

"Of course, some one else," he jerked out bitterly, after a few moments of silence. "Lucky chap, anyhow; only, don't take too much on trust in that quarter," with a sneer.

She half started up in her hammock, and her eyes flashed. The compression of her lips, together with the hardening of the lower half of her face, was not now attractive; to an impartial spectator, it would have bordered on the repellent. But Lambert was not an impartial spectator, being madly in love.

"That's right," she retorted. "Pray go on. Just like all you men," with bitter, stinging emphasis. "When you can't have everything as you want it you swing round and become insulting."

"Oh, I had no intention that way," he returned quickly, half cowed by the lash of her anger. "I made the remark simply and solely in your own interest."

"My own interest is very well able to take care of itself." Then relenting, for she felt mercifully disposed towards this fresh victim. "Never mind. You are very much upset. I can see that. We will think no more about it."

He made no reply, but sat looking straight in front of him. The molten glare of afternoon was merging into the slanting rays of approaching sunset. From the scorching stoniness of the hillside the screech of crickets rang out in endless vibration—varied now and again by the drowsy hum of winged insects, or the "coo" of a dove from the willows overhanging the dam. A shimmer of heat lay over the wide veldt, and a thundercloud was gathering black upon the craggy turrets cresting the distant spurs of the Stormberg mountains.

"You are right. I am rather—er—well, not quite myself," said Lambert jerkily. "I think I had better go."

Mona's face softened. She had refused him, it was true, but she was not going to dismiss him altogether. That was not her way, being a young woman who thoroughly believed in proving the fallaciousness of the proverb about not being able to eat your cake and have it too.

"Don't go away angry," she said, throwing a deft plaintiveness into her pleading. "We have been such good friends—why should we not continue to be? You will come and see us as usual?"

The melting wistfulness of her eyes, even the lingering pressure of the hand which she had extended—half dropped—to him out of the hammock, had their effect on Lambert, who in a matter of this kind was as easy to make a fool of as most men.

"Well, I think I'll go now," he said unsteadily. "Yes, I hope we'll continue to be friends—for I must go on seeing you," he added with a kind of desperation. "Good-bye."

"Not good-bye. Only 'so long' as they say here," she answered kindly. And with a hurried assent he tore himself away.

Mona, left to herself, felt regretful, but it was a regret dashed with a kind of triumph; which exultation in turn gave way to a feeling bordering on fierce resentment. Not against Lambert, though; for before his horse's hoofs were out of hearing along the Doppersdorp road she had almost forgotten her dejected and discomfited adorer. No, it was evoked by his parting insinuation, which had so aroused her anger at the time, and now moved her to an exultation which made all her pulses stir, and, alone as she was, caused her to flush hotly.

Not long, however, was she destined to be left to her own thoughts, such as they were, for presently Mrs Suffield invaded her solitude. At her the latter shot a quick, curious glance.

"Well, Mona; and what have you done to him?"

"To him? To whom?"

"You know who well enough: the doctor, of course. He could hardly bid me good-bye coherently, and went away with a face as if he were about to hang himself."

"Well, he wouldn't be going *away* to do that; because he could hardly find a tree big enough for the purpose in the whole district except here. He'd have to do it here or nowhere."

"What a heartless girl you are, Mona! Why did you play with the poor fellow like that? Of coarse its all fun to you—"

"And death to him, you were going to say. But it isn't. He's glum enough now—but wait a year or two and see. He'll brag about it then, and go about hinting, or more than hinting, that there was a stunning fine girl down Doppersdorp way—this, if he's changed his abode—who was awfully smashed on him, and so on. Wait and see. I know them, and they're all alike." And the speaker stretched herself languidly, and yawned.

Grace Suffield hardly knew what to say, or whether to feel angry or laugh. But she was spared the necessity of replying, for Mona went on—

"By the way, we never see anything of Mr Musgrave now. Its ages since he's been here."

"I was nearly saying, 'small wonder, after the way you treated him.' But I won't, for there, at any rate, is a man whom even you can't make a fool of. He's built of sterner stuff."

"Is he?" with a provoking smile. "But what on earth do you mean, Grace, by 'the way in which I treated him'?"

"Oh, you know very well what I mean. You did nothing but encourage him at first; then you cold-shouldered him, and launched out in a fast and furious flirtation with the new doctor, because he *was* new, I suppose."

"So was the other. But, Grace, I didn't cold-shoulder him. I liked the man. If he was so weak as to become jealous of the doctor, I can't help it."

"Weak!" flashed out Grace. "Weak! I don't think there's much weakness about Mr Musgrave, and I'm certain he's not the sort of man to indulge in anything so—so—feeble as jealousy."

"Then he won't do for me," rejoined Mona, with a light laugh. "I don't care about a man who can't be jealous. I like them to be jealous. Makes one more valuable, don't you see."

"All right, Mona, my child. I can only say what I've said more than once before, and that is, Wait until your own time comes, as come it assuredly will; then we shall see."

Furious with herself for doing so, Mona was conscious of colouring ever so slightly at this prediction, often uttered, but coming now so close upon her former meditations. She took refuge by the bold expedient of running in right under the enemy's guns.

"Far be it from me to disparage your knight errant, Gracie," she replied, with a mischievous laugh, and a slight emphasis on 'your.' "So he is made of sterner stuff, is he?"

The only answer was a sniff of contempt.

"Very well," she went on adopting this as an affirmative; "what will you bet me I don't bring him to my feet in a fortnight, Gracie?"

"I won't bet on anything so ridiculous—so atrocious," was the tart reply. "Roden Musgrave is too far out of the ordinary specimen of a man to be twisted round even your finger, Mona."

It was the speaker's turn to colour now. She had spoken with such unconscious warmth that Mona was gazing fixedly at her with the most mischievous expression in the world.

"Oh!" was all she said. But the ejaculation spoke volumes.

It was a curious coincidence, but a coincidence, that Lambert, about halfway on his road to Doppersdorp, should encounter—or rather, so absent and self-absorbed was his mood, run right into—a couple of horsemen riding in the direction from which he had just come. Indeed, it was the cheery hail of one of the latter that first made him aware of their presence.

"Hi! Hallo, Lambert! You're riding in the wrong direction, man. Turn round, turn round and come back with us. We are going to have a rhybok shoot to-morrow."

But Charles Suffield's hospitable suggestion only made Lambert scowl, and mutter something about having to be back. For the second of the two horsemen was the objectionable Musgrave himself, who carried a gun. The sight almost made him hesitate. He had no mind to leave the field open to his rival, for so, in his soreness and jealousy, he considered the other. His excuse, however, was not altogether a bogus one. Of late, quite an alarming proportion of his time had been spent at Quaggasfontein, and his patients were beginning to grumble, notably those who had ridden or driven some three or four hours to find him, and found him absent. His practice would suffer; for, apart from the possibility of the importation of a rival medico, there was a large proportion of people who would speedily find out their ability to do without treatment, from the mere fact that they had to. So he stuck to his intention as first expressed.

"Lambert looks a trifle off colour," said Suffield, with a comical glance at his companion when they had resumed their way.

"Does he? I'm not sorry he didn't leap at your suggestion. I don't particularly care for the fellow."

"He seems awfully gone on Mona, and I suppose she's playing the fool with him, as usual. She's a most incurable flirt, that girl, and she certainly does manage to bring them all to their knees. I tell her she'll end her days an old maid."

The other smiled drily over Suffield's artless ramblings, for the two men had become very intimate by this time. It occurred to him that Mona had thought at one time to pass him through the same mill.

The warmth of welcome Roden met at the hands of his hostess was about equal to the warmth with which she scolded him. What did he mean by such behaviour? It was nearly a month since he had been near them. Busy? A great deal to do? Nonsense! She knew better than that. Doppersdorp Civil Servants were not the most hard-worked of their kind, there was always that redeeming point in the Godforsakenness of the place, and so on, and so on.

"That's right, Mrs Suffield; crowd it on thick! Nothing like making up for lost time," he laughed.

"Well, but—you deserve it."

"Oh yes. I won't make that bad excuse which is worse than none, and which you have been discounting before I made it. Besides, you owe me a blowing-up. I'm afraid I dragooned you far harder, when you were handed over to my tender mercies, crossing the river in the box."

"Well, you were rather ill-tempered," she admitted maliciously. "I wonder how Mona would have stood it."

"Stood what? The crossing or the temper?" said Mona. "I've got a fine old crusted stock of the latter myself."

"You have," assented Roden.

"That's rude."

"Your own doing," was the ready rejoinder. "You left me the choice of two evils, though, Miss Ridsdale. Wouldn't it be ruder still to contradict a lady?"

"Go on, you two hair-splitters!" laughed Grace. "Mr Musgrave, I've put you in the same room you had last time. You know your way. Supper will be ready directly."

"And you'd better turn on a fire in the sitting-room, Grace," said Suffield. "The days are hot for July, in this high veldt, but the nights are nipping. Besides, like a nigger, I'm keen on a fire to smoke the evening pipe beside, when one can invent the shadow of an excuse for lighting one. It's more snag, you know."

And so it was. Seated there at the chimney-corner smoking the post-prandial pipe, while the burning logs crackled brightly, and conversation flowed free and unrestrained, varied by a song or two from Mona, as also from Suffield, who was no mean vocalist, and the prospect of some sport on the morrow, it occurred to Roden that life as at present constituted was a fairly enjoyable thing. That illustrious, if out-of-the-world township, Doppersdorp, might not have been precisely the locality he would have chosen as an abiding place; but even it contained compensating elements.

Chapter Eight
Concerning the Chase

"Well, you two Sabbath-breakers!" was Grace Suffield's laughing greeting to her husband and guest on the following morning, as she joined the two on the *stoep*, where they were cleaning and oiling a rifle apiece preparatory to the day's doings. "So you're not to be persuaded into abandoning your wicked enterprise?"

"It's the only day a poor hard-worked Civil Servant has the whole of, Mrs Suffield," answered Roden.

"Oh yes! I daresay. As if you couldn't have as many days as you chose to ask for. But come in now. Breakfast is ready."

They entered, and were immediately beset by the glum face and wistful entreaty of the eldest hopeful, begging to be allowed to come too.

"Not to-day, sonny; not to-day," answered his father decisively. "You can go out any day; you're not a hard-worked Civil Servant. Besides, we shall hardly get anything; we're only going just for the sake of the ride. Where's Mona?" he added. "Late, as usual?"

"Oh yes. We needn't wait for her."

Well that they did not, for breakfast was nearly over when she sailed in, bringing with her—surprise; for she was clad in a riding habit.

"Hallo, young woman! What's the meaning of this? Going to ride into Doppersdorp to church?" sang out Suffield.

"Not to-day, Charlie. I'm going to see you and Mr Musgrave shoot a buck."

"Eh!" said Suffield, with a blank stare at Roden.

"Oh, you needn't look so disappointed, or you might have the civility not to show it. I'm going with you, and that's all about it," said Mona, with nonchalant decision, beginning upon her tea.

"Well, upon my word! But we are going into the very dev—er—I mean, all sorts of rough places, right up among the *krantzes*. Who on earth is going to look after such a superfine young party as you?"

"Wait until somebody is asked to. Meanwhile, I flatter myself I'm old enough and ugly enough to look after myself."

"Father, you said just now you were only going for the sake of the ride," struck in the disappointed hopeful.

"Um—yes, did I though? So I did, Frank. I say, though. Did you ever hear the saying, that small boys should be seen and not heard? If you're ready, Musgrave, we'll go round and see about the horses." Under which somewhat cowardly expedient Suffield rose to effect a timely retreat. "By the way, what are you going to ride, Miss Independence?" he added, turning on the threshold.

"Oh, I've arranged all that," replied Mona, indifferently.

And she had. When they reached the stable they found the ragged Hottentot groom already placing a side-saddle upon one of the horses, a steady-going sure-footed bay.

Now, Roden Musgrave was a real sportsman; which, for present purposes, may be taken to mean that, whatever might be lovely woman's place, in his opinion it was not out buck-shooting among more or less dangerous slopes and crags. Nevertheless, when Mona's glance had rested momentarily upon his face as she made her surprising announcement, he flattered himself that he had done nothing to show his real opinion. Nor had he, actively, but there was not the slightest sign of brightening at the news, such as would have lit up the countenance of, say, Lambert, in like case. And this she, for her part, did not fail to note.

It was a lovely morning as they rode forth along the base of the great sweeping slopes, terraced at intervals with buttresses of cliff. The air was as clear and exhilarating as wine, and the sky one vivid, radiant, azure vault. High overhead a white fleecy cloud or two soared around a craggy peak.

"Isn't it a day?" cried Mona, half breathlessly, as they pulled up to a walk, after a long canter over the nearly level plain. "Grace thinks we are an out-and-out sinful trio."

"So we are, Miss Ridsdale," said Roden. "But you're the worst. Woman—lovely woman—is nothing if not devout. Now, with Suffield and myself it doesn't matter. We are the unregenerate and brutal sex."

"Well it isn't our fault, anyway," said Suffield. "We are Church of England, and that persuasion is not represented in Doppersdorp. And, at any rate, it's better to be doing something rational on Sunday than to sit twirling one's thumbs and yawning, and smoking too many pipes all day because it is Sunday."

"Why don't you agitate for a church, then?" asked Roden.

"Oh, the bishop and the dean are too hard at it, fighting out their battle royal in Grahamstown, to spare time to attend to us. There's a Methodist meeting-house in Doppersdorp and a Catholic chapel, as well as the Dutch Reformed church, but we are left to slide."

"Have you been to the Catholic church, Mr Musgrave?" said Mona. "I go there sometimes, though I always have to fight Grace before and after on the subject. But I don't see why I shouldn't go. I like it."

"That surely should be justification enough."

"Don't put on that nasty, cynical tone when I want you to talk quite nicely."

"But I don't know how."

"I'm not going to pay you the compliment you're fishing for. What were we talking about? Oh, I know. Isn't Father O'Driscoll a dear old man?"

"I suppose so, if that means something in his favour."

"That is just like you," said Mona, half angrily. "Why don't you agree with me cordially instead of in that half-hearted way, especially as you and he have become such friends? They are already saying in Doppersdorp that you will soon turn Catholic."

"One might 'turn' worse. But Doppersdorp, as not infrequently happens, is wide of the mark. When the old man and I make an evening of it our conversation is not of faith, but of works. We talk about fishing."

"What? Always?"

"Always. Don't you know that the votary of the fly when, after long abstinence, he runs against another votary of the fly, takes a fresh lease of life. Now, Father O'Driscoll and myself are both such votaries, the only two here. Wherefore, when we get together, we enthuse upon the subject like anything."

"It's refreshing to learn that *you* can enthuse upon any subject," Mona rejoined.

"Oh, I can. Wait till we get up yonder among the rhybok."

"This way," cut in Suffield, striking into a by-track. "We must call in at Stoffel Van Wyk's. That long *berg* at the back of his place is first-rate for rhybok."

"Most we?" expostulated Mona. "But we shall have to drink bad coffee."

"Well, the berry as there distilled is not first-rate."

"And try and make conversation with the *vrouw*?"

"That too."

"Well, don't let's go."

"Mona, are you in command of this expedition, or am I? The course I prescribe is essential to its success. Hallo! Jump off, Musgrave! There's a shot!"

They had turned off from the open plain now, and were riding through a narrow *poort*, or defile, which opened soon into another hill-encircled hollow. The passage was overhung with rugged cliffs, in which ere and there a stray euphorbia or a cactus had found root. Up a well-nigh perpendicular rock-face, sprawling, shambling like a tarantula on a wall, a huge male baboon was making his way. He must have been quite two hundred yards distant, and was looking over his shoulder at his natural enemies, the while straining every muscle to gain the top of the cliff.

Roden's piece was already at his shoulder. There was a crack, then a dull thud. The baboon relaxed his hold, and with one spasmodic clutch toppled heavily to the earth.

"Good shot!" cried Suffield enthusiastically. "It's not worth while going to pick him up. I wonder what he's doing here all alone, though. You don't often catch an old man baboon napping."

"Don't you feel as if you had committed a murder, Mr Musgrave?" said Mona.

"Not especially. On the other hand, I am gratified to find that this old Snider shoots so true. It's a Government one I borrowed from the store for the occasion."

"Murder be—um!—somethinged!" said Suffield. "These baboons are the most mischievous *schelms* out. They have discovered that young lamb is good, the brutes! Sympathy wasted, my dear child."

But when they reached Stoffel Van Wyk's farm they found, to Mona's intense relief, that that typical Boer and all his house were away from home. This they elicited with difficulty between the savage bayings of four or five great ugly bullet-headed dogs, which could hardly be restrained from assailing the new arrivals by the Kaffir servant who gave the information.

"We'll go on at once, then, Musgrave," said Suffield. "Stoffel's a very decent fellow, and won't mind us shooting on his farm; though, of course, we had to call at the house as a matter of civility."

The place for which they were bound was a long, flat-topped mountain, whose summit, belted round with a wall of cliff, was only to be gained here and there where the rock had yawned away into a deep gully. It was along the slopes at the base of the rocks that bucks were likely to be put up.

"We'll leave the horses here with Piet," said Suffield, "and steal up quietly and look over that ridge of rocks under the *krantz*. We'll most likely get a shot."

The ridge indicated sloped away at right angles from the face of a tall cliff. It was the very perfection of a place for a stalk. Dismounting, they turned over their horses to the "after-rider."

"Hold hard, Miss Ridsdale. Don't be in such a hurry," whispered Roden warningly. "If you chance to dislodge so much as a pebble, the bucks down there'll hear it, if there are any."

Mona, who was all eagerness and excitement, took the hint. But a riding habit is not the most adaptable of garments for stalking purposes, and she was conscious of more than one look, half of warning, half of vexation, on the part of her male companions daring the advance.

Lying flat on their faces they peered over the ridge, and their patience was rewarded. The ground sloped abruptly down for about a hundred feet, forming, with the jutting elbow of the cliff, a snug grassy *hoek*, or corner. Here among boulders and fragments of rock scattered about, were seven rhybok, two rams and five ewes.

They had been grazing; some were so yet, but others had thrown up their heads, and were listening intently.

They were barely two hundred yards distant. Quiet, cautious as had been the advance, their keen ears must have heard something. They stood motionless, gazing in the direction of the threatened peril, their ringed black horns and prominent eyes plainly distinguishable to the stalkers. One, a fine large ram, seemingly the leader of the herd, had already begun to move uneasily.

"Take the two rams as they stand," whispered Suffield.

Crash! Then a long reverberating roar rolls back in thunder from the base of the cliff. Away go the bucks like lightning, leaving one of their number kicking upon the ground. This has fallen to Roden's weapon; the other, the big ram, is apparently unscathed.

"I'll swear he's hit!" cried Suffield, in excitement and vexation. "Look at him, Musgrave. Isn't he going groggily?"

Roden shaded his eyes to look after the leader of the herd, whose bounding form was fast receding into distance.

"Yes, he's hit," he said decidedly. "A fine buck too. He may run for miles with a pound of lead in him, though. They're tough as copper-wire. We'd better sing out to Piet to bring on the horses, and try and keep him in sight anyhow."

The fleeing bucks had now become mere specks, as, their stampede in no wise abated, they went bounding down the mountain-side more than half a mile away.

"Look there, Suffield," went on Roden, still shading his eyes; "there are only the five ewes. Your ram's hit, and can't keep up, or else has split off of his own accord. Anyway, he's hit, and will probably lie up somewhat under the *krantz*."

Away they went, right along the base of the iron wall, which seemed to girdle the mountain for miles. And here Mona's boast about being able to take care of herself was put to a very real and practical test, for the ground was rough and stony and the slope here and there dangerously steep.

Suddenly an animal sprang up, right in front of them, apparently out of the very rocks, at about a hundred yards.

"That's him!" shouted Suffield, skimming past his companions, bent on diminishing the distance to get in a final shot. But this was not so easy, for a full-grown rhybok ram, even when wounded, is first-rate at; and this one was no exception to the rule, for he went so well and dodged so craftily behind every stone and tuft of grass that his pursuer would have to shoot him from the saddle, or not at all. Suffield, realising this, opened fire hastily, and of course missed clean.

"We've lost him!" he growled, making no effort to continue the pursuit.

But the quarry here suddenly altered its tactics. Possibly suspecting danger in front, it turned suddenly, and doubling, shot down the steep slope at lightning speed, and at right angles to its former course. There rang out a heavy report at some little distance behind. The buck leaped high in the air, then, turning a couple of somersaults, rolled a score of yards farther, and lay stone dead.

"By Jove, Musgrave, but you can shoot!" cried Suffield, as they met over the quarry. "Three to four hundred yards, and going like an express train. *Allamaagtag!* I grudge you that shot."

"He's yours, anyhow. First blood, you know."

They examined the animal. Roden's ball had drilled clean through the centre of the heart, but the first wound would have sickened anything less tenacious of life. The bullet had struck far back in the flank, passing through the animal's body. Leaving the after-rider to perform the necessary rites and load up the buck upon his horse, together with the first one, which was already there, they moved up to a snug corner under the rocks for lunch.

"We haven't done badly so far," quoth Suffield, with a sandwich in one hand and a flask in the other.

"We must get one more," said Roden, "or rather, you must. That'll exactly 'tie' the shoot; one and a half apiece."

"Well, and have I been so dreadfully in the way, Mr Musgrave?" said Mona.

"I am not aware that I ever predicted that contingency, Miss Ridsdale."

"Not in words, perhaps; but you looked so glum when I announced my intention of coming, that, like the pack of cards instead of the Testament in the wicked conscript's pocket, which turned the fatal bullet, it did just as well."

"Did I? If so, it was inadvertently. But I daresay my conscience was pricking me in advance over that baboon I was destined to murder. That might account for it."

The fact was that, however dubious had been his reception of the said announcement, Roden was in his heart of hearts conscious that the speaker's presence with them that day, so far from being a drawback, had constituted rather an attraction than otherwise. Indeed, he was surprised to find how much so. When Mona Ridsdale chose to lay herself out to make the most of herself, she did not do it by halves. A good horsewoman, she looked splendidly well in the saddle, the well-fitting riding habit setting off the curves and proportions of her magnificent figure to every advantage. Moreover, she was in bright spirits, and to-day had laid herself out to be thoroughly companionable, and, to do her justice, had well succeeded; and more than once, when the pace had been too great, or the ground too rough, or a dark, haunting terror of her saddle turning had smote her, she had manfully repressed any word or look which might be construed into an appeal for consideration or aid. She had even been successful beyond her hopes, for Roden, silently observant, had not suffered this to escape him, though manifesting no sign thereof. So the trio, as they sat there under the cliff, lunching upon sandwiches in true sportsmanlike fashion, with a vast panorama of mountain and plain, craggy, turret-like summit, and bold, sweeping, grassy slope, spread out beneath and around for fifty miles on either hand, and the fresh, bracing breeze of seven thousand feet above sea-level tempering the golden and glowing sunshine which enveloped them, felt on excellent terms with each other and all the world.

"The plan now," said Suffield, when they had taken it easy long enough, "will be to separate and go right round the *berg*. It is lying under the *krantz* we shall find the bucks, if anywhere."

"Where does my part come in in that little scheme, Charlie?" said Mona. "Who am I to inflict myself upon?"

"Upon me, of course," said Roden.

She shot a rapid glance at him as though to see if he were in earnest, and her heart beat quick. This time she was sure that no dubiousness lurked beneath his tone.

"Just as you like," she rejoined; for her, quite subduedly. Then Piet, the after-rider, having received his instructions—viz., to start off homeward with the two bucks already slain—they separated accordingly.

Chapter Nine
"Love that is First and Last"

"Now you will have to take care of me," began Mona, after some minutes of silence, as they started slowly to ride round beneath the cliff.

"A heavy responsibility for any one man during a whole hour or more."

"You have not found it so hitherto?"

"Oh, then there were two of us. We took the risk between us. Hallo!" he broke off, "that's a fine specimen!"

She followed his upward glance. A huge bird of prey had shot out from the cliff overhead and was circling in bold, powerful sweeps, uttering a loud, raucous scream.

"As good a specimen of a *dasje-vanger* as I ever saw," went on Roden, still gazing upward. "Now, I wonder if a Snider bullet would blow it all to pieces at that distance!"

"You'll never bring it down with a bullet?" said Mona eagerly.

"Not, eh? Perhaps not."

The great eagle, jet black save for her yellow feet standing out against the thick dusky plumage, floated round and round in her grand gyrations, her flaming eye visible to the spectators as she turned her head from side to side. Roden, without dismounting, put up his rifle. Simultaneously with the report a cloud of black feathers flew from the noble bird, who, as though with untamable determination to disappoint her slayer, shot downward obliquely, with arrow-like velocity, and disappeared beyond the brow of the cliff overhead.

"You were right," said Roden, slipping a fresh cartridge into his piece. "I did not bring it down, for with characteristic perversity, the ill-conditioned biped has chosen to yield up the ghost at the top of the cliff, whereas we are at the bottom."

"Oh, can't we go up to it? This is much better game than those poor little rhybok. But, wherever did you learn to shoot like that?"

"We can go up!" he replied, purposely or accidentally evading the last question. "That gully we passed, a little way back is climbable. But you had better wait below. It will be hard work."

"So that's how you propose taking care of me—to leave me all alone? Not if I know it. The place looked perfectly safe."

Safe it was: a narrow, staircase-like *couloir*, consisting of a series of natural steps; the rocks on either side heavily festooned with thick masses of the most beautiful maidenhair fern. Leaving the horses beneath, they began the climb, and after a couple of hundred feet of this they stood on the summit of the mountain.

The summit was as flat as a table, and covered with long coarse grass, billowing in the fresh strong breeze which swept it like the surface of a lake. Around, beneath, free and vast, spread the rolling panorama of mountain and plain.

"Ah! this is to live indeed!" broke from Mona. "I don't know that I ever enjoyed a day so much in my life."

The other did not immediately look at her, but when he presently did steal a keen, but furtive glance at her face, there was something there, which, combined with the tone wherein she had uttered the above words, set him thinking.

"I don't see anything of the *dasje-vanger*," he said, at length; "and yet this is about the place where it should have fallen. It may have fluttered into the long grass, but couldn't have gone far with that bullet hole through it. Now, you search that way, and I'll search this."

For a few minutes they searched hither and thither; then a cry from Mona brought him to her side.

"This is the place," she said. "Look!"

She stood as near as she dared to the brow of the cliff, pointing downwards. On the very verge, fluttering among the grass bents, were several small feathers, jet black, and such as might have come out of the breast of the great bird. Roden advanced to the brink.

"This *is* the place!" he declared, leaning over. "And, look! there lies our quarry, stone dead. The spiteful brute has chosen a difficult place, if not an inaccessible one."

"Where? Let me see. Hold my hand, while I look down, for I don't half like it."

This he did, and shudderingly she peered over. From where they stood the cliff fell for about twenty feet obliquely, but very steep, and grown over with tufts of grass, to a narrow ledge scarcely two feet wide; below this— space. But upon this ledge lay the great eagle, with outstretched wings, stone dead, its head hanging over the abyss.

"I can get at it there, fortunately," muttered Roden.

"What are you going to do?"

"I'm going down to pick up the bird."

"You are not."

He stared.

"But I want it," he urged. "It is too fine a specimen to be left lying there."

"Never mind; you can shoot another. Now, don't go, don't!"

Again he recognised the expression which came into her face, as with startled eyes and voice which shook with the very *abandon* of her entreaty, she stood there before him. What then? He had seen that look in other faces, but what had come of it!

"I am going down," he repeated.

"You cannot; you shall not. It is too horrible. You will be killed before my eyes. Won't you give it up because *I* ask you?"

"No."

There were men who would have given a great deal to have heard Mona Ridsdale speak to them in that tone, who would willingly have risked their lives, rather than have refrained from risking them, at her request. This one, however, answered short and straight and with brutal indifference, "No."

They looked at each other for a moment, as though both realised that this was a strange subject for a conflict of will, then she said,

"So you will not give it up?"

"No. It is an easy undertaking, and for me a safe one."

She turned away without another word, and he began his descent.

This, however, was less simple than it looked, as is usually the case, or rather, so appallingly simple that a slight slip, or the loosening of a grass tussock, would send the average climber whirling into space. But Roden Musgrave was an experienced hand on mountains, and thoroughly understood the principle of distributing his weight. In a very short space of time he was standing on the ledge, and had picked up the dead bird.

"I can't throw it up," he cried, for the benefit of his companion, who, once he had began his descent, had not been able to resist watching its progress, and lying flat on the brink was marking every step. "It's too heavy. I shall have to sling it around me somehow."

"Make haste and come out of that grisly position," was all she replied.

And her definition of it was not an unmerited one. The ledge was hardly wide enough to turn upon, and from beneath they had both seen the great rock wall, in its unbroken smoothness, considerably upwards of a hundred feet in height.

Then with the dead eagle slung around him, he began his return, inch by inch, step by step, holding on by every tuft of grass or projecting stone, carefully testing each before trusting any portion of his weight to it—she the while watching every step with a fearful fascination.

All of a sudden something gave way. One moment more, and he would have been in safety. Roden felt himself going—going. Still, with consummate presence of mind, he strove to distribute his weight. All in vain. He could not recover his lost footing. He was sliding with increased momentum, sliding to the brink of the terrible height.

Mona's blood turned to ice within her. She was too stricken even to shriek, in the unspeakable horror of the moment. Her fingers dug into the ground, instinctively clenched, as she lay there, gazing down, an appalled and powerless spectator.

He, for his part, did not look up. The dust and stones slid in streams from beneath him and leaped over the ledge into space—then his descent stopped. He seemed to be flattening himself against the height, clinging for all he knew how. And then, as if to add to the gloomy depression of this horrible peril, there stole up a dark, misty cloud, spreading its black wings around the summit of the mountain, shedding a twilight as of fear and disaster. Mona found her voice.

"Oh, try and rest a little while and collect yourself," she said; "then make another attempt!"

"I can't move," came the response; "and—I can't hold on here much longer. I believe my left wrist is broken. I am suffering the torments of hell."

Mona was almost beside herself. Roden Musgrave was in a bad way indeed when such an admission could be wrung from him.

"Dear, don't give up!" she cried, in a wail of despairing tenderness, such as had never been wrung from her lips before. "Make one more effort;

this time, because *I* ask you. A yard or two more, and I shall be able to reach you."

Was this the woman who had stood shrinkingly to gaze over the brink, and had quickly retreated with a shudder? Now, as she lay there, extending her arm down as far as it would go, in order to afford him the necessary hand-grasp, all fear on her own behalf seemed to have left her. But the man, flattened against the face of the cliff with the dead eagle slung to his back, seemed not able to move, and as she had said, it was but a yard or two farther.

But the effort must be made. Roden was only resting for one final struggle. It was made. Reaching upward he grasped the extended hand, then let go again.

"Hold it! hold it!" cried Mona, appalled by the awful whiteness which had spread over his face, evoked as it was by the agony he was suffering.

"No, I won't, I should only drag you down."

"You would not. I am very firm up here," she replied. "I can hold you till—till help comes."

He wriggled up a little higher, then with his uninjured hand he grasped hers. A sick faintness came upon him. The world seemed to go round. The brink of the cliff, the brave, eager face and love-lit eyes, the swaying grass bents, now rimy with misty scud, all danced before his vision. He felt cold as ice, that deathly numbness which precedes a faint. But for the strong, warm clasp of the hand which now held his, Roden Musgrave's days were numbered. Well indeed was it for him, that the splendid frame of its owner was not merely the perfection of feminine symmetry, but encased a very considerable modicum of sheer physical strength.

"Roden, darling!" she murmured. "Save yourself if only that you may do so through me. You have surprised my secret, but it shall be as though you had not, if you prefer it."

It was a strange love-making, as they faced each other thus, the one overhanging certain death, the other raised entirely out of her physical fears, resolute to save this life, which after all might not belong to her. Thus they faced each other, and the dark whirling blackness of the glooming cloud lowered thicker and thicker around them.

"Let me go, Mona!" he gasped forth wearily, in his semi-faint. "I may drag you down. Good-bye. Now—let go!"

She almost laughed. The strong grasp tightened upon his hand firmer than ever.

"If you go, I go too. Now I am going to shout. Perhaps Charlie will hear." And lifting up her voice she sent forth a long, clear, ringing call; then another and another.

No answer.

Then, as the minutes went by, the bolt of a wild despair shot through Mona's brave heart. Strong as she was, she could not hold him for ever, nor was he able, in the agony of his broken wrist, to raise himself any farther. Her brain reeled. Wild-eyed with despair she strove to pierce the opaque grey curtain which was crusting her face and hair with rime. It was winter, and this table-topped mountain was of considerable elevation. What if this thick chill cloud was the precursor of a heavy snowfall? Charlie, acting on the idea that they had missed each other in the mist, might have gone home. Every muscle in her fine frame seemed cracking. The strain was momentarily becoming greater, more intense, and again she sent forth her loud, clear call, this time thrilling with a fearful note of despair.

It was answered. Eagerly, breathlessly she listened. Yes—it came from below the cliff. Charlie had arrived at the spot where they had left their horses. She shouted again. The answer told that he was climbing the gully by which they had ascended.

"Do you hear that? We are safe now. A few minutes more, and Charlie will be here."

"It is you who have done it, Mona," he murmured.

Then she spoke no more. Now that succour was near at hand, she found herself actually revelling in the position, and a delight in making the most of it while it lasted was qualified by the agony Roden was suffering, as also by a strange feeling of jealousy that she had not been able to carry out the rescue alone and unaided; of resentment that she should be driven to call in the help of another.

"That's it, is it?" said Suffield, prompt to master the situation at a glance. "Now, Mona, I'll relieve you of this amount of avoirdupois, and when you have rested for a minute you hold on to me for all you know how, and I'll lug him up in a second."

The while he had got hold of Roden by the hand and wrist; then in a trice had, as he said, dragged the sufferer over the brink and into safety, for he was a powerful man.

"So that's what it was all about?" he went on, as he cut loose the dead eagle. "The *dasje-vanger* nearly revenged itself. How do you feel, Musgrave, old chap?"

"Like an idiot," said Roden faintly, as he took a liberal pull at the flask the other had been swift to tender him, and began to feel the better therefor. "I never could stand being hurt. Though hard enough in other ways, anything in the way of pain turns me sick. But, Suffield, if it had not been for Mona I should have been a dead man."

"Oh, 'Mona,' is it?" thought Suffield, with an internal grin. Then aloud, rather anxiously, "Anything else besides the wrist?"

"I've banged up a knee a good bit; but I expect it's only bruised. Now we'd better start. I seem to be getting all right."

He was ghastly pale as he tottered to his feet, evidently still in great pain.

"No, never mind," he went on; "I don't want any help, I can walk all right."

But as they began the descent of the gully, Suffield, carrying both rifles and the dead eagle, leading the way, he felt faint and dizzy. In an instant Mona's hand had closed upon his. Hitherto she had stood silently aloof in the revulsion of feeling. He was safe now. The words which had been wrung from her by the extremity of his peril must be regarded as unsaid. So she resolved—but was it a revolution that came within her power to keep? The volcanic fires of her strong, passionate, sensuous temperament had lain dormant beneath an egotistic and inconsiderate vanity, had lain dormant, unknown even to herself. Now they were to burst forth with a force, and to an extent, unsuspected by herself, and as startling as they had been hitherto unknown. But on one point there was no room for any more self-deception. Whatever half-truth there might have been in Grace Suffield's oft-uttered prediction, now it had become all truth. Mona realised that her tarn had indeed come—for good and for ill, for once and for ever.

Chapter Ten
"I Have Won You!"

The alarm and concern felt by Grace Suffield on the return of the trio, Roden with his arm in a sling, and looking rather pale and, as he jocosely put it, interesting, almost beggars description; and the way in which her concern found expression in rating, womanlike, the person whose chief *raison d'être* was to be rated—viz., her husband, was beautiful to behold.

Why had he allowed his guest to ran such risks—to go into dangerous places by himself? He could not be expected to know the country as they did; and so on, and so on. And Roden listening, stared and then laughed—first, as he looked back to a few experiences of "dangerous places" that would make them open their eyes wide did he choose to narrate them; secondly, at the idea that he needed to be taken out in leading-strings. And this idea brought him promptly to Suffield's aid. The accident was his own fault entirely, he declared, and it was lucky it was no worse. And then, glad of the opportunity, he launched out at length upon the topic of Mona's courage in the emergency, and how he owed his life entirely to her. A new light seemed to dawn upon Grace as she listened to this recital, and she glanced narrowly at Mona, who, however, lost no time in taking herself out of the room, remarking rather petulantly that there was no need to trumpet her praises quite so loudly.

Roden's injuries, when carefully examined, were found to consist of a severe sprain of the left wrist, which was not broken as he at first believed; a bruise on the side of the head, which had had not a little to do with his incapacitation at the time of the occurrence; and a contused knee. He vigorously, however, opposed the idea of sending for Lambert. The whole thing was simple enough, he declared. A mere question of bandages and fomentation. He would be all right in the morning.

"You ought to say, 'See what comes to wicked people who go out buck-shooting on Sunday,' Mrs Suffield," he concluded.

"I won't strike a man when he's down," she answered. "I'm waiting until you're well again. Then the lecture is coming. Don't flatter yourself you are going to escape it."

The bandaging and fomentation were most effectually carried out. Strangely enough, however, Mona held aloof. She seemed in no way anxious to do anything for the sufferer now. She was abnormally silent, too, throughout the evening; but that might be due to reaction from the shock and fright she had received.

Although at bedtime Roden had made light of his injuries, yet they were sufficiently painful to keep him awake during the best part of the night. After a couple of hours of unrestful slumber he started up, feeling feverish and miserable. A burning thirst was upon him, together with a strange sinking sensation, begotten of the constant throbbing of his sprained wrist, and the dull, dead ache of his bruised knee. He would have given much for some brandy-and-water, but it was unobtainable by any means short of disturbing the household in the dead of midnight, and this he did not care to do. Stay, though! There was his flask. It might still contain a little of the ardently desired stimulant. Quickly he found it, and a shake resulting in a grateful gurgle, announced that it was nearly half full.

But alas for the uncertainty of human hopes! The stopper was jammed, and flatly refused to be unscrewed. With both hands he might have managed it, but with the use of only one the thing was impossible. In vain he tried every conceivable device for holding the flask, while with his uninjured hand he twisted frantically at the stopper. It would not yield.

"Tantalus, with a vengeance," he growled wearily. "If it were made of glass instead of this infernal metal, I'd knock the head off."

Faint and sick, he staggered back to bed, feeling about as miserable as a man can under the circumstances. It was a cool night, almost a cold one, still, in his feverish unrest, Roden had thrown the window wide open. As he lay, he could see the loom of the great hills against the star-gemmed vault, which was cloudless now, and there floated ever and anon the cry of a night-bird, or prowling animal from the wild mountain-side. The sight, the sounds, carried his meditations back to the strange and well-nigh tragic events of the day. A kind of fate seemed to have overhung them from the very beginning. Why had Mona suddenly and unexpectedly insisted upon joining the party? But for her, he would have met with a terrible death, crushed to atoms at the foot of the great cliff. There had been no exaggeration in his statement to that effect, and now, lying there in the darkness and silence of night, when the mind, in a state of wakefulness, is most active, he realised it more fully than ever. But for her strong courageous handgrip, he could not have maintained his position two minutes. Had she been of the kind of women who faint and scream, and altogether lose their heads, his fate had been sealed. But no. She had behaved grandly, courageously, heroically. Was it ruled that her fate was to be bound up with his? he wondered, as he reflected upon the strangely spontaneous manner in which her secret had escaped her. And here the inherent cynicism, the verjuice drop of suspiciousness engendered by a life of strange experiences, injected itself upon his reflections, and he began steadily to review all the circumstances of their acquaintanceship.

He remembered how she had first attracted, then repelled him; how she had first been disposed to make much of him, only to turn suddenly, in the most capricious and irresponsible manner, to lavish her favour upon Lambert. Well, that had in no way troubled him. Lambert was a newer arrival; Lambert was young, and he himself was not exactly young, but a tolerably jaded and experienced victim of circumstances; and while disliking him, never for a moment had he dreamed of regarding the doctor in the light of a rival. He had merely stood by and watched this new development of her preferences with a whole-hearted amusement not undashed with contempt. To-day, however, his eyes were opened. She had merely been resorting to the stale device of playing off Lambert against himself. But now—? The better, truer, nobler side of Mona's nature had flashed forth in that moment of peril. She had displayed a glimpse of her true self in yielding up possession of the secrets of her innermost heart; and up till that day he would not have believed that she had a heart.

But the enlightenment? What was to be the upshot of it? She had saved his life—could she not therefore claim it? *Would* she not therefore claim it? And at the thought his mind stirred uneasily. For he did not return her love.

How should he? Again drawing upon the stores of his experiences he could recall that same look in other eyes, could recall even the same utterances—the latter far more impassioned, far more self-oblivious than hers had been—all perfectly genuine at the moment. *At the moment*! For how had it ended? A year or two of absence, of separation—new interests surrounding—the gradual dimming effects of time, and all that warm, real, live passion had cooled down into the dry ashes of worn-out memories— had faded into extinction. How should he, we repeat, credit with any more lasting properties the fervour of this latest instance?

He tossed restlessly from side to side, the same feverish thirst tormenting him. Suddenly his room grew light—he could distinguish objects quite plainly. The moon had risen, suffusing the heavens and the black loom of the mountain-top across the vista of the open window with golden light. Wearily, hopelessly, he flung himself out of bed and made another attempt at unscrewing the flask. Once more in vain. Well, he did not want to disturb the household, but even consideration had its limits. He would go and knock up Suffield.

Sick with pain and exhaustion, he made for the door; but before he reached it, to his surprise it opened—opened softly.

"Roden, darling! Where are you?" whispered a voice.

"Good God!—Mona!" was all he could ejaculate, in his unbounded astonishment.

"Something told me you were in pain, and wretchedly ill," she whispered, her voice shaking with a thrill of tenderness. "And you are. I came to see what I could do for you."

"Just this, Mona," was the firm reply. "Go back to your room at once. Good God! Only think! Supposing any one were to hear you! Heavens! it would be too awful."

In the light of the newly risen moon he could distinguish the soft, velvety gleam in her eyes, that wondrous kindling of her face into a love-light which rendered it strangely beautiful. She wore a white clinging dressing-gown, which set off the lines of her splendid form, and as she stood thus before him, Roden Musgrave would not have been human if he had remained unmoved.

"Mona, Mona, why are you doing this?" he whispered, his voice slightly thrown off its balance. Then encircling her with his uninjured arm, he kissed the lips uplifted to his. And at the same time, while her eyes closed, and she nestled against him with a long, shuddering sigh of contentment, he recognised that on his part this was not love.

"But—how selfish I am, keeping you standing like this!" she said suddenly. "I can tell by your very voice that you are in pain."

"I am that. But go back at once to your room."

"Not yet. I am here now; and I want to do something for you, and I will."

"Then see if you can unscrew this infernal flask. I've been trying hard at it all night, but can't do anything with only one hand."

She took the recalcitrant flask. A firm hold, a vigorous grip with her strong, lithe fingers—the stopper came off in the most provokingly easy manner.

"Ah, I feel better now!" he said, after a liberal admixture of its contents with a little water. "And now, Mona, having done guardian angel to very considerable purpose, you must go."

"Not even yet. I am going to do guardian angel to more purpose still. You must try and get some sleep. You are hot and feverish; but see, I have brought a fan. I am going to sit by you and cool your forehead. You will soon drop off then."

"Mona, you are too self-sacrificing," he whispered. "Do you think I could sleep knowing the ghastly risk you are running? Now, to please me, do go back at once. It is still safe, but you can't tell how long it may remain so. One of those brats of Suffield's might wake at any moment and yell, and set the house generally agog. Go while it is safe. You have already done a great deal for me, and I feel immensely the better for it."

But his adjurations fell on deaf ears, and he was really feeling very feverish and exhausted; far too much so to continue to urge the point. So she sat by his bedside, softly fanning his burning and aching brow, and presently he dropped off into a delicious state of restfulness and ease, such as he had not known since first receiving his injuries. Was it the helplessness engendered by weakness and suffering and exhaustion that rendered his mind more amenable to her sway? Was there a languorous, all-pervading mesmerism in the very force and power of her love, which drew him beneath its spell in spite of himself? Whatever the cause, he was soon sleeping soundly and peacefully.

For upwards of an hour Mona sat there watching him, but he never stirred. At last she rose, and gazing intently for a few moments upon the sleeping face, she bent down and imprinted a long kiss upon the unconscious forehead.

"Darling love—*my* love! I have won you from Death, and I claim you," she murmured passionately. "You *shall* be mine. You *are* mine."

And still turning to look at him as though she could not tear herself away, she moved to the door, and was gone—gliding forth as softly and silently as she had come.

Chapter Eleven
"I Hold You!"

On the morning following his misadventure Roden Musgrave was far too bruised and feverish to undertake the journey back, and accordingly a note was sent in to his official superior asking for a day's leave, which missive Suffield undertook to deliver in person, and supplement with his own explanations; and not only was the application readily granted, but Mr Van Stolz, full of concern, must needs ride out with Suffield in the afternoon to see his damaged subordinate, and to impress upon the latter that he was not to think of returning until he felt thoroughly able to do so.

"Don't you break your neck about anything, Musgrave, old boy," he said, on taking his leave. "We shall manage to get along all right for a day or two. I can put Somers on to copy the letters, and even to write some of them. When a fellow is bruised and shaken about, he wants to lie quiet a little. I wouldn't mind swapping places with you, to have Miss Ridsdale as a nurse," he added waggishly, as Mona appeared on the scene. "Take care of him, Miss Ridsdale; good men are scarce, at any rate in Doppersdorp. Well, good-bye, everybody; good-bye, Mrs Suffield. Suffield, old chap, give us a fill out of your pouch to start on; mine has hardly enough in it, I find, to carry me home."

And amid a chorus of hearty farewells, the genial R.M. flung himself into his saddle and cantered off townwards.

"What a delightful man Mr Van Stolz is!" said Mrs Suffield, gazing after the retreating horseman.

"I agree entirely," assented Roden. "And now I shall feel bound to go back to-morrow, if only that one is sensitive on the point of seeming to take advantage of his good-nature."

"Well, wait till to-morrow comes, at any rate," rejoined his hostess. "Meanwhile, whatever you have to suffer you have richly deserved, mind that. Wicked people, who break the Sabbath, are sure to suffer. I told you I had a severe lecture in store for you when you were well enough, and now you are."

"Then all I can say is the moral you want to draw is no moral at all, or a very bad one at best," laughed Roden. "For I am 'suffering' for it in the shape of indulging in the most delicious and perfect laze, and, better still, being made such a lot of, that I feel like Sabbath-breaking again, if only to ensure the same result. For instance, it's rather nice sitting here taking it easy all day, and being so efficiently taken care of."

"Ah, you didn't find it such fun in the night, when you couldn't unscrew the flask top. Do you know, I'll never forgive you for such foolishness. The idea of being afraid to knock anybody up!" said Mrs Suffield tartly.

He dared not look at Mona. The joke was too rich, and he was inwardly bursting with the kind of mirth which is calculated to kill at the longest range of all—mirth of a grim nature, to wit. He had told his tale of Tantalus, when asked what sort of a night he had had. The sequel to that episode, we need hardly say, he had not told.

"I never like disturbing anybody's hard-earned slumbers. Don't you think I'm right, Miss Ridsdale?"

Mona, who was watering flowers just below the *stoep*, thus appealed to, looked up with a half-start. He had relapsed into the formal again. But she understood.

"It depends," she said. "No one would grudge being disturbed for such a reason as that."

There was a caress in the tone, latent, subtle, imperceptible to any but himself. The voice, the attitude, the supple grace of her beautiful form, emphasised by the occupation she was then engaged in, as indeed it was in almost any and every movement she made, stirred him with a kind of enchantment, an enchantment that was strange, delicious, and rather intoxicating. He thought that he could lie there in his long cane chair, amid the drowsy hum of bees and the far-away bleating of sheep upon the sunny and sensuous air, and watch her for ever.

But a very much less soothing sound now rose upon the said air, in the shape of a wild yell, quick, shrill voices, and a series of vehement shrieks.

"My goodness! what on earth are those children about?" cried Mrs Suffield, springing to her feet, and hurrying round to the back of the house, where the tumult had arisen, and whence doleful howlings and the strife of tongues still continued to flow.

"They've been scratching each other's faces, or got stung by a bee, or something of the kind," said Mona composedly, her figure drawn up to its full height in an attitude of unconscious grace, as she rose from her occupation and stood for a moment with one foot on the lower step of the *stoep*, looking half over her shoulder at the flower bed, while calculating how much more watering it needed. Then she put down her watering can and came up the steps.

"Hot for the time of year," she said, sweeping off her wide-brimmed straw hat, which became her so well, and drawing off her gardening gloves.

"Perhaps; but you looked such a vision of coolness, moving about among the flowers, that it made up a sort of Paradise. Now, come here, Mona, and talk to me a little. There is something about you which is the very embodiment of all soothing properties."

A soft light grew in the hazel eyes. With a pleased smile she stepped to the head of his couch, and placing a cool hand on his forehead for a moment, bent down and kissed him.

"You poor invalid!" she murmured, looking down at him tenderly. "I feel responsible for you now—you seem to belong to me—until you are well."

"In that case I am in no hurry to get well, dear," was the answer, in a tone strangely soft as coming from the man who, not much more than a dozen hours ago, had been haunted by an uncomfortable dread, lest she should claim and exact this very proprietorship in the life she had saved. And indeed, if Roden Musgrave was in some danger of losing his head it is little to be wondered at—remembering time and place, his own weakened but restful state, the warm and sensuous surroundings, and this magnificent creature bending over him, with the light of love in her eyes, a caress in every tone of her voice. With all his clear-headedness and cynical mind, his was by no means a cold temperament; indeed, very much the reverse. But what kept his head level now was the ice-current of an ingrained cynicism flowing through the hothouse temperature, the intoxicating fragrance of what was perilously akin to a long-forgotten feeling—namely, love. The present state of affairs was delightful, rather entrancing; but how was it going to end? In but one way of coarse—when she was tired of it, tired of him. This sort of thing never did last—oh no! He had seen too much of it in his time.

To his last remark, however, Mona made no direct rejoinder. There was nothing unduly effusive about her, and this went far towards enhancing her attractiveness in his eyes. In the tendernesses she showed him there was nothing overpowering, nothing of gush; and keenly observing her every word, every action, he noted the fact, and was duly impressed. About her there was no jarring note; all was in perfect harmony.

A Veldt Official A Novel of Circumstance | 79

Now sitting there they talked—talked on matters not limited by the boundaries of the district of Doppersdorp, or those of the Cape Colony, but on matters that were world wide. And on such Mona loved to listen; for of the world he possessed far greater knowledge than falls to the lot of most men, and of human nature likewise—this man who at middle age, for some reason, found himself compelled to fill a position usually occupied by youngsters starting in life. But while delighting in his keen, trenchant views upon men and matters, Mona failed not to note that there was one subject upon which he never dwelt, and that subject was himself.

"You give me new life," he said, dropping his hand upon hers as she sat beside him. "What a pity we did not come together before—before I had made such a hash of the old life. But," with a queer smile, "I am forgetting. You would have been in short frocks then, in very short frocks. I am quite an old fogey, Mona."

"You are not," she replied closing her fingers upon his with something of the strong supple grip, in which she had held his hand when to relax her grasp of it meant death—his death. Now it seemed as though that same grasp was in accord with her thoughts, holding him back from something else; from the Past, perhaps; from the effects of that marring of his life to which he had made so direct an allusion. Yet to what nature did that allusion apply? A chill seemed to hold her heart paralysed for the moment. Should she ask him? Here was her opportunity. Would it not be wiser—nay only in accord with the very first dictates of common sense? Confusion to the dictates of common sense! Let the past take care of itself, and the future too. The present was hers—was theirs, and the present was very good, very fair, very sunny; glowing, golden, enchanting with the strong wine of love. Do we refuse to take advantage of a cloudless day because the morrow may be black and overcast, and furious with rolling thunder and volleying squalls of rain? No. The cloudless day was hers—was theirs. Let the morrow take care of itself.

"You are nothing of the sort," she continued. "So I give you new life, do I? Roden dear, I might say the same—I love to talk with you like this. I knew I should from the first moment we met. And Grace had said the very thing you have just said of yourself, when I asked her what you were like, 'Quite a middle-aged fogey.'"

"Oh, the mischief she did! I shall have a row with Mrs Grace about that."

"Ah, but wait. She only said she had heard so, for she hadn't seen you, and of course had no idea of your identity with her knight errant during the post-cart journey. In the latter capacity you should have heard all the nice things she said about you. Charlie declared himself sick of the very name of the unknown, only he didn't know it, for that she seemed to have got him on the brain; which I amended by saying I rather thought she had got him on the heart. Then Grace was cross."

Roden laughed queerly.

"Well, Mona, and so ought I to be, for that was the very way to prepare me the most unfavourable reception. Come now, isn't it an invariable rule that the individual much-belauded in advance turns out a sure disappointment on acquaintance?"

"It is the rule. But every rule has its exceptions."

"Meaning me. Thank you. I can appreciate the delightfulness of the compliment, for I believe it is sincere. Nevertheless, my dear child, you will find few enough people to agree with you—precious few."

"I know, Roden. You are one of those whom a few people would like very much indeed, but whom the general run would rather dislike."

"Perhaps. And now, disclaiming all idea of being ungracious, how about quitting so profitless a topic as my own interesting self? And indeed here comes that which will assuredly divert all attention from it, or any other matter."

Mona subtly and imperceptibly somewhat widened the distance between them—indeed, in whatever situation or dilemma she had been surprised, she might have been trusted to get out of it gracefully—just as the whole brood came running up. Their mother, having pacified the disturbance, and forthwith taken the whole lot for a walk, whence they were returning.

"Well, what was all the grief about?" said Mona. "Frank, I suppose, teasing somebody again."

"It wasn't me, Cousin Mona," said the accused urchin resentfully. "I had nothing to do with it. Bah! It was Alfie, as usual. He'd let another slate pencil fall on his toe, I suppose." And the wrongfully accused one marched off in high dudgeon.

Roden laughed unrestrainedly.

"That fellow's a wag, by Jove!" he said. "You'll have to entrust him with the care of the humour of the family, Mrs Suffield," as Grace came up, and was delighted with the answer repeated for her benefit, for Frank was rather the favoured one in her eyes, probably because he was the most mischievous and unmanageable. The while Mona was watching with a jealous eye lest any of the small fry in their restive exuberance should come near imparting to the invalid chair a sudden and unpremeditated shake.

"I saw that, Mona," he said, after they had all cleared out. "I have seen the same kind of watchfulness, though in different ways, before, since I have been lying here. Believe me, dear, I keenly appreciate it."

Her eyes lighted up. She seemed about to reply, but thought better of it and, said nothing. In her heart, however, she was echoing gladsomely that resolute, passionate murmur which she had uttered in the silent midnight as she stilled his pain in slumber by the very restfulness of her presence; echoing it with such a thrill of exultation as to tax all her powers of self-command, "Darling love—my love—you are mine! I have won you, and now I hold you!"

Chapter Twelve
Breathing of War

The town of Doppersdorp was in the wildest state of excitement and delight. We say delight, because anything which tended to stir the soporific surface of life in that centre of light and leading was productive of unqualified satisfaction, and the tidings which had now arrived to effect this result were of no less importance than the announcement that hostilities had actually broken out in the Transkei.

At the street corners men stood in knots discussing the news; in the stores, swinging their legs against counters, and blowing out clouds of Boer tobacco, this was the topic of conversation, while semi-nude and perspiring natives rolled the great wool bales in and out, and those at the receipt of custom dispensed wares or took payment in listless, half-absent fashion; of such enthralling interest was the turn events had taken. But it was in the bars, where glasses filled and emptied to-day with abnormal briskness, that the Doppersdorp tongue wagged fast and free.

True, the Transkei was a long way off, but the ruction would never stop there. It was bound to spread. The Gaikas and Hlambis in British Kaffraria were bound to respond to the call of the Paramount Chief. The contagion would spread to the Tembus, or Tambookies, within the Colonial territory, and were there not extensive Tembu locations along the eastern border of the district of Doppersdorp itself? This was bringing the matter very near home indeed. The enterprise of Doppersdorp was aroused, its martial spirit glowing at white heat. This indeed has its disadvantages; for at such a rate, with every citizen burning to sally forth and distinguish himself in the tented field, Doppersdorp would be deserted; and it was clear that with all its male inhabitants occupied at a distance, subduing Kreli and his recalcitrant Gcalekas, that illustrious Centre of the Earth would be left at the mercy of all comers.

At Jones' hospitable board, as the shades of evening fell, the tidings were discussed far more eagerly than the painted yellow bones and rice to which allusion has been made. From Jones himself in the pride of office at the head of the table, through the manager of the local bank and a storekeeper's clerk or two, down to the journeymen stonemasons and waggon-maker's apprentices at the lower end, the same topic was on every tongue. The Gcalekas had attacked and routed a strong body of Police in the Transkei, and had killed several men and an officer. Indeed, the Inspector in command had undergone a narrow escape, having turned up at a distant post the following day without his hat. Such was the report which had come in; every word of which, especially the latter circumstance, being implicitly believed by the good burgesses of Doppersdorp—probably because Inspectors in that useful force, the Frontier Armed and Mounted Police, did not at any time, when on duty, wear "hats." But it was all the same to Doppersdorp.

"Any more news, Mr Musgrave?" said Jones eagerly, as Roden entered.

"If there is, for the Lord's sake wait until we've all done," struck in Emerson, the bank-manager, who was of a grim and sardonic habit of mind. "As it is, we can scarcely any of us get through our oats, we are all in such a cast-iron hurry to start for the Transkei."

"There isn't any."

"Good. Then we needn't prepare for the siege of Doppersdorp just yet—we poor devils who can't rush forth, to death or glory."

"We could hold out for ever, for we should always have Emerson's Chamber of Horrors to fall back upon," laughed a storekeeper opposite; "that is, if it is not already dead of fright from the *schrek* it got last week."

While others guffawed the bank-manager grinned sourly at this allusion. It happened that the premises provided by his Corporation for the housing of its employé's contained a spacious backyard, with an open shed and some stabling. This yard Emerson had seen fit to populate with the most miscellaneous of zoological collections, comprising a young *aasvogel*, two or three blue cranes, an owl and a peacock, besides a few moulting and demoralised-looking fowls, a tame meerkat, a shocking reprobate of a baboon—whose liberty and influences for evil were only restricted by a post and chain—several monkeys; item, Kaffir curs of slinking and sinister aspect; and, in fact, innumerable specimens which it was impossible to include within the inventory with any degree of assurance, for the inhabitants of the menagerie were continually being added to, or disappearing, the latter according to the degree of watchfulness maintained on their own part, or that of aggression on the part of their neighbours. This collection was known in Doppersdorp as Emerson's Chamber of Horrors.

"You weren't here that night, Musgrave. Away at Suffield's place, I think," went on the last speaker, with a wink at the others. "Well, some fellow got hold of a cur dog in the middle of the night, and thinking it had escaped from Emerson's Zoo, reckoned it a Christian duty to restore the wanderer. So he took it to the street leading to the bank-yard, tied one of those detonating squibs to its tail, and headed it for the gate. Heavens! you never heard such an awful row in your life. Phiz! bang! went the cracker, and there was the mongrel scooting round and round the yard, dragging a shower of fiery sparks, and every now and then bang would go the cracker like pistol-shots. You can just imagine the result. Everything kicked up the most fearful clamour—the dogs, and the cats, and the peacock, and the *aasvogel*, and the monkeys, all yelling at once; and the more they yelled, the more the thing seemed to bang off. It didn't hurt the cur though, for it was a long way behind him. But the best of the joke is that the banging of the crackers started the notion that the town was being attacked, and Lambert and some other fellows—myself among them—came slinking up gingerly with rifles. The squib had long burnt out by the time we got there; but the sight that met our astonished gaze was magnificent. Emerson was standing on the top step, clad in a short nightshirt, emptying all the furniture into the backyard, and, oh, his language! Well, I can only give you some idea of it by saying that it was so thick, that the chairs and tables he was hurling out stuck in it. They could not even reach the ground."

"It looks as if you had a finger in the pie yourself, Smith. You seem to know all the details," said Roden. But Emerson merely grinned sardonically. He did not think the recital worthy of comment. Besides, he had heard it so often.

"I? Not I. It only came in at the end, as I tell you," protested Smith.

At this juncture a note was handed to Roden. It was from Mr Van Stolz.

"Here's a little more excitement for Doppersdorp to-night," he said when he had read it. This was its burden. "One hundred and thirty-three mounted men from Barabastadt, *en route* for the front, are passing through. They will camp here to-night. Volunteers and band going out to meet them. Tell everybody."

This was news indeed. In a trice the table was deserted. All who heard it were in first-rate spirits—those who belonged to the newly formed Volunteer Corps, because it would afford an opportunity for a lively game of soldiers; those who did not, because it meant more excitement; while Jones, perhaps, was in the greatest feather of all, for would there not be a prodigious consumption of drinks in the bar of the Barkly Hotel that night? Roden and Emerson were left alone at the table.

"Come along, Musgrave; let's go and have a look at these Barabastadt heroes," said the latter. "The Light Brigade is nothing to them. We are sure to see some first-class fun."

"Not a doubt of it," was the reply. And these two cynics rose to follow the crowd, but with a different motive.

Outside, in the starlight, the whole town was astir. The two men who had ridden in to notify the arrival of the main body were beset with questions—and drinks. What was the latest news? Had Government called out the burgher forces all round; and if not, would it do so? and so on, and so on. Meanwhile the local Volunteer Corps, numbering about sixty of all ages and sizes, had formed in marching order, and, preluded by a few sounding whacks on the big drum, the band struck up, and that doughty force marched off to quick-step time, accompanied by a moving mass of humanity; even the inhabitants of Doppersdorp and its 'location'—some mounted, the larger proportion on foot, amid much talking and laughing and horseplay and lighting of pipes; a squad of ragged Hottentots of both sexes, chattering shrilly, hanging on the rear.

"Here come the heroes," said Emerson satirically, as, having proceeded about a couple of miles out, a cloud of dust and a dark, moving mass came indistinctly into sight. So the Volunteers were halted, eke the civilians; and Mr Van Stolz rode forward to welcome the leaders of the Barabastadt burgher force. Then forming into double file, and preceded by the band, the new arrivals resumed their route for Doppersdorp.

Now it happened, unfortunately, that the band of that doughty corps, the Doppersdorp Rifles, was very much in a state of embryo. Its available repertory consisted of but two tunes, for the simple reason that it knew no others. These were "Silver Threads among the Gold," and "Home, Sweet Home." The first of these had enlivened the march out; and although it was started to effect the same object on the return, it would hardly last over a space of two miles. The second, though admirably adapted for welcoming the returning warriors, as a God-speed was clearly inappropriate. The bandmaster—our old acquaintance Darrell, the attorney, whose persuasive eloquence had not availed to save the mutton thief, Gonjana, from the just reward of his crime—was in a quandary. Music they must have. Music, however, repeated to endless iteration point, was worse than none. In this dilemma he bethought him of "John Brown." Surely they could play that. The inspiration was a happy one. No sooner did the well-known air bray forth—with somewhat discordant and quavering note it is true—than those nearest seized upon the chorus. It was caught up, and went rolling along the whole line. Then it occurred to somebody to alter the chorus to, "We'll hang old Kreli to a sour apple-tree," an idea received with the wildest enthusiasm, having the effect of redoubling the volume of song.

But over and above, and throughout all this rollicking jollity, there was a something about those dark, mounted figures filing here in the starlight, the gleam of the rifles, the sombre simplicity of the accoutrements, which told of the sterner side, which seemed to bring home the idea that this was no toy contingent; that the task of quelling a barbarian rising was not all child's play; and that some of these might return with strange experiences, while some might not return at all.

The weeks that followed this passing through of the first band of defenders of their "'arths, 'omes, and haltars," as their spokesman graphically put it, while returning thanks for attentions received during their sojourn, constituted to Doppersdorp a period of the most delicious excitement. Some startling and sensational report was of daily occurrence, borne mainly on the wings of rumour and impracticable of verification; for that centre of light and leading, notwithstanding its huge importance in the eyes of its citizens, was yet without such an appliance of modern civilisation as telegraphic communication. What mattered it, as long as things were kept alive, and everybody was happy! And things were kept alive, with felicitous results.

To begin with, there arose a large demand for firearms of all sorts. This was good for the store-keepers, who booked orders briskly; for the farmers in the district, Dutch or English, were particular as to the quality of their weapons, but at such a juncture were less so as to price, as long as they were quickly supplied. So great consignments of rifles, and revolvers, and ammunition, were slowly and painfully hauled up to Doppersdorp from the coast ports, and the store-keepers were delighted. So too were the Government contractors; for the Barabastadt contingent, if the first, was not the only mounted corps to pass through the township; and did not each and all require forage and rations? Again, the martial ardour gave a great impetus to volunteering, distinctly to the advantage of the community at large, in that this afforded an outlet to the energy of the local youth in the shape of nightly drill. Such energy was thus better utilised than in taking to pieces the vehicle of some unoffending and unsuspecting Boer, which might be standing unguarded in an accessible spot, or in balancing a beam of wood with murderous intent against the door of some unpopular citizen. Further, it had the effect of drafting off a selection of volunteers upon active service to the front; and, whereas these consisted, for the most part, of rowdy and undisciplined spirits, their absence could not fail to be advantageous to Doppersdorp. What their respective commanders at the seat of hostilities might be found to say on the matter was another thing. Even the Resident

Magistrate was bitten with the prevailing death-or-glory fever; but alas! his proposal to turn out the whole district under arms at a day's notice, and to lead it in the field at the service of the Government, provided the requisite leave and Field-commandant's commission were granted him, was met on the part of that unappreciative entity with signal ingratitude—curt refusal, to wit, bordering on snub. So having sworn for about five minutes upon the perusal of this reply, cheery little Peter Van Stolz lounged into the clerk's office, and having once more delivered himself of his views on the subject of Governments in general, and that of the Cape Colony in particular, lighted his pipe, declared that he didn't care a damn, and that, after all, he'd be the same sort of fool to fling away his accumulation of leave, roughing it in the veldt and feeding on unvaried trek-ox, instead of running down to Cape Town to put in the same period among his relatives and old friends, and having a particularly good time. So he stayed at home perforce, to direct the labours of the Civil establishment of Doppersdorp, which, in common with most of those in the border districts, were very much swelled by the outbreak of hostilities.

Chapter Thirteen
A Limed Twig

Roden Musgrave was seated in his quarters, alone.

It was a dark, rainy night, and rather a cold one. A snug wood fire burned in the grate, and this he was loath to leave, although it was midnight. Yet the one more pipe which he had humbugged conscience into allowing would prove the necessary sedative, was smoked out; nor was there any further excuse for delaying bed. But just as he had risen to carry out that intent, there came a knock at the back door.

The house, we have said, was a very small one—two rooms in front, which its occupant used as bedroom and sitting-room, and two at the back, a storeroom and kitchen, which latter he did not use, save for stowing away lumber. There was no hall, the front and back doors opening into the sitting-room and kitchen respectively. Towards the latter Roden now made his way, wondering the while; for the knock had been a stealthy one—unmistakably so—and of as faint a nature as was compatible with audibility at all. As he paused to listen, Roden laughed grimly to himself, deeming he could guess at its meaning, and was just turning away to leave it unanswered when it was renewed, and with it, his ear caught the bass whisper of a Kaffir voice. This put another light on the case. A matter of duty might be involved.

"What do you want?" he said, suddenly throwing open the door. The light he carried fell upon the form of a single Kaffir, who grinned.

"Why, it's Tom," went on Roden, holding the lantern to the man's face, and recognising a particularly civil and good-humoured store-boy, in the employ of the abominable Sonnenberg. "Well, Tom, what the deuce do you want with me at this time of night? If it's another complaint against your *baas*, you'll have to wait till to-morrow, my boy."

This, in allusion to a past case of disputed wages, wherein Tom had summoned his Hebraic employer before Mr Van Stolz, and had won. Yet Sonnenberg had still kept him in his service. Now the Kaffir grinned and shook his head. It was no case of the kind, he declared, and his manner was mysterious. Would the *baas* let him come in for a little while and talk, and above all things shut the door? He had something very important to discuss.

Roden, impressed by the mysteriousness of his manner, complied without hesitation. Yet, in all probability, it was some commonplace trifle. Natives were prone to blow out a frog into an ox.

Seen in the light of the room, this mysterious midnight visitor was a sturdy, thick-set Kaffir, of medium height, with a peculiarly open and honest countenance. He was dressed in the ordinary slop clothes of a store or stable-boy, more or less tattered, and more or less ingeniously repaired with twine or bits of *reimpje*. He was a Tembu from Umfanta's location, and knowing this, Roden was prepared for some revelation of a possibly startling character—if true, that is—for there were extensive Tembu locations in the district, which, though peaceful on the whole, were not impervious to the wave of restlessness contingent upon hostilities in the Transkei, and radiating among the tribes within the Colonial borders.

No revelation of a dark and bloody plot, however, no intelligence of a secret midnight rising, was destined to fall upon Roden's official ears; for speaking in Boer Dutch with a little indifferent English, his knowledge of both tongues being too limited to admit of the vast amount of parable and circumlocution wherewith he would have approached the subject in the fluency of his native language, the Kaffir readily came to the point.

The *Baas* had a gun, not the beautiful new one which he took out to shoot bucks with, explained Tom, with avidity, but an old one which loaded in the old-fashioned way. The *Baas* wanted to sell that gun, yet no one would buy it. He, Tom, had seen it more than once on *Baas* Tasker's auction sale, but nobody would bid so much as a pound for it.

Now, all this was perfectly true. Roden did own such a piece, a heavy, old-fashioned muzzle-loader, double-barrelled, an excellent gun of its day, and shooting true as true could be with rifled or shot-barrel. But its day had gone by. While there was a brisk demand in Doppersdorp at that time for firearms, such must be breech-loading weapons; at muzzle-loaders nobody would so much as look.

Even as the other had said, he had made more than one attempt to sell that gun, but in vain. A Boer now and again would pick it up as it lay in Tasker's auction room, and after eyeing it critically for a moment would replace it with a melancholy shake of the head. "A good *roer*" would be his verdict, his experienced eye taking in that much. "An excellent *roer* in its day, but its day is passed; we want breech-loaders now." While some Briton of the baser sort, being a shop-boy or waggon-wright's apprentice, with no experience whatever of firearms, would superciliously bid "five bob for the old gas-pipe." Remembering all this, Roden stared; for now he began to see through this fellow's drift.

"The *Baas* wanted to sell this gun," continued the Kaffir, but nobody would offer anything for it. Now, why not sell it to him? No one would be any the wiser. It was night; no one had seen him come in. That was because he had come so late, and on a dark and rainy night.

"And what do you want to do with it, Tom, when you've got it?"

Au! It was not for himself. He was not in want of it. It was for his brother. He would give ten pounds for it, ten pounds down in hard cash.

"That settles the matter, then," said Roden, decisively, intent on drawing him on. "If it's for your brother, I won't have any more to say. Two in an affair of this sort is one too many. But three; oh no! That deal won't come off, Tom."

The Kaffir looked profoundly disappointed, then muttered a little. Then he said, with a shamefaced laugh—

"It isn't for my brother, *Baas*. That was not true. I want the gun myself. I will give twelve pounds for it. See, I have the money."

He produced a tied-up rag, an exceedingly dirty and greasy rag, and shook it. The result was a clinking sound, the solid, metallic, comfortable clink of hard gold.

"I can't sell it to you, Tom," said Roden again, thinking the while how he only wished to the Lord he could.

"Look, *Baas*," went on the Kaffir eagerly, his fingers quivering nervously in their hurry, as they struggled with the knots of the greasy rag. "Here is the money; I will give it all. I will give fifteen pounds for the gun; but I can offer no more, for I have no more. Here it is—all."

He had untied the knots of the rag, and was eagerly counting forth its contents upon an old packing case. There they lay, fifteen bright sovereigns, glittering in the light of the lantern.

Roden Musgrave wanted money just as much as the average junior Civil Servant habitually does, or for the matter of that the average senior either. He had repeatedly tried to realise the old muzzle-loader, and had at length given it up in disgust. As the other had said, nobody would bid so much as a pound for it. And here was an offer of fifteen sovereigns for it—fifteen sovereigns in hard cash, lying there to be picked up. Of course he knew perfectly well what it was wanted for, but equally did he know that the average Kaffir is so wretched a shot as to be unable to hit a house, unless he were first dropped down the chimney thereof. If this fool, bursting with martial ardour, chose to steal away and join the hostile tribes, he was pretty certain to get bowled over himself, but it was a hundred to one against him being marksman enough to inflict any damage upon the Colonial ranks. Indeed, were it otherwise, what was it to him, Roden? No unit of the extremely limited number in whose well-being he had the faintest interest was at that moment at the front, or was in the least likely to go. "Why should he refuse a good offer, a very good offer?"

He looked at the fifteen sovereigns lying there in a row, and he looked at the Kaffir who was eagerly watching him. The boy had an open, honest face, and might safely be trusted to hold his tongue. Besides, Kaffirs usually keep faith in a fair and straightforward transaction between man and man. A moment more, and he would have concluded the deal, when his instincts of prudence and caution put before him one consideration. He dared not.

Looked at from the lowest grounds, he dared not. Were the transaction brought home to him, it would mean his ruin. He would be ignominiously dismissed his post, and probably proceeded against criminally, into the bargain: result, a ruinous fine, the possibility even of imprisonment without that doleful option. Even the suspicion of such a thing would mean a bar to all his official prospects. Fifteen golden sovereigns were good, but not good enough as a set-off against so tremendous a risk, and the same would apply to six times the sum were it offered.

"I can't do it, Tom," he said, his mind now as thoroughly made up as ever it had been in his life. "The fact is, I dare not."

The other was woefully disappointed. He could not offer more for he had not another farthing in the world. As for any risk he said, he would rather die than break faith by letting out one word on the subject of the transaction to any living soul—white, black, or yellow. Let the *Baas* cast his eyes backward. Who was there who could say anything against his character, or adduce one single instance of him ever having broken his word? He had been long in Doppersdorp, and had served more than one master; yet no one had anything but good to say about him, except, perhaps, the one he was then serving.

"I tell you, Tom, I can't do it," repeated Roden. "Do you know you are asking me to break the law, which I am here to help administer? Look, now! If you can get the magistrate to give a permit, it's another thing, though even then I should bring a pretty hornet's nest about my ears were the matter known. But you are about as likely to find a magistrate who will consent to sign a permit for the sale of a gun to a Kaffir, while there's war going on between the Colony and that Kaffir's fellow-countrymen as you are to find a Bushman Hottentot who would refuse to get drunk if you made him a present of a bucketful of brandy. I can't do it, Tom. Wait, though; why don't you get your master, *Baas* Sonnenberg, to sell you one. He'd sell you a grin of a sort—or his immortal soul, if he's got one—for fifteen sovereigns cash. Try him. Besides, I should be delighted to have him chocked into the *tronk* for 'gun-running.' Try him, Tom," he went on, banteringly sneering, as he saw the other start and his face light up eagerly at this reference to Sonnenberg. "Well now, that deal is off, clean off, you understand, so pick up your money again and clear, for it's getting precious late. Here's a bit of tobacco for you."

The Kaffir picked up the coins in silence, tying them up in the greasy rag as before.

"Fifteen pounds is a lot of money," went on Roden, "and to-morrow you'll be only too glad I didn't take your offer when you find you still have the money, instead of going away to get shot like the rest of your people."

"*Au!*" exclaimed the fellow half to himself, yet looking up briskly as though a new and bright idea had dawned upon him in the words. "When I find I still have the money," he repeated, as he took his leave.

But as he went out, a dark figure, which had been crouching outside against the door throughout the whole of this interview, rose and glided rapidly round the corner, unperceived by Roden Musgrave.

Outside, in the black and rainy street, the Kaffir made his way swiftly towards his master's dwelling, which was odd at that time of night, because he slept at the town location half a mile in the contrary direction, and as he went, closely followed by the stealthy figure, he kept repeating in his own language the words: "When I find I still have the money in the morning... Only too glad. *Yau!*"

With this ejaculation he stopped short. In the dark and rainy silence the full force of the idea flashed upon him in all its brightness. The result was that he turned, and bent his steps in the direction of his habitual sleeping quarters.

Hardly had he gone ten yards before he was met by the figure which had been following him. Seen in the gloom it was that of a man, a Kaffir, of about the same height and build as Tom himself. The latter, however, showed no surprise or alarm at this sudden meeting, for the two walked together side by side, the low rumble of their bass voices mingling in converse, together with frequent bursts of half-suppressed but clearly inextinguishable laughter.

Now in the office or den devoted to the shadiest of his transactions—and he was wont to deal in some very shady transactions—sat Adolphus Sonnenberg, with an expectant, but very evilly exultant expression of countenance, and this increased as the minutes went by. With him also sat Lambert.

Between them was a bottle of grog, glasses, and a biscuit tin, eke a box of cigars. The expression of Lambert's face was akin to that on the more abominable countenance of the Jew. Both were waiting, for something, for somebody; the most casual spectator might have seen that at a glance.

"Do you think he'll tumble?" the doctor was saying—not for the first time. "Do you think he'll fall into the hole?"

"Tumble? Fall into de hole? I should rather think he would," was the emphatic reply. "These beggarly Civil Servants are all so damn hard up, they'd sell their souls for fifteen pounds. And I know Musgrave would."

"Steady, steady! No names," warned the other, glancing furtively around.

"I don't care a damn. Ha, ha! we shall see who will sing small now! Ha, ha! Musgrave, my boy, we shall see who has de crow this time. We shall see you in your own dock to-morrow, or de next day. Then de *tronk*, for he'll never be able to pay de lumping fine they'll have to put on him; a beggarly out-at-elbows rip, for all de side he crowds on." And the expression on the face of the evil Jew was now simply demoniacal. "That devil, Tom, ought to be back by now!" he went on, glancing again at the time. "A quarter to one, by Jove!"

Both sat on, ill at ease and talking constrainedly, the one gloating over the sure accomplishment of a diabolical revenge, the other anticipating his chances when this all-powerful rival should be once and for all removed from his path. Still the hands of the clock moved on and on; still nobody came.

"I can't stand this any longer," said Sonnenberg at last, jumping from his seat, when nearly another hour had gone by. "Have another liquor, doctor, and then we'll prowl out and see if we can see anything of Tom."

"Is it wise? Apart from the possibility of missing him, is it wise, in view of the tremendous rumpus this affair will make, for us to be seen prowling around together at this time of night? Remembering, too, that Tom is your boy?"

The Jew answered with a snarl of rage, recognising the force of what the other said. Then, after a little further waiting, he could stand it no longer, and the pair sallied forth.

Carefully, in the darkness they reconnoitred Roden Musgrave's modest abode, but all was quiet, all as usual. Then they patrolled the township, no lengthy task. But of the defaulting Tom, not a sign.

"I feel like ripping his black hide off him in the morning," snarled Tom's master savagely. "Well, he may have mistaken my orders about returning to report to-night, and if he's brought the job off all right, that'll put things more than square. And I'm certain he has."

"Let's hope so, anyhow," replied Lambert. And hoping being all they could do for the present, the worthy pair separated for the night.

Chapter Fourteen
Hoist With His Own Petard

When Tom, the store-boy, reached his master's premises at an early hour on the following morning, early as it was, his said master was there to meet him.

"Well, Tom?"

"Morrow, *Baas!*"

"Did you get what you wanted?"

"*Ja, Baas.*"

"You got it all right?"

"*Ja, Baas.*"

Sonnenberg could hardly conceal his delight.

"And, Tom, what did *he* say," with a nod in the direction meant, "when he gave it you?"

"What did he say?"

"Yes, you fool. What did he say? That was what I asked."

"Say? say?" repeated the Kaffir, as though to recollect. "*Au!* he said I would be glad in the morning to find what I wanted most."

"Was that all?"

"*Ja, Baas.*"

"And your brother, Ndimbi, he saw the whole affair?"

"*Ja, Baas.*"

"All right, Tom. Get to your work now," said Sonnenberg, turning away. The bird was trapped now. As pretty a case as ever was proved in broad daylight. It was early yet, but no longer able to conceal his impatience he went to knock up Lambert.

It was close upon the breakfast hour at the Barkly Hotel, and a knot of men were collected on the *stoep* waiting for the bell. There came strolling up Roden Musgrave and Emerson, the bank-manager.

"Wish to the Lord you'd go and shoot some game, Musgrave," the latter was saying. "Jones has been giving us more than enough of his rag yard of late."

"His what?" said a man who was within earshot.

"Oh, old bones, and heads and tails, and all that kind of ill-assorted refuse. Now a young rhybok or so—or a few partridges would come in well."

"Musgrave doesn't give much of his spare time to buck-shooting now. Higher game, don't you know," chaffed another, with what was intended for a very meaning wink.

"Talking of shooting," said Lambert, getting up from where he sat, "I wish you'd lend a fellow one of your guns, Musgrave. I want to go out this afternoon somewhere."

"I've only got two," answered Roden, "and you don't want the old muzzle-loader, I suppose?"

"That's just the one I do want," rejoined the other eagerly. "At least— er—I mean, I couldn't of course think of asking for your other one—your best."

"All right. It's a very true shooter, although, a trifle heavy. Look round at the office about twelve, Lambert, and you shall have it."

"At the office? Is it there then?" quickly asked the doctor, again giving himself away, and causing his precious confederate, who was intently listening, to swear almost audibly.

"You look round about then," was the careless rejoinder.

"What does he mean? What the devil does he mean?" whispered Sonnenberg, excitedly, beckoning the doctor back after the others had gone in. "Tom swears it's all right, yet you're to have the gun about twelve o'clock. Now, I believe he's going to try and get it back again. Yes; that's it. I'll keep an eye on Tom till then and stop that little game."

This the amiable Jew accordingly did. But that sable servitor, though never out of his master's sight, was more good-humoured than ever, and trotted about the store and the yard, doing his work thoroughly and well, and notwithstanding that he never left the premises, by the time Lambert appeared at the public offices, according to direction, Roden reached the gun from the corner—the very weapon supposed to have been sold to Tom. Lambert could hardly believe his eyes. There it was, however; the identical piece. There had been no substitution, as he had at first suspected. Every one knew it; for the peculiar rifling of its long-range barrel was unique in Doppersdorp. No, there could be no mistake.

"I'm sorry, Lambert," said Roden, in the indifferent tone of a man speaking to another whom he disliked but had never quarrelled with, "but I find the old shooter has broken down. It'll want some tinkering before it'll be good for anything."

There could be no mistake as to the truth of this; the locks were off, and Roden seemed to be piecing them together with his hand. Lambert stared. He was lost in amazement. Had not Sonnenberg assured him jubilantly that all had gone well, that the bait had taken, that their mutual enemy was safe within the net? Yet here was the gun still in its owner's possession, and the diabolical plot had clean broken down.

Replying confusedly and at random to certain remarks on the part of Mr Van Stolz, who had at that moment entered, Lambert finally broke away, and betook himself post-haste to his confederate. The latter's rage was a sight to witness. He went out there and then to the yard. Tom was at work in the stable, and alone.

"Tom."

"Baas."

"Didn't you tell me this morning that it was all right—*that it was all right*?" repeated the Jew in his fury hissing the words through his set teeth.

"*Ja, Baas.*"

"But it isn't all right, you *schepsel*!" Then lowering his voice to a whisper, "Where is the gun?"

"*Yau*! What gun, *Baas*?"

Sonnenberg nearly choked with fury, and made a step forward as though to strike the Kaffir. The latter, however, moved not a muscle, standing there as imperturbably as though there were no infuriated white man within a mile of him.

"Look here!" stuttered the Jew, "if you don't drop this infernal fooling I'll—I'll—kill you. Didn't you tell me you had got the gun all right? Didn't you?"

"Childlike and bland" hardly expresses the mild open reproachfulness which sat upon Tom's broad and sable countenance. He shook his head with a pleasant smile.

"Nay what, *Baas*. I said no word about any gun. You asked me if I got what I wanted, and I replied that I did."

The Jew fairly danced; to the vast but veiled amusement of his retainer, who would have a delicious incident to relate from kraal to kraal, from hut to hut, in his wanderings for many a long day; for Kaffirs are keen mimics, and the reproduction of Sonnenberg in his wrath would throw crowds into roaring, rolling, riotous laughter, whenever he should feel like bringing it forth.

"You damnable black scoundrel!" hissed the Jew. "Give me back my money, and then go—g-go to hell."

"Nay what, *Baas*. You gave me some money to buy a gun, and now you ask it back. Besides, I have not got it. My brother Ndimbi is taking care of it."

"I'll have you both in the *tronk* for theft. You'll get five years at least, the pair of you infernal thieves."

"Theft? Thieves?" repeated the Kaffir, in magnificent surprise. "*Au!* You are joking, *Baas*. Did you not give me money to buy a gun with, and tell me even where I could most likely get it? My brother Ndimbi was by, and heard it all. And now you ask for it back again. Nay, *Baas*, I can't return it, for Ndimbi has it. I owe him nearly all of it, so as I could not get a gun I thought I had better pay it."

Sonnenberg turned perfectly livid, and fairly gasped for breath. He saw now how completely he had been done. Tom had not the slightest intention of returning the money. He detested his master, and now here was a glorious chance of being even with the latter for many a past meanness. In all good faith he had intended to make the purchase, and then depart for the seat of war. But Roden's uncompromising refusal, and the words he had used in reference to Sonnenberg, had thrown a new light on the matter. Tom and his brother had talked it over during their walk home, and had concluded to keep the money, fully assured that Sonnenberg would never dare to make a stir about it.

And, in fact, it was so. Standing there, mad with helpless wrath, the shrewd brain of the Jew had already realised that much. If he prosecuted Tom, the other Kaffir would prove being present when the money was given, and for what purpose it was given. Roden Musgrave, too, would testify that the boy had made the proposal to him on the very night, which would be so far circumstantially corroborative. On his side he had only Lambert; but although Lambert had been present at the transaction he understood hardly any Dutch, in which tongue the affair had been negotiated. Besides, Lambert was weak, and a good bit of an ass, and under cross-examination might be counted upon to give himself—to give both of them—away. Again, to substantiate the charge of theft he would have to show how and when he had missed the money, and what opportunity the boy had of appropriating it. Tom was known, too, as a particularly honest and well-conducted boy, while he, Sonnenberg, laboured under the disadvantage of being a very shady sort of customer. Moreover, his hatred of Roden Musgrave was well known—and his vows of vengeance against the latter had been made often and publicly. No, it would never do. The combination of coincidences would have far too fishy a look. Besides, the very suspicion of having endeavoured to supply a native with firearms, no matter with what object, would be more than likely to draw down upon him most unpleasantly practical demonstrations of popular wrath, and that there were many who would be only too glad of a pretext to foment, and take part in such he was well aware. There was no harm in trying a little bluff though.

He might as well have spared himself the trouble. At all his threats and promises Tom merely laughed good-humouredly. Then Sonnenberg, shaking his fist in the boy's face, ordered him to clear out, to leave his service there and then, which request was met with an equable consent, and a demand for wages up to date.

"I'll see you in hell before I'll pay you a cent, you damned black thief," screamed the Jew. "You've robbed me of more than enough already. Get out of this, now, at once, or I'll kick you out."

"*Au!*"

"Do you hear?" screamed the Jew, advancing a step. But the other did not move. He merely reiterated his demand for wages.

"You'll get nothing from me. Now go, before I kick you out. What—you will have it? All right. Take that."

But "that" fell upon empty air. A very ugly look had come into the Kaffir's ordinarily good-humoured face, as he deftly dodged the blow aimed at him. Still, he did not return it. Sonnenberg, reading weakness in this abstinence, rushed at him again.

To assert an intention of kicking a person out of anywhere may constitute a tolerably resonant threat; but to render it in any way an efficacious one, it follows that the kicker must be of a vastly more powerful habit of body than the kickee, of which salutary consideration Sonnenberg had completely lost sight as, foaming with rage, he returned to the charge. Now, Tom was an extremely thick-set, muscular Kaffir, who thought nothing of carrying a muidsack of mealies or other stuff on his back as often as required, in the process of loading or off-loading waggons in front of the store, whereas his employer was weedy and "soft" all through, and took a precious deal more bad liquor than good hardening exercise; consequently, when these two closed, the tussle could have but one result. That result was Sonnenberg on his back in the dust of the yard, and the Kaffir sitting upon him, the while lecturing him on the advisability of promising to refrain from further violence if permitted to rise. This the Jew, at length, help not arriving, had no alternative but to do, whereupon his servitor was as good as his word, and in a trice Sonnenberg was standing upright again, the back of his coat and trousers bearing a strong family likeness to Lot's wife subsequent to her "conversion," shaking his fist wildly, and rolling out curses thick and marvellous in many languages. Then he fished some coins out of his pocket, and flinging them at Tom, ordered him to quit that instant, and that he would want every farthing of it and more to pay the fine that would be put upon him for this assault.

The Kaffir, whose face had resumed its normal good-humour, picked up the money with native imperturbability, and having satisfied himself that it represented every farthing of his wages, coolly pocketed it, and took his departure.

Scarcely were the public offices open than Sonnenberg came rolling in to prefer his charge of assault against Tom, a proceeding which that astute child of nature met by taking out a cross-summons, and in the result both were dismissed before half heard, Mr Van Stolz remarking on the very strange circumstance of Lambert witnessing the affair through a window, and yet not going to render assistance. And Sonnenberg had the pleasure of paying a guinea to the law-agent, Tasker, having—unwisely—employed that astute practitioner, in the hope of rendering Tom's conviction doubly sure.

Tom, however, was the gainer by the full amount of his wages, over and above the sum of fifteen pounds which his ex-master had so generously presented him with, in order to compass an enemy's ruin. Nothing more, however, was said about this, and a few days later he disappeared from Doppersdorp. But greatly did the malevolent Jew rage and swear, as he reflected how he had been done, and, thinking to recognise his hand in the matter throughout, more than ever did he vow the most deadly vengeance upon Roden Musgrave.

Chapter Fifteen
A Shake of the Dice

Time stood not still, even at Doppersdorp, and on the whole it went by merrily. There were always mounted contingents proceeding to the seat of war or returning thence, the latter quicker that they went, as the misanthropic Emerson cynically, but we believe libellously, put it. This kept things lively, especially for such good Doppersdorpers as had anything to sell, and was a state of affairs likely to last indefinitely, for, although actual hostilities were confined to the Transkei, Kreli was scotched, not killed, and as long as the Paramount Chief was at large and unconquered there was no telling how far the rising might spread. Indeed the tribes within the Colonial border, Gaikas, Hlambis, and a section of the Tembus, were reported more and more restless, and ominous rumours filled the air, of a preconcerted rising, of signal fires flashing their dread message nightly from the most prominent mountain heights, of war-dances on a large scale, and the sending of cattle away to places of concealment.

For all these alarms, Doppersdorp, secure in its comparative remoteness from the theatre of strife, cared but little. Still, it must draw some entertainment out of the prevailing excitement, wherefore its already existing Volunteer Corps was promptly remodelled, and many recruits poured in. It was a most important institution was this Volunteer Corps, for did it not confer military rank on more than one of the most prominent store-keepers, with whom Solomon in all his glory was not in it, what time these majors and captains were swaggering around in a silver-grey uniform adorned with a shining shoulder strap and a whistle and jingling chain, the while striving hard to be at their ease and yet not stumble over the sabre, which was the proudest adornment of all? Further, did it not form a convenient outlet to the martial ardour of many a waggon-wright's or blacksmith's apprentice, and perchance a shopman or so—hight a store-clerk in local parlance—who, rising suddenly from their hard-earned slumbers, to the sound of a bugle ringing out the wildest of alarm, would fall into rank for a nocturnal forced march along the waggon road, and, hearts beating high with heroism, effect the surround and capture of three or four amazed and perfectly harmless natives camped for the night? Then it was deemed necessary to place a guard over the nocturnal safety of the township, with periodical patrols, during which some warrior might perchance distinguish himself by spitting with his bayonet a more rashly aggressive cur than ordinary. These heroes found nightly asylum in a "guard-house," devoted to the custody of many fleas and a few insignia of the order of Good Templars, to whom the structure in fact belonged; and when upon his round of inspection one of the newly gazetted majors or captains aforesaid heard the ringing order, "Guard—turn out!" why then indeed he felt he had not lived in vain. But that doughty corps the Doppersdorp Volunteer Rifles had its uses, and in the fulness of time its band learned to play more than two tunes.

Further, there would appear sporadically in Doppersdorp at this time certain warlike individuals, arrayed in nondescript uniform, high boots, and very bright spars, eke helmet, immaculately white. These warriors would swagger around, tapping the boots aforesaid with a chowrie—a weapon which, for some occult reason, they much affected—and giving out darkly that they were recruiting for native levies, of which they were to have command when a sufficient number of recruits had been raised. In some few instances these "colonels," as the misanthropic Emerson termed them, were *bond fide*, and able to produce credentials at the public offices empowering them to receive rations and assistance in the furtherance of their plans. Of such, the above misanthrope would predict that, the next time they were heard of would be in connection with "cooking" pay-sheets, or something of the kind. And, alas! for the frailty of human nature, ministering to the triumphant laughter of the cynic, in one or two such instances Emerson's sardonic predictions were fulfilled.

Turning from public affairs to those of private persons, Mona Ridsdale's behaviour, as regarded a certain one of such private persons, had become, all things considered, strange. We say "all things considered" advisedly, because the change in her demeanour was unaccountable, to say the least of it. The sweet, subtle charm of those days of convalescence, seemed, with the accomplishment of that convalescence, to come to an abrupt termination. Her patient fairly off her hands, Mona seemed to encase herself with a cold reserve, as in a shell. Had she mistaken her feelings after all? Had she given herself away too much, and now desired to draw back before it was too late? Her behaviour puzzled those around her. Suffield noticed it, but like a wise man held his tongue. His wife noticed it, and being a woman, did not hold hers. She remonstrated, giving her relative what she termed a little bit of her mind—result, anger, and a lively passage of arms.

There was one whom this behaviour did not puzzle, and that was Roden Musgrave himself. To him it afforded no surprise; for it was precisely such as might have been expected. The only thing that did surprise him was that he himself should have been temporarily lulled into believing in, not so much the genuineness, as the durability of the feeling Mona had shown; that a cool, practised head, such as his, should have been thrown off its level, even for the moment. He had been ill, which might account for it. Well, he was well now, and awakened from that fantastic dream. Mona had undoubtedly saved his life by her cool, ready courage; yet now he hardly felt grateful to her. Possibly, she herself regretted she had done so now, in that the failure of her efforts would have spared her the small degree of vexation which might attend her sudden change of front. Those words, those acts at the time, had been wrung from her by a certain warm, hysterical superabundance of feeling which must find an outlet somewhere. This it had found, and the volcano was quiescent again—until the advent of some fresh cause of eruption; some *freak* cause, be it understood. Clearly hers was one of those surcharged, excitable temperaments, which, craving a new sensation, will conceive an ardent passion, flaming with fiercely consuming brilliancy and heat, only to sink, like a burnt-out building, as quickly as it flared—to die into dark, cold, unprofitable ashes. He had seen such before—not once, nor twice—and the outcome was ever the same.

He remembered his first instincts with regard to her. Why had he suffered himself, even partially, to lose sight of them? Well, fortunate that it was only partially, and there was no harm done. Yet, after all, he was human.

Few and far between now were his rides out to Suffield's farm, and then for a visit of but short duration. His spare time he spent mostly in buck-shooting among the mountains, and his ordinary working time was now, since the war, pretty full. For her part, Mona seldom came into Doppersdorp.

But if Roden's visits to the Suffields were infrequent, the same could not be said for those of Lambert. Quick to perceive the state of affairs, the young doctor judged his own opportunity to have come round again, and was not slow to improve it. If Musgrave was out of the running, now was his own time to chip in, as he put it; and truth to tell, his efforts in that direction were received very graciously.

"I'm surprised at you, Mr Musgrave," said Mrs Van Stolz one evening. "You are letting the doctor cut you out most completely."

"Cut me out?"

"Yes. He is always at the Suffields' now. I thought when you were invalided there, your chance had come, but you seem to have thrown it away again, somehow."

"My chance! My dear Mrs Van Stolz, what on earth 'chance' are you alluding to?"

"Oh, how very innocent we are!" she rejoined archly, while her husband chuckled. "Well, it may not be true, but they say Miss Ridsdale and the doctor take moonlight walks together."

This shaft, meant to be deadly, seemed to fly utterly wide. Roden, who was engaged lighting his pipe at the moment, continued to do so with unmoved countenance and hand as steady as a rock.

"And if it is true, I don't see what earthly business it is of mine," he answered, in so perfectly equable a voice as to astonish his hearers. "Really I have no more right to challenge Miss Ridsdale's acts than, say, Lambert himself has."

"Perhaps he has by this time, Musgrave," struck in Mr Van Stolz mischievously.

"In that event, still less can it be any business of mine," was the perfectly good-humoured rejoinder. As a matter of fact, Roden disliked this form of chaff; but he liked the utterers of it more than a little, and knew that they meant it as nothing but sheer fun; moreover, he was far too thorough a student of human nature to afford prominence to a distasteful topic by appearing to shrink from it. Nor was his unconcern in any degree forced. It was not in him to be jealous of Lambert, or indeed, of anybody. Jealousy was a word which, done into a definition, meant going begging to a given person for a consideration beyond what that person felt—a despicable lowering of himself, towards which Roden Musgrave felt no temptation. He rated himself at far too high a value for that.

If Mona's apparently unaccountable conduct were of set design, if her distant reserve were intended to draw him the more ardently to her feet, to bind him more closely in her chains, if she were really making use of the rather stale and transparent trick of playing off one against the other, why then she was indulging in a very risky game. With nine men out of ten that sort of thing might answer; with this one, never. He was beginning to think of her with something of aversion, bordering on contempt.

So the weeks went by and Christmas had come, but there was a sullen, boding, uneasy feeling; for the restlessness of the border tribes had been growing apace. Doppersdorp, however, managed to make merry, after its kind, and got up rifle matches, and athletics, and balls, of a mixed and republican sort, and the band made a nocturnal round from house to house, discoursing from its limited repertory much bad music, which grew worse in proportion to the cumulative hospitality of those serenaded. Then vast numbers of natives swarmed in from the locations, drawn by a big tab of the worst kind of grog, broached by Jones of the Barkly Hotel, and on tap for all comers; and by midday the township was overran by such racing, whooping blackfellows as were not too drank for that form of seasonable exuberance; yet in view of the novel reflection that Christmas occurred but once in a year, these and other little irregularities were winked at.

Then, with the closing days of the year, the thunderclap burst, the pent-up electricity so long in the air blazed forth. The tribes within the border had risen, and that with a spontaneity and fixity of purpose which should have been gratifying to all overs of the thorough-going, and the hot, Southern midsummer nights of the closing year echoed the fierce thunder of the war-song, where crowds of excited savages danced fiend-like in the lurid glow of flaming homesteads.

The news of the outbreak, grim as it might be, was received by Doppersdorp as by no means an unmixed evil; for did it not mean more excitement, and was not excitement a most blessed boon to that slow-going community? First, there was the delight of discussing the news, and, on the part of each citizen, the inestimable joy of carrying on the whole campaign exactly as it should be carried on—from Jones' bar-room. Then, there was the exhilaration of many Volunteer parades, and the sounding of wholly strange and uncalled-for alarms at all hours of the day and night, not to mention midnight swoops into the town location in quest of potential spies, and the rude disturbance of the slumbers of its population, resulting in two or even three decrepit and otherwise inoffensive natives, unable in the scurry and alarm to produce their passes, being marched off to gaol, triumphantly and securely escorted by some three-score fixed bayonets. All these, and many more doughty deeds of valour, were achieved by the armed manhood of Doppersdorp daring those trying times.

Perhaps, however, the acme of jubilation was attained when the Burgher law was put in force in the district. Then a monster meeting was convened, and to it swarmed a vast number of armed Boers of all sorts and sizes, and the atmosphere of the Court-house was terrific, even with all the windows wide open, in its combined reek of humanity and general unwashenness, and honest sweat, and gun-oil, and seldom-changed corduroy, and hoarse, uncouth, clamouring voices. For the enthusiasm was intense, so that, with all the excuses and prayers for exemption, Mr Van Stolz had no difficulty in enrolling a good solid command some three hundred strong, and when this was mustered on the following day in front of the Court-house, and marched out, duly armed and mounted, to the usual accompaniments of the Volunteer band and "God save the Queen," and the whole population of Doppersdorp, reputable or ragged, yelling itself hoarse with patriotism and enthusiasm, all felt that very great things had been done, and that even a Kaffir war had its bright side—for those who stayed at home.

After this, things quieted down a little, and just then, on Mr Van Stolz' recommendation, Roden found himself placed on the Commission of the Peace, and nominated Assistant Magistrate; for the district was a large one, and there was a periodical Court held at an outlying township.

"You see, Musgrave," said the former, "it will get you on quicker, even if it means precious little more pay. You can go and hold the periodical Court at Luipaard's Vlei, and that'll get you into practice; and then, if I go on leave, as I want to do soon, I'll make them appoint you to act here. It all helps you on, betters your chances. I like to help a fellow on all I can, when he's the sort of fellow to help; and I've often been able to. The only one I'm damned if I've been able to help is myself," he broke off, with a jolly laugh, careering away down the Court-house to stop somebody passing in the street, whom he more or less particularly wanted to see.

Just before these matters took place, Mona's demeanour underwent a further change. She showed a disposition to revert to the old state of things. Yet the bird was too scared to return at once to the lure. As we have said, Roden Musgrave set too high a value upon himself to give vent to so commonplace and vulgar an emotion as jealousy, and as a matter of fact he had felt none. But he had undergone a mental shaking up, so to say, had had time to pull himself together and think. Yet, we know not now it happened, so imperceptibly, so gradually, but the sweet, subtle spell was beginning to weave itself around him again, and the worst of it was he knew it.

He began to find reason in her former reserve. She had said too much at first. She wanted an opportunity of drawing back. She had mistaken her own feeling, her own heart—had been too impulsive. Well, such an opportunity she should have, and accordingly he had left her undisturbed. And now once more she had broken down the barriers, and how it came about he knew not any more than we do. Her image began to hover around him during his official work, to accompany his long solitary rides, taken for purposes of business or pleasure. Yes, the chains were weaving themselves about him again, and somehow or other he seemed not unwilling that they should.

In due time glowing reports arrived as to the doings of the Doppersdorp Burghers, who had met the enemy more than once with dire results to that barbarous entity, both in slaughter and the capture of numerous head of cattle. Presently, too, arrived, on a few days' leave, our old acquaintance, Darrell, the attorney, whose practice being of a precarious, not to say hand-to-mouth nature, might profitably be neglected for a while in favour of the more certain pay of a Field-captain in the Doppersdorp Burghers, to which office he had been duly elected. He, his leave expired, returning to the field of glory, pressed Roden to accompany him to the Main Camp for a few days, and go on a patrol or two, and see something of the war; which invitation Roden, with the sanction of his official superior—for there was a lull in the extra work just then—decided to accept.

Chapter Sixteen
"Within the Veins of Time"

"Then you won't give up going to this wretched war?"

"Well, no. You see I've got it all arranged now. I can't throw up the plan. Besides, I want to see how they work a war of this kind. My mind is made up."

No one knew better than Mona that when the speaker said his mind was made up, why, then it *was* made up. Still she continued to plead.

"Ah, don't go! Besides, it is a paltry affair, and hardly worth a man's while to touch. It is quite sickening to hear these Doppersdorp 'heroes' brag. They go away nearly three hundred strong, and come back again with three men slightly scratched, and talk big about 'terrible hand-to-hand conflicts lasting all day,' 'assegais flying as thick as hail,' and so forth. Dear, don't go; I have a presentiment something will happen."

Roden laughed.

"How does that pan out for a lovely bit of feminine consistency?" he said. "After labouring to show that the whole thing is child's play, and the merest walk over, you adjure me not to go, on the ground that I shall come to grief if I do."

"And that day on the cliff; was my warning right or wrong then?"

His face softened at the recollection. For a moment they stood gazing into each other's eyes.

"You saved a strange sort of life, Mona."

Instead of replying, she moved to the window and declared, in a commonplace way, that there was a big dust-cloud whirling up the road; for the place they were in was a certain staring and fly-blown apartment, which did duty for "drawing-room," at the Barkly Hotel, and now steps were approaching the door. The latter opened, admitting the head and half the person of Sonnenberg.

"Beg pardon. Thought Suffield was here." Then meaningly and with an impudent grin, "Sorry to interrupt. 'Two's company,'" and the door closed behind him.

"See now," went on Roden, "it isn't a case of going to the front. I'm only going to ride over to the Camp for three or four days. It's a good opportunity. Darrell wants to go too, so we are going together."

"Only two of you?"

"Oh, we may pick up others on the way."

"And what about getting back?"

"Must chance that."

Mona looked as if about to renew her pleading, but just then Suffield's voice, and the voices of others were heard coming up the stairs; for it was just before the one o'clock dinner at the Barkly. So she whispered hurriedly:

"Dear, you will ride out with us this afternoon?"

"H'm! there are a lot of things to be put straight, and I start the first thing in the morning. I don't like to shirk. What'll the Chief say?"

"Mr Van Stolz? I'll ask him myself."

"No, no," he said, laughing at her eagerness, and locking his fingers in hers, for her hands had crept into his after the interruption on the part of the objectionable Jew. "I'll work it somehow. But, dear, you must make Suffield wait, for I can't in conscience shut up shop this side of four, at the earliest."

This side of four! Why, she thought about seven was going to be the hoar named. Make Suffield wait! Why, Charlie should wait till midnight if she chose. And the voice, the tone! When Roden spoke thus he could make her do whatever he liked. Was he beginning really to care a little for her at last? Her heart beat tumultuously as she went down the stairs, laughing and talking commonplace with her companion. Could he ever love her as she loved him? Was it not all a one-sided affair and therefore despicable? Ah! but—she told herself—there was a possibility; and this it was which underlaid the strange wellspring of new-born happiness which had sprung up in Mona's heart, completely transforming her. Now and then a corner of the curtain which hid his inner nature was lifted—lifted just enough to convince her that the capabilities which lay behind were those which it was in her power to call into play, and that the day might come when her love should be returned tenfold.

After all, thought is swift, and can cover a great deal while the thinker is descending one flight of rather rickety and not very well-swept stairs.

Nothing was said during dinner about Roden's impending trip, for an absence from duty of upwards of two days was irregular, to say the least of it, on any other terms than a formal application to headquarters, which, at that distance from the Colonial Office, would necessitate a couple of weeks' correspondence and a due expenditure of red tape. When Roden returned to the office he found Mr Van Stolz already there, letting off steam in a few harmless "cuss words," for the post had just arrived, bringing with it from headquarters an unusually large batch of circulars, desiring information of no conceivable utility; also some returns.

"Musgrave, old chap, look at all this damn nonsense," said the jolly little R.M., with a mischievous laugh, shoving away the obnoxious papers and lighting his pipe. "What, the devil! do they think we've got nothing better to do—and with all these troops of burghers pushing through to the front, and knocking us up in the middle of the night to find rations for them? These stoopid returns 'll take at least a week of turning out dead-and-buried records to make up."

"Then I won't go down to the Camp to-morrow, sir," said Roden, thinking how he would quietly chaff Mona as being in league with the people at headquarters to knock his trip on the head.

"No, no, Musgrave. It isn't so important as all that. I'll get them together, somehow, and Somers can give a hand. Besides, we needn't hurry. It doesn't do, either, to break one's neck being over zealous. You don't get any the more appreciation for it, or promotion either; at least, that's what I've learnt after my twenty odd years in the Service, though of course it wouldn't do to say that to every sort of a youngster who happened to be one's clerk. And, I say, Musgrave, old fellow, that pony of yours has had quite his share of work of late, after Stoffel Van Wyk's rhyboks. Why not take my horse to go down there on? He's a young horse, but a good one, and he'll stand fire like an armchair, as you know, though he does shy like a fool now and again at a *schuilpaat* (Dutch. The small land tortoise common all over South Africa.) the size of a snail."

"It's awfully good of you, Mr Van Stolz, but—"

"Tut, tut! What's a horse for, if not to be ridden? Any fellow knows he can always have mine when I'm not using him, and I'm not often."

"Rather—why, you keep the whole township going in riding material."

"Ha! ha! I believe I do!" was the jolly reply. "Why, no less than three fellows wanted to borrow Bles to-day, but I thought it might be as well if you took him to go and have a shot at the Kaffirs, instead of your own, Musgrave, so I let him have a rest to-day."

"Well, as a matter of fact, I shall be very glad to accept the offer," said Roden. "My pony is perhaps a little in want of a rest. Upon my word, though, Mr Van Stolz, there may be more good-natured people in the world than yourself, but with some experience of that orb I don't believe there are."

"Pooh, pooh!" laughed the genial little man, not ill-pleased with such a spontaneous outburst on the part of his self-contained, cynical, and generally somewhat unpopular assistant. "Why, man, you'd do such a trifle as that for me, wouldn't you?"

"Rather. But I'll be hanged if I would for the whole of Doppersdorp."

"Ha! ha! But poor old Doppersdorp isn't such a bad place. There are a lot of people in it who are damn sweeps; but I can always pull with everybody—even damn sweeps. When I'm on the Bench it's another thing. I don't care for anybody then. But when you've got to be in a place, Musgrave, you may as well make the best of it."

"And that I flatter myself I do. What with yourselves, Mr Van Stolz, and the Suffields, and one or or two more, I am not particularly discontented with the place."

"Ha! ha! And one or two more!" laughed the magistrate mischievously. "What did the wife say when you first came up here, Musgrave? And wasn't she right? Own up, now. When is it to come off?"

From anybody else this sort of chaff would have more than annoyed Roden—indeed, hardly anybody else would have ventured upon it with him. Coming from whom it did, he merely laughed, and said that, if for no other reason, he did not see how anything real or imaginary could "come off," in the light of the munificent rate of pay wherewith a paternal Government saw fit to remunerate the labours of the junior members of its judicial service. Then he turned the conversation into other channels, and thus, alternately subsiding into silence as the nature of their work required, and smoking a pipe or two and narrating an anecdote as something suggested one to either, this happily assorted brace of officials got through the first half of an afternoon, until the tread of a pair of heavy boots on the boarded floor of the Court-room without was heard drawing near.

"Some confounded Boer, I suppose, who'll extend a clammy paw, and put his hat on the ground and spit five times, preparatory to beginning some outrageous lie," growled Roden, thinking it was about time to take himself off.

"May I come in?" sang out a voice.

"Hallo! It's Suffield. Come in, Suffield!" cried the magistrate, jumping up.

"Busy, I see!" said Suffield, having shaken hands, and looking rather awkward, for what with Mona worrying his life out for the last half hour, and what with the confounded cheek, as he reckoned it, of suggesting that Musgrave should knock off work and come along, he felt himself in that figurative but highly graphic predicament known as between the devil and the deep sea. But the eyes of the most good-natured man in the world read and interpreted his look.

"Going to take him away with you, Suffield?" he said.

"Well—um—ah—"

"Off you go, Musgrave; I expect Miss Ridsdale will comb your hair for you for keeping her waiting, and it's nearly five. And I say, Suffield," he called out after them when they were leaving; "don't let him try to tumble over any more cliffs, eh! So long!" and chuckling heartily, the genial official turned back to light a fresh pipe and do another hoar of his own work, and that of his assistant too.

Ambling along the dusty waggon road which led up to the grassy *nek* about a mile from the township, preparatory to striking off into the open veldt beyond, the trio were in good spirits enough.

"Well, and why haven't you blown me up for keeping you waiting?" said Roden.

"Do I ever blow you up? Besides, you couldn't help it," answered Mona.

"Ah, 'To err is human' says the classic bard. He might have added, 'to blow a man up for what he can't help is feminine.'"

"Don't be cynical now, and sarcastic. And it's our last day."

"Why, hang it, the chap isn't going to be away for a year," cut in Suffield, who was at that moment struggling with a villainously manufactured lucifer match, which gave him rather the feeling of smoking sulphur instead of tobacco. And then there was a clatter of hoofs behind, and they were joined by a couple of Boers of the ordinary type, sunburned and not too clean of visage—one clad in "store-clothes" the other in corduroy, and both wearing extremely greasy and battered slouch hats. These, ranging their wiry, knock-kneed nags alongside, went through the usual ceremony of handshaking all round, and thereafter the swapping of pipe-fills with the male element in the party.

Boers, in their queer and at times uncouth way, are, when among those they know, the most sociable of mortals, and never dream that their room may be preferable to their company; wherefore this accession to the party was heartily welcomed by Mona, for now these two could ride on ahead with Charlie and talk sheep and ostriches, and narrate the bold deeds they had done while serving in Kreli's country, in Field-Commandant Deventer's troop, which had just returned covered with laurels—and dust—from that war-ridden region. But alas! while one carried out this programme to the letter, his fellow, the "store-clothes" one, persisted in jogging alongside of Roden discoursing volubly, of which discourse Roden understood about three words in twenty.

"*Ja, det is reegt, Johannes,*" ("Yes. That is right.") the latter would assent in reply to some statement but poorly understood. "Darn the fellow, can't he realise that two's company, three's a bore—in this instance a Boer! Nay what, Johannes. *Ik kan nie Hollands praat. Jy verstaand,* (I can't talk Dutch. You understand?). Better jog on and talk to Suffield, see? He can talk it like a Dutch uncle; I can't."

"*Det is jammer?*" ("That's a pity.") said the Boer, solemnly shaking his head. Then after a moment's hesitation he spurred up his nag and jogged on to join the other two.

The open veldt now lay outstretched before them, and Suffield and the two Dutchmen were cantering on some distance ahead. Rearing up on their left rose the great green slopes and soaring cliff walls of the mountain range, and, away on the open side, the rolling, grassy plains, stretching for miles, but always bounded nearer or farther by mountains rising abruptly, and culminating in cliff wall, or jagged, naked crags. Here and there in the distance, a white dot upon the green, lay a Boer homestead, and a scattered patch of moving objects where grazed a flock of sheep or goats. The slanting rays of the afternoon sun, now not far from his western dip behind yon cluster of ironstone peaks, shed upon this bright, wavy, open landscape that marvellous effect of clear and golden radiance which renders the close of a cloudless day upon the High Veldt something like a dream of enchanted worlds.

They were rather silent, these two. The thrilling, vivid happiness of the one, was dashed by a certain amount of apprehensive dread on behalf of the other, who was going quite unnecessarily to expose himself to danger, possibly great, possibly small, but at any rate unnecessary. On the part of that other, well, what had he to do with anything so delusive as the fleeting and temporary thing called happiness, he whose life was all behind him?

Yet he was very—contented; that is how he put it; and he owned to himself that he was daily growing more and more—contented.

"I can't make out what has come over us," he said, as though talking to himself, but in his voice there was that which made Mona's heart leap, for she knew she was fast attaining that which she most desired in life. Then they talked—talked of ordinary things, such as all the world might have listened to; but the tone—ah! there was no disguising that. Thus they cantered along in the sweet, pure air, over the springy plain, against the background of great mountain range, and soon the walls of the homestead drew in sight, and Mrs Suffield came out to greet them, and the dogs broke into fearful clamour only equalled by that of the children, and the two Boers dismounted with alacrity to go in, sure of a good glass of grog or two beneath Suffield's hospitable roof, ere they should resume their homeward way.

Chapter Seventeen
"It is Sweeter to Love—It is Wiser to Dare"

Now night had fallen, and at Quaggasfontein the sounds of household and nursery were alike hushed, and these four sat out upon the *stoep*, enjoying the still freshness; discussing, too, Roden's trip to the nearest seat of hostilities, on which topic Grace Suffield was inclined to be not a little resentful.

"How can you go out of your way to shoot a lot of wretched Kaffirs, who haven't done you any harm, Mr Musgrave?" she said.

"That holds good as regards most of the fellows at the front," he replied.

"No, it doesn't. Many of them are farmers, who have had their stock plundered, perhaps their homes destroyed. Now, nothing of the kind holds good of yourself. I call it wicked—yes, downright wicked, and tempting Providence, to throw oneself into danger unnecessarily. Your life is given you to take care of, not to throw away."

"I don't know that it's worth taking such a lot of care of," he murmured queerly. But she overheard.

"Yes it is, and you've no right to say that. Putting it on the lowest grounds, don't you come out here and help amuse us? That's being of some use. Didn't you help me splendidly when we crossed that horrible Fish River in flood? I believe you saved my life that night. Isn't that being of some use?"

"Here, I say, Mrs Suffield, are you all in league to 'spoil' a fellow?" he said, in a strange, deep voice that resembled a growl. For more forcibly than ever, her words seemed to bring back to the lonely cynic, how, amid the whole-hearted friendship of these people, he had been forced again to live his life—if indeed he could—if only he could!

"Don't know about 'spoiling.' You seem to be catching it pretty hot just now, Musgrave, in my opinion," laughed Suffield.

"And he deserves to," rejoined that worthy's wife, with a tartness which all her hearers knew to be wholly counterfeit. "Doesn't he, Mona?"

"I don't know. As you're so savagely down upon him, I think I shall have to take his part."

"Hear, hear!" cried Roden. "Well, Mrs Suffield, you have mistaken your vocation. You ought to have been a preacher—a good, out-and-out, whole-souled tub-thumper. However, you seem determined I am destined to glut the assegai of John Kaffir, and as you are so savage on the subject, it is to Mona I shall impart my last will and testament—orally, of course. So, come along, Mona, and give it, and me, your most careful attention."

Left alone on the *stoep*, the husband and wife laughed softly together, as they watched Mona's white dress disappear in the darkness.

"All is coming right, as I told you it would, Grace. Musgrave is a precious careful bird; but he's limed safe and sound at last. Mark my words."

"You needn't be so awfully vulgar about it, Charlie. That's quite a horrid way of putting things."

Now in the silence and darkness those two wandered on—on beneath the loaded boughs of the fruit garden, and on by the low sod wall, then out in the open, and finally into gloom beneath the drooping, feathery branches of the willows. It was a silence unbroken by either, unless—unless for a soft shuddering sigh, which followed upon a long kiss.

In the dark and velvety moonless vault great constellations flashed as though they were fires, throwing out the black loom of the distant mountains away beyond the open waste, and flaming down into the smooth mirror of the water, upon which the willow boughs trailed. Even beneath the shadowy gloom their light pierced; shining upon the white dress, and throwing the large, supple figure of the girl into ghostly relief.

"I love you, Mona. Here on the very spot where we first beheld each other, I tell you I love you. And you had better have let me fall to my death, shattered to atoms that day, than that I should tell it you."

The tone, a trifle unsteady, but firm and low, was rather that of a man unfolding a revelation of a painful but wholly unavoidable nature than the joyous certainty of a lover, who knew his passion was returned in measure as full as the most ardent could possibly desire. But the girl for a moment made no answer. Her lips were slightly parted in a smile of unutterable contentment, and the light in her eyes was visible under the stars. Again he kissed the upturned lips, long and tenderly as he had never done before.

"Yes. This is the spot where we first met," she said at last, with a glad laugh in her voice. "My hammock was slung there—and look, there it is still. I remember so well what we were talking about that day. Grace was predicting that my time would certainly come, and I said I didn't believe anything of the kind, but I rather hoped it would. And I had hardly said so when—oh, darling! *you* came up! And it has all been so entrancingly sweet ever since. Life has been entirely different, and I am quite a transformed being."

Thus she ran on—almost rattled on, so airy, so bright and joyous was her tone. But it was so with a purpose; for all her pulses were thrilling; her very mind seemed to reel beneath the surpressed strength of her feeling. She felt giddy. The great stars in the dark vault overhead seemed to be whirling round. With heart panting, she leaned heavily upon the arms which encircled her, then tried to speak, to whisper, but could not.

"Dear, I ought not to have told you—ever at all," he went on. "But I am going away to-morrow—"

Then she found her voice.

"Why *are* you going away to-morrow? Give it up, my heart's love, and stay near me."

"That is just why I am going away—to be away from you for a few days. Wait," seeing she was about to interrupt. "This was my idea. I wanted to be at such a distance that it would be impossible to see you merely by taking one hour's short ride. I wanted to try if I could break the influence which you were so surely weaving round me."

"Ah, why would you try?"

"For the good of us both; but especially for your good. Listen, Mona. I am no longer young, and my experience of the world is not small. Well, nothing lasts. We are both of a strong nature. Two strong natures cannot fuse, cannot intertwine. Then comes disillusion."

"Now, I wonder if, since the world began, any living woman was ever convinced by such reasoning as that," said Mona decisively. But not heeding her, he went on—

"To every one of us the cup of life is filled but once. The contents of mine are nearer the dregs than the brim; whereas you are but beginning to sip at yours."

"Which dark syllogism I quite grasp, and fully appreciate—at its proper value," she returned. "But come; have we not had about enough solemn wisdom beneath the stars? Why, just before we first saw you—here, on this very spot—Gracie was trying to make me believe you were quite a sober and middle-aged fogey. Those were her words; and if you go on a little longer in this strain, I shall begin to think she was right. I remember, too, how I answered her. I said I was about tired of boys. So let's hear no more about 'cups of life' and 'dregs,' but repeat what you said just now—just before—my beloved one!"

The glad, laughing voice changed to one of tenderest adjuration. And it may be that he did repeat it.

"Now," he went on, "would you rather I had told you this before going away, or after my return?"

"But you are not going away, now?"

"I am—more than ever, I was going to say. I want a few days to think."

"Roden!" she exclaimed suddenly, with a catching in her voice; "this is not an artifice? You are coming back—coming back to me?"

"If John Kaffir allows me—certainly. Dwelling a moment upon which consideration, perhaps that is why I told you before I left, what I have just told you. Would you rather I had not?"

"Would I rather forego one moment of the life, the soul, those words have given me? Love of my heart, I know it is of no use to try and persuade you to give up this plan now. But be careful of your life. You are mine, remember. I won you when I held back your life that awful day upon the brow of the cliff; and that consciousness, and that alone, enabled me to do it. Whatever will and strength was given me then was through that alone. Now, say, are you not mine? mine for ever—throughout all the years?"

"Dear, 'for ever' is a long time. Had we not better put it, 'as long as you think me worth keeping'?"

"Why do you say such a thing, and in such a voice?" This with a shiver, as though she had received a sudden stab.

"Mona, what was it I was trying to impress upon you but a minute or so back? I have got my life all behind me, remember. Nothing lasts. I have seen eyes melt, as those dear eyes of yours are melting now—have heard voices tremble in the same sweet intensity of tone. Well, it did not last. Time, separation, new interests, and it was swept away; nor did the process take very long, either. Nothing lasts! Nothing lasts! It may be my curse; but, child, I have reached a stage at which one believes in nothing and nobody."

"Did they—those of whom you speak—love you as I do? Was their secret wrenched from them at the very jaws of death?"

"No. Never did I hear words of love under such, strange circumstances. And yet, Mona, the fact that it was so, nearly turned me against you, for I seemed bound—bound to you in common gratitude. If you had left me to myself, I believe that feeling would have changed into strong dislike."

"And when did the change come—the change for the better?" she said softly.

"I don't know. It has all been so gradual. But there is something, some magic about you, dear, that drew me to you in spite of myself—and kept me there."

"Then one can love, really love, more than once in a lifetime?"

"Of course. The notion to the contrary was invented for the purposes of fiction of the most callous sort. More than once, more than twice. But the difference is that through it all runs the interwoven thread of misgiving, that the thing is ill-judged and destined to end in blank—or worse."

"Mine throughout all the years, did I not say just now?" she whispered, again drawing down his head. "This seals it," and again speech was stilled in a long, clinging kiss. "This is our farewell—only for a few days—and oh, my heart's life, how slowly they will drag! I will go to the place where I held you up from death, and there—on that, to me the sweetest, spot on earth—pray, and pray with all my soul that no danger may come near you."

Were his very senses slipping away from him in that warm embrace? Was it indeed upon him that this love was outpoured, or upon somebody else? The thought passed with jarring hammer strokes through his brain. And like the distant echo of gibing demon-voices, came that old, grim, cynical refrain, "Nothing lasts! Nothing lasts!"

And as a little later he rode homeward through the stillness of the night, on the puffs of the fresh night breeze billowing up the grass, sighing through the coarse bents, still that goading, tormenting refrain kept shrieking in his ears, "Nothing lasts! Nothing lasts!"

Chapter Eighteen
The Hostile Ground

Doppersdorp was some distance behind the two horsemen by the time the sun shot up, a wheel of flame, into the cloudless beauty of the blue vault, flooding the great plains and the iron-crowned mountain heights with waves of gold; and the air, though warm, was on these high tablelands marvellously pure and clear. It was the morning for reflections of a dazzling nature to the man who could enjoy the rare luxury of such; and to Roden Musgrave seemed a fitting continuation of the strange, wondrous enchantment of the past night.

He had persisted with a purpose in this expedition, he had told Mona, because he wanted to be out of reach of her for a brief while, to think. And now that every hoofstroke was bearing him thus out of reach, the strange prescription was indeed taking effect. Now he realised to the full what she was to his life. He had often been for days without seeing her. But then any day, any hour almost, he might have been at her side. His retrospect went to the time when he had looked upon her with something akin to dislike, even dread—dread lest the subtle power of her influence should steal him from himself, should drown his hard cold reason—the fruit of hard experience—in the sweet fumes of its intoxicating spell. But even through all this had run the misgiving that such dread was not ill-founded; for he knew that she possessed the power to do this, did she but choose to exercise it—knew it from the moment he had first looked into her eyes, and had gazed upon her exquisite grace of form and movement. And she had exercised it, and he—well, he had struggled with all the instinct of self-preservation, yet had struggled in vain. He was bound, and the bonds were of a captivity that was very, very sweet.

Yet, nothing lasts. This love of his latter-day life stirring up into a volcanic blaze of activity feelings not only dead and buried, but which he had been wont to scoff at as impossible of existence—how was it to end? In the prosaic, hard-and-fast knot of a legal bond? That, then, would be the beginning of the end. Nothing lasts. The prose, even the vulgarity, of a commonplace tie would be the beginning of disenchantment, disillusion. What then? Thus a sure and certain foresight into the future ran through the glowing, lotus-eating dream of the present, yet, with all its dark and neutral-tinted shades, only seemed to throw out the warm sun-waves of the present into greater contrast.

"I say, Musgrave, I can't congratulate myself on having the liveliest of travelling companions," said Darrell, with a grin. "Do you know that it's exactly forty-seven minutes since you've let fall a word? I've been timing you."

Roden started.

"The deuce you have! Excuse me, Darrell, I sometimes get that way. I believe you're right. Well, I'll make up for it now, anyway."

The other grinned again, but said no more on the subject, and the two men pursued their way at a quick, easy pace, now halting to off-saddle at some farmhouse, now in the veldt. But Roden afforded his companion no further pretext for rallying him on account of his silence.

That night they slept at a Boer's farm on the border of the hostile ground. The worthy Dutchman and his numerous progeny were in a high state of alarm, for rumours had come through his native hands that whole locations of Gaikas, hitherto peaceful, had risen in arms and joined Sandili, who was now trying to break through the not very closely drawn cordon of patrols, and take refuge in the dense forest fastnesses of the Amatola. He and his were going to trek into laager at once, and when he learned the destination of the two Englishmen, he stared at them as though they were ghosts already.

"Nay what. You'll never get through," he said, as they took their leave. "Your lives are not worth that," flinging away a grain of salt, "if you try. Besides, it is very wrong. It is laughing in the face of the good God. You will come to harm, and you will deserve it."

But Darrell's laugh was loud and irreverent as he bade the utterer of this comforting prognostication farewell. He was a harum-scarum, dare-devil sort of mortal, who was afraid of nothing, yet could be cool enough when occasion arose.

Throughout the day they pursued their journey, passing now and then a deserted farmhouse, whose empty kraals and smokeless chimneys, and unreaped crops standing in the mealie lands, spoke eloquently to the desolation that reigned. "The land was dead" indeed, as the native idiom expressed it.

They had taken a straight line across the veldt, avoiding roads and beaten tracks as likely to be watched by outlying parties of the enemy. And now the farther and farther they advanced, the brighter the outlook they kept.

"You'd better note the lay of the ground well, Musgrave, if you still intend to carry out that lunatic idea of returning alone," said Darrell.

"That's the very thing I have been doing. It's easy country, this of yours, to find one's way about in, Darrell. As for returning alone, I shall have to do that, failing an escort. Can't stretch my rather irregular leave to straining point."

It was late in the afternoon. They were riding along the side of a slope which was irregularly sprinkled with clusters of thick bush. Below ran a nearly dry river-bed, and beyond this rose a ragged ascent covered with spekboem scrub. Suddenly both men looked at each other, gently checking their steeds.

A sound was heard in front, at first faint, as of the displacement of a stone, then nearer, till it resolved itself into a clink of shod hoofs upon the stony veldt. Then the whistling of a popular air.

"Now what damned fool can this be kicking up all that shillaloo?" exclaimed Darrell.

The horseman appeared round the corner of a cluster of scrub. On finding himself thus unexpectedly confronted, he reined in instinctively, with a startled movement. Then seeing that the others were friends, he broke into a loud, jolly laugh.

He was a strongly built, broad-shouldered individual, bearded and sunburnt. He was clad in a nondescript uniform coat, cord trousers, and high boots, and on his head a pith helmet surmounted by a spike. He bestrode a powerful chestnut horse with a white blaze. But—and this was the first point that struck these two—he carried no firearm, not even the inevitable revolver, unless it was in his pocket.

"Where's your gun?" said Darrell, with a grin, as soon as the first greetings and explanations were over.

"Haven't got one."

"But haven't you got a revolver?"

"Devil a bit of a revolver. Look here, though, I've got a pipe," producing that comforting implement. "Give us a fill."

This was soon done. Then Darrell, whom the situation struck in its wholly comic light, laid his head back and roared.

"You fellows must have swept this side quite clear of Kaffirs—patrolled it within an inch of its life, I suppose—that you can afford to ride about the veldt in dead war-time unarmed?" he said.

The other looked up quickly; an idea seemed to strike him.

"No; now you mention it, this is just the very side that hasn't been much looked after. Let's off-saddle. I want to get to Cathcart before dark."

"See there now, Musgrave," said Darrell. "Here you have a type of the species of lunatic this country can produce. At least, I can't imagine any other turning out a man who might be met with four hours from the Main Camp in a country swarming with hostile Gaikas, armed with nothing but a whip."

"And a pipe," laughed the stranger. "You've forgotten the pipe."

"Well, counting the pipe even. What do you say, Musgrave? Do you know any other part of the world where they manufacture such lunatics?"

"I never heard of any," said Roden gravely.

The jolly stranger laughed, enjoying these comments as the best possible of jokes. They had off-saddled together, and were foregathering after the manner of casually met campaigners. Roden had a very substantial flask which was not half emptied yet, and this was drawn upon for the occasion. Their new acquaintance gave the other two all the latest information. There had been a good deal of patrolling, and taking of stock, and hustling the rebel Gaikas, but just lately not much in the killing line. The Gaikas were rather fighting shy of coming to close quarters, and when run too hard, would retreat across the Kei into Kreli's country only to swarm back again when the coast was clear.

Thus they chatted until it became time to saddle up. But just as the last strap was buckled there rang out the sharp crackle of dropping shots. It came from about half a mile lower down the kloof.

"Hallo!" cried the stranger. "My fellows are having a row with somebody."

"Your fellows? I thought you were alone," said Darrell.

"Pooh! they don't count. Only four chaps going back to their billets. They've been volunteering and don't like it, so they're going back. Store-clerks, or something of the kind. A poor lot, anyway. Why, I'm doing escort to them rather than they to me, if anything. Let's go down and see what's the row, anyhow."

As the three, now mounted, made their way down to the scene of strife, the shots, which had ceased for a few moments, rang out again with renewed vigour. From the sound, it was evident that two parties were engaged. Darrell laughed aloud over the delightful prospect of a certain battle, and the stranger, who was unarmed, seemed just as eager to be there as the other two.

"Lend us one of your six-shooters," he said. "I don't suppose they'll come close enough to be hurt by that. Still they might."

This remark was addressed about equally to either. Roden, however, was not over anxious to respond. If this fool chose to ride about without weapons, it was rather too much to expect those who were less idiotic to partially disarm themselves for his benefit. He'd see the fellow hanged before doing anything so feeble, he thought. Darrell, however, handed over his revolver.

Now they came upon the combatants—the white ones, at any rate. In a small ravine, which ran down at right angles to the river-bed, four men were lying behind stones and bushes. Opposite, puffs of blue smoke were issuing from the dense scrub, and the whizzing screech of potleg or slug hummed viciously over the beleaguered four, and unpleasantly near their newly arrived allies.

Clearly, as the stranger had said, his men were not up to much, for, as they lay there behind their scant cover, they were pumping in shots at large, with the whole dense forest-clad slope for a target. For of an enemy, beyond the jetting smoke puffs, and the very unpleasant screech of the missiles overhead, there was no outward and visible sign.

"Cease firing, men!" sang out the strange. "Do you want to use up all your darned ammunition at nothing at all?"

They looked round, evidently relieved at this fresh accession to their very slender fighting strength. And now the firing from the opposite bank suddenly ceased.

The three had secured their horses behind a clump of euphorbia, where they would be protected from stray shots as much as possible. The steeds of the others stood saddled and bridled beside their riders, for the men had been suddenly fired on while advancing along the hillside, and, acting upon their first impulse, had flung themselves from the saddle and rushed into cover. The place was about as bad for defensive purposes as it could well be, for it was commanded at the rear by a horseshoe-like range of rocks.

"A real rotten place to 'stand off' a war-party from," muttered Roden. Then louder: "Do you see that bare patch of riverbank, Darrell?" pointing to a rocky shelving bit of shingle just visible where the slope of the hill shut out farther view, some four hundred yards below the left front. "Well, keep your eye brightly upon that, for I have an idea that's where they'll try and cross. Ha! I thought so—" he broke off. And with the words his piece was at his shoulder, and through the long jagged stream of smoke and flame Darrell could see a dark form leap with extended arms, and fall in a heap upon the spot indicated.

"*Maghtaag!* What a shot!" cried Darrell, amazed at the other's quickness and accuracy of aim.

"That'll hold them back a little," went on Roden rapidly. "Now, you watch all the approaches. I'm going up yonder," pointing to the overhanging ridge. "That's where they'll try next, I know. This isn't the first time I've been in this sort of thing." And before the other could get in a word, he was gone.

Crawling, climbing with the agility of a cat, and the craft of the savages against whom he was pitted, Roden was not long in gaining his self-chosen position. Half-sunk in a cranny, his head hidden by three or four large spiky aloes, he peered forth upon the whole plan of battle. Just then the fire of the concealed Kaffirs broke out afresh, their missiles humming among the rocks beneath.

"That means a change of plan," he said to himself. "They are going to cross below, out of sight, and gain this ridge. Ah!"

Bound the slope of the hill, and invisible to the beleaguered ones, was a drift, with something of a waggon track leading up from it. Into this, dark forms were quickly plunging, one by one, then disappearing in the thorn-brake which lined the river on this side. Quite a number had crossed, and meanwhile the fire in front was being kept up hotter than ever.

The thorn-brake ended about two hundred yards from the crest of the ridge, and that distance of stony open ground had to be passed in order to gain the latter. Lying there now, with his finger on the trigger, Roden's glance was fixed upon this area, and there was a hard, set frown upon his brows, as of a man who knew that he had a very stern undertaking indeed upon his hands.

There was a stir on the edge of the thorn-brake; a bird or two dashed out in wild alarm. Then there emerged a crouching shape, followed by another and another. These beckoned backward, and soon others stepped forth, till there must have been a score. Roden's heart beat quick. This game of hide-and-seek was becoming interesting. It was exciting.

He gazed upon the advancing Kaffirs—brawny, athletic savages, glistening with red ochre. The roll of their white eyeballs was plainly visible to him as they glided forward a few paces, then halted to listen, then glided on again. There was a gleam of triumph in their cruel eyes, for they knew that, did they once gain that rocky ridge, they would hold the little handful of whites below very much at their mercy. And they were coming straight for it, little knowing the reception that awaited them.

Drawing his breath hard, he still waited, letting them come on nearer and nearer. He did not mean more than he could help of that score of warriors to regain the cover of the thorn strip, and the nearer they were to him, the longer they would take to reach it.

They were now just within a hundred yards. Carefully sighting the foremost, so as to get two in line, he let go. The effect was startling. Of the two warriors, one dropped on his face, stone dead; the other lay kicking and struggling. The survivors sent up a wild yell of dismay and alarm. Some halted for a moment irresolute, while others dropped down flat, even behind mere pebbles, in their instinctive seeking for cover. But immediately a second ball hummed into their midst, drilling through the heart of another, and spinning him round to the earth. Again from the roar on the smoke-crowned ridge came another messenger of death, and at the same time, by way of keeping up the illusion of numbers, though at too long range to take effect, Roden poured his shot-barrel, loaded with a heavy charge of *loepers*, into the disconcerted assailants. The latter waited no longer. Some leaping and zigzagging to render themselves an uncertain mark, others, gliding and crawling like snakes, they made their way back to the cover they had left, just as fast as they could get there.

Even then they were not all to escape. For he who held that rock-crowned ridge had learned the art of quick-loading, and that in a hard and sharp school. In a twinkling the smoking shell was out of the breech, and a fresh cartridge in its place; in less than a twinkling an unerring sight was again taken, and an enemy fell. Two more were dropped before the security of the thorns was gained, one dead, the other badly wounded.

The crisis over, Roden's pulse began to beat with excitement. He had driven back a score of enemies with the loss of a quarter of their number, in something less than three minutes; he—single-handed. He had saved the position, and, in all human probability, the lives of his companions. No wonder he felt a little excited. And then immediately he became deadly cool.

Was it instinct—second sight—what? Wheeling round, with lightning rapidity, he discharged his piece almost without aiming. The glistening, sinuous frame of a savage heaved itself up from a point of rock not ten yards behind, and toppled heavily over into the hollow beneath. Roden had turned only in the very nick of time. The Kaffir was aiming full at his back, and at that distance could not have missed. He was settled, anyhow; but what about the rest?

For contrary to expectation the savages had designed to seize this position from both sides at once. While he had been playing such havoc with one division the other had crept up to occupy the ridge on the side he could command least—for it was a little above him—and indeed had occupied it; for he could see a movement or two among the rocks in the rear of the spot where he had dropped the last enemy.

And now he began to realise that he was in a hard, tight place. The newly arrived force of Kaffirs was already beginning to fire down into the hollow beneath. Those whom he had driven back into cover, on learning that they had only one enemy to deal with, would soon find a way of coming up.

And indeed this promised to be the case, for now the savages began to shout and call to each other; and all the while the fire upon those in the hollow beneath grew hotter and hotter. Ammunition was probably not profusely plentiful with those four homeward-bound whites, and might soon be exhausted.

Just then the enemy's fire suddenly ceased. What did it mean? Away down the river bank, Roden from his elevated perch could see the stirring of the bushes; and his quick practised eye, following the movement, could see it was a *retreating* one. Then against the now declining sun something gleamed and shone forth again in many a sparkle of glittering light. It was the gleam of arms.

Away across the plain, advancing at a hard canter, came a number of mounted figures. A glance was enough. It was a patrol, and a strong one. They were saved.

But only just in the nick of time.

Chapter Nineteen
A Dark Mystery of the Veldt

The predominating impulse in the mind of Roden Musgrave when he awoke the next morning in Darrell's tent, in the Main Camp, was to saddle up his horse, and betake himself back to Doppersdorp as quickly as his steed could convey him thither; and as he stepped forth, and his eye wandered over the array of tents, and waggons, and fires, and cooking pots, and accoutrements, and men of all sorts and sizes, Dutch burghers and town volunteers, and Fingo and Hottentot levies, the impulse grew stronger still. Here was a huge mass of different phases of humanity, hundreds strong, and now that he was here the associations of the place failed to interest him, for he was familiar with them all. The sort of adventure which held any fascination for him was of the nature of that which he had gone through the day before; but all this organised crowd under arms was devoid of attraction for him. He had seen it all before.

Darrell, whose tendency never inclined to minimising any exploit in which he had borne a part, had spread the account of the day's scrimmage far and wide; and how Roden had saved the position, and shot down half-a-dozen Kaffirs in less than that number of minutes. This soon grew to a full dozen, and so on, which to Roden himself was mightily distasteful. For, the affair over, and he and his comrades in safety, his wish was, if anything, that he had not shot anybody at all. He would gladly have brought back the slain Kaffirs to life again, if that were possible; but anyhow, he saw nothing to brag about in the fact of having shot them. He was thoroughly sick of all reference to the matter.

Conquering, however, his homing impulses, he suffered Darrell to persuade him into taking part in a two days' patrol, which turned out a deadly monotonous affair; for no sign of an enemy did they see, and a cold, drizzling rain fell the whole time. Mightily glad was he when it was over, and they returned to the Main Camp, and more than ever was he resolved to start back for Doppersdorp on the following morning.

"Where on earth did you pick up your ideas of arranging a fight, Musgrave?" said Darrell, as, having finished their supper of ration beef and

Boer brandy, they and two or three others were taking it easy in the tent of the former, their pipes in full blast. "Any fool could see you were no new hand at that sort of thing, by the way in which you grasped the ins and outs of the position the other day."

"Oh, I saw something of the Indian wars out West a few years ago. By the way, Darrell, what was the name of that lunatic we picked up the other day, armed with only a quince switch?"

"Bolton. He's a law-agent, and broker, at Barabastadt. And, confound him, he forgot to give me back the revolver I lent him."

"Serves you right for being such a fool as to lend it him. Now that's a thing I'd never do. I'd see him hanged first. If the fellow had lost his gun by accident, it would be another thing; but to go about without one, out of mere swagger and bounce, and then come down on the first sensible cuss he meets, to rig him out with his! No, no. It's a little too thin."

"That's how fellows come to grief in war-time," struck in another man. "They get so confoundedly careless, and at last they do it once too often. It always happens. I say, Musgrave, tell us something about that Indian business. Are the redskins as good at a fight as Jack Kaffir?"

"They're just as good at one as any fellow need wish. But now, if you don't mind, I'm most confoundedly sleepy, and would as soon turn in as not." And in a very few minutes, in spite of the talk and discussion going on around him, he was fast asleep.

Roden held to his resolve and, notwithstanding all persuasion to the contrary, he started soon after sunrise. To many a man, not more timid than his kind, that return journey of seventy or eighty miles, the bulk of it over the hostile ground, might well have seemed a formidable undertaking, the more so that it was a solitary journey. This one, however, entered upon it with no great concern. He had brought off riskier things than that, he said in his casual way, in reply to misgivings more than once expressed by Darrell and the rest. As for the solitary side of the matter, he rather preferred it. Fighting was out of the question. It would be a case of leg-bail entirely, and that was a game at which one could play better than two. Again, the presence of one was more likely to pass unnoticed than that of two.

"You keep your weather eye skinned, Musgrave, and a particularly bright look-out for small gangs," was Darrell's last injunction having ridden a few miles out from camp with him. "Sandili is trying to slip through into the Amatola at one rush, but sending that, he's sending his chaps through in driblets. Shouldn't wonder if you fell in with a patrol or two. But if you're spotted by the niggers, no matter how few, leg it; do you hear? leg it; for you never know how many more are close by."

"Pho! They ain't mounted, and if they were, wouldn't know now to ride. I've raced a whole day in front of a wild, mad, yelling war-party of Sioux devils; and if your John Kaffir can make things warmer than that, Darrell, he's welcome to try."

"Eh? The deuce you have!" said Darrell in amazement. "Here, I'll come a mile or two farther, and let's have the yarn."

"No, no. I don't feel like yarning—anyway just now. Well, so long. No fear about me. I'm not going to turn up missing."

The ride, though lonely, was a delightful one. The day was of unclouded loveliness and the air fresh and exhilarating as a cordial. Away on either hand stretched the grand open country, rolling in wide grassy plains, heaving up into rugged and stony ranges, here and there deepening into a bush-grown river-valley. The life of the wild veldt was never still—the cheery whistle of spreews, glinting from spray to spray in sheeny flashes of light, and the metallic, half-grating note of the yellow thrush; the soft shout of the hoopoe, echoing from the distance, mingling with the softer voices of doves, which were dashing alarmed from the grotesque heads of the plumed euphorbia, disturbed by the horse's tread. Great webs lay spread from bush to bush, each containing several huge spiders, black and horny; and of these the horseman would now and again receive a shower right in his face—not being always able to guide his horse so as to clear them. But the insects, though hideous, were quite innocuous, and, relishing the encounter as little as the human party to the same, dropped off immediately upon contact. Buck, too—the wary bushbuck and dainty little duiker—would rustle up with a mighty disturbance, to bound away in the scrub or long grass, flashing a white flag of defiance.

"Game lies close—that's a good sign," meditated the horseman. "But it goes like the devil once it is up—that's a bad one. Well, it may be a good one too, meaning only that this section has been well patrolled."

It was tantalising, very, as he watched the animals bound away in gracefully flying leaps, affording the sweetest of shots from the saddle. But he who now rode there dared not pull a trigger, for it might easily cost him his life, and that was a possession he did not want to lose just then.

It was an exciting ride withal—keenly so; for every turn of the way might bring him face to face with an enemy. If he topped a rise of the ground, might he not run right into the teeth of a hostile band on the other side? As he rode along the slope of a bush-clad hill, for he avoided the bottom of defile or ravine, he more than half expected the "whizz" of missiles from the ambushed savage lurking concealed above. Yes, it was an exciting ride, a perilous ride, yet he travelled at an easy pace, knowing better than to fall into the blunder of pressing his steed in order that it might the more quickly be got over.

At first he enjoyed the exciting possibilities of the journey—the strong dash of peril—as, keenly on the alert, he urged his steed forward. It reminded him of old times. But each and every excitement has its limits, and as the hours went by the tension relaxed, the strain upon his nerves subsided. He began to think upon other matters than potential danger. That last farewell under the stars—the recollection of it coursed sweet and warm through his being; his pulses bounded with the very gladsomeness of living. Soon they would meet again, and—what a meeting!

For this voluntary absence of his had borne its fruit. But a few days; yet it had seemed to need only this to consolidate and weld this strange, bewildering love of his latter-day life. In the rough duties he had voluntarily undertaken during that brief period—the patrolling, the tireless bivouac under the stars; the shots exchanged with the lurking enemy; the jovial, but not very boisterous revelry of camp life—that image was ever-present, sweet, smiling, radiant-eyed; and try as he might, he could not banish it.

Now the shadow of a cloud swept across his path, together with a gleam of blue lightning. Creeping stealthily up, their jagged outlines gradually obliterating the blue arch, leaden cloud-piles were spreading, and puffs of hot wind set the grasses singing. In sharp, staccato boom, the electric voice spoke overhead, but no rain fell. It was a dry thunderstorm, often the most perilous.

He was riding just beneath the apex of a long, sparsely-bushed ridge. Already, as he began to descend, the lightning was darting down upon the height in vivid streams, which the sharp, startling thunder-crack seemed to accompany rather than to follow.

"This is getting a trifle sultry, and the veldt here is crusted with ironstone," he said to himself. Then turning his horse, he held ever downward. Half-darkened, the scene was now desolate enough—the long slopes of the kloof, and the ridges cut clear against the livid thundercloud. Down in the hollow several "bromvogels," the great black hornbill of South Africa, were strutting amid the grass, uttering their drumming bass note. These flapped away heavily on the near approach of the horseman, and rising high overhead, were soon winging their aerial course seemingly to the thundercloud itself.

Suddenly the horse stopped short, and, with ears cocked forward, stood snorting, with dilated eyes gazing upon the dark line of bush in front. Roden's meditations took to themselves wings, and drawing his revolver, as more convenient at close quarters than the rifle, shifted the latter into his bridle hand, and sat for a moment intently listening.

Not a sound.

It was a nerve-trying moment. The savage war-shout, the crash of firearms, the "whiz" of assegais—that was what it would only too likely bring forth. Still silence, save for the bass grumblings of the thunder.

Then there was a winnowing of wings, and a huge bird arose. Roden knew it for a vulture, of the black and non-gregarious kind. A vulture! That meant the presence of death.

So far reassured, for the bird would not have been there had the scrub concealed living men, he cautiously made his way between the bushes to the spot whence he had seen the funereal scavenger arise, and again the horse started and shied, spinning half round where he stood. One glance, and the secret was out. In the long grass lay the body of a man—a Kaffir.

It had been that of a savage of splendid proportions—tall, broad, thick-set, and muscular. It lay upon its back, staring upward with lacerated eyeless sockets, their contents torn out by the black vulture. Otherwise it was untouched.

Stay—not quite. From a great jagged hole in the chest a very lake of blood had welled, staining the long grass. It was a bullet hole; the sort of gap made by a heavy Snider missile. The man had been shot. But how? when?

The body was quite naked, and whatever it might have owned in life, in the shape of weapons or other requisites, had disappeared. From its aspect, not many days could have elapsed since death. It was a ghastly find, this black, rigid corpse, with its eyeless sockets and teeth bared and set; a ghastly find in the subdued gloom of the shadowing thundercloud, with the blue lightning playing down upon the lonely veldt. But there was worse to follow.

For, exploring farther, Roden came with equal suddenness upon several corpses, half a dozen at least. All were contorted as in the agonies of a violent death, and all were riddled more or less with bullet wounds. What was the secret of this conflict here, he wondered? Who had been engaged in it? Whose the victory? Would he next come upon the bodies of those of his own colour? Looking up suddenly his eyes fell upon a most melancholy object. It was the charred remnant of a burned house.

Now the mystery stood explained. Those whose remains he had found had been shot down by the inmates; slain in self-defence. But, those inmates! Clearly the savages had been victorious; and—what of the inmates?

The walls stood, the dirty whitewash showing livid in contrast to the black, charring action of the names. The roof had fallen in, and the empty apertures, where the windows had been, gaped wide like the staring, sightless sockets of the corpse. The house had been of no great dimensions, and was clearly the dwelling of some small farmer. A low, crumbling sod wall shut in a sorry-looking "land," containing now only a few trampled cornstalks; and hard by were the broken-down fences of a sheep kraal.

Strong-nerved as he was, Roden Musgrave could not repress a quickening of the pulses, a shrinking of the heart, as he drew near to explore the interior of the ruin. What further dread secret was he about to light upon? The mangled corpses of the white inmates, entombed beneath their own roof-tree, a prey to the devouring assegai of the savage? He expected nothing less.

But a very few minutes' search convinced him that the place contained no human remains. He was puzzled. What had become of the unfortunate settlers? That there had been a fierce and sanguinary battle was evident, but it was impossible that the savages could have been beaten off, else would the house not have been fired. Herein was a mystery.

The situation of the place was gloomy and forbidding to the last degree, the black rain standing deep within that lonely kloof, and, lying around, the grim earthly remains of those who had assailed it. Opposite rose a rugged cliff, whose brow was crowned with a grove of fantastically plumed euphorbia; and then as his eye caught a stealthy movement amid the gloom of the straight stems, Roden gave a slight start, and immediately was as ready for action as ever he had been in his life.

Yes, something was stirring up there. The moment was rather a tense one, as standing amid those weird ruins he bent his gaze long and eagerly upon the darkness of the straight euphorbia stems, round, regular as organ pipes. Shadowy figures were flitting in and out. Were others creeping up to assail him in the rear, signalled by these? Was he in a trap, surrounded? Then he laughed—laughed aloud; for there went up from the euphorbia clump a strong, harsh, resounding bark:—

"Baugh-m! Baugh-m!"

"Only baboons after all!" he cried, feeling more relieved than he cared to own. And seeing nothing to be gained by further lingering, by extended investigation, he once more mounted his horse and took his way out of this valley of desolation and of death.

And as he gained the opposite ridge, he found that the storm was clearing away, or rather travelling onward. Before him lay a series of grassy flats, fairly open, but dotted with *clompjes* of bush here and there. The sun had broken forth again, and, the cloud curtain now removed, was flooding the land with dazzling light. The change was a welcome one, and had the effect of restoring the traveller's spirits, somewhat depressed by the grim and gruesome scene he had just left. And now, as the sun wanted but an hour to his setting, Roden decided to off-saddle for that space of time. Then his steed, rested and refreshed, would carry him on bravely in the cool night air, and but a very few hours should see him safely over the hostile ground, if not among inhabited dwellings once more. So, choosing a sequestered hollow, Roden off-saddled and knee-haltered his steed, and then betook himself to a little clump of bush which grew around a stony *kopje*, and which afforded him a secure hiding-place and a most serviceable watch-tower, for it commanded a considerable view of the surrounding veldt.

Chapter Twenty
Mona's Dream

Notwithstanding the splendid courage and quickness of resource she had shown upon a certain critical and, but for those qualities on her part, assuredly a fatal occasion, Mona Ridsdale was by no means free from that timidity under given circumstances, which seems second nature with most women. She preferred not to be left alone in the dark if possible to avoid it, and, in fact, had as dread a realisation of what it meant to be "unprotected" as the most commonplace and unheroic of her sex: consequently, when Suffield found it unavoidable to be absent from home a night or two, Mona was apt to conjure up terrors which interfered materially with her peace of mind. Now, just such an absence on the part of her male relative befell some few nights after Roden's departure for the Main Camp.

"Oh, Grace, I do feel so nervous this evening!" she exclaimed, starting, not for the first time, as one of the ordinary nocturnal wild sounds from veldt or mountain-side came floating in through the open windows. "Feel my hands, now cold they are; and yet it is such a hot night that one wants every square foot of air the windows will admit."

"That is foolish, Mona," replied her cousin. "Yes, your hands are indeed cold. Why, to-morrow will ring back not only Charlie, but perhaps somebody else."

"God grant it may!" was the eager rejoinder. "But do you know, Grace, I have a horrible presentiment on that score too; I believe that is why I feel so shivery to-night. It is like a warning—I feel as if something were going to happen to him—were happening!"

There was a wildness in the glance of the dilated eyes, a quick, spasmodic catch of the voice, which disconcerted the other, who, in ordinary matters, was the less timid of the two.

"Mona, dear, don't, for Heaven's sake, give way to such fancies. They grow upon one so. And how you will laugh at them—at yourself—in the morning, when Charlie comes back, and perhaps somebody else."

"I can't help it. I wish the night was over. I am sure something is going to happen before the morning."

The two were sitting together, the supper over, and the nursery department tucked up, snug and quiet for the night. Suffield had ridden away to attend a sale at a distance, and would hardly return before the following afternoon. It was, as we have said, a hot night, and both windows of the room were open; indeed, it would have been well-nigh impossible to breathe had they been shut. At the black spaces thus framed Mona would stare ever and again, with a quick glance of apprehension, as though expecting, she knew not what, to heave into view from the gloom beyond. It was a still night, moreover, and every sound from without was wafted in with tenfold clearness—the weird shout of a night-bird from the mountain-side; the yelp of a jackal far out upon the plain; the loud and sudden, but musical twanging note of the night locust, whose cry can hardly be credited to a mere insect, so powerful, so bird-like is it. Even the splash of a mud-turtle waddling into the dam was audible.

A rushing, booming, buzzing sound swept past the open window. Mona started again, and her face paled. It was only some big flying beetle, blundering past the oblong of light which had half-attracted, half-scared him; yet so overwrought were her nerves that she could hardly repress a startled scream. Now, this sort of thing is catching, and Grace Suffield felt that a little more of it would probably end by unnerving herself.

"My dear Mona," she said; "this is more than nervousness. You have caught cold somehow. Come now, you must go to bed; and I will make you something hot."

"I can't go to bed, Grace, and I couldn't sleep if I did," she answered. "Let's go out on the *stoep*. The air may make one feel better."

To this the other agreed, and they went forth. It was a grand and glorious night. A faint moon hung low down in the heavens, and the great planets gushed their rolling fires in the star-gemmed blackness. Such a night had been that other, when only the dark willows had overheard those whispers—deep, pulsating, passionate—welling from the overcharged hearts and strong natures of those who uttered them.

"Look, look! That is almost bright enough for a meteor!" cried Mona as a falling star darted down in a streak of light, seeming to strike the distant loom of the mountain range in its rocket-like course. "There is something weird, to my mind, about these falling stars. What are they, and where do they go to?"

"Everything is weird to your mind to-night, dear. Come in now, and go to bed."

"Not yet, Grace. I feel better already. I knew the air would do me good. Look there! what is that—and that?"

Her tone now belied her former words—her limbs shook. And now both stood listening intently.

For there floated upon the still night air a sound—an eerie, wailing, long-drawn sound—faint, yet clear; very distant, yet plainly audible; rising and falling; now springing to a high pitch, now sinking to a muffled, rumbling roar—yet so faint, so distant. Far away over the darkened waste where the great castellated pile of the Wildschutsberg rose gloomy beneath the horned moon, there hovered a strange reddening glow. At the sound the dogs lying around the house sprang up, baying furiously.

"Grace, I believe the Tambookie locations out yonder are up in arms. That is the war-cry—they are dancing the war-dance. Listen!"

Here indeed was a potential peril, a tangible one, and removed from the spheres of mere bogeydom. There had been uneasy rumours in the air of late—that the Tembu locations on the confines of the district were plotting and restless, and more than ready to rise and join their disaffected fellow-tribesmen now in open rebellion beneath the slopes of the Stormberg. No wonder if these two unprotected women felt a real apprehension chill their veins, as they stood upon the *stoep* of their lonely homestead gazing forth with beating hearts, listening to these ominous sounds rising upon the stillness of the night. The distance which separated them from the disaffected savages was not great, hardly more than half a score of miles.

"Even if it is so, I don't think we have anything to fear," said Grace at last. "They would go in the other direction if they moved at all; either cross over to join Gungubele's people, or Umfanta's, or perhaps move down to league forces with the Gaikas. They would hardly venture so near the town as this."

"Move down to league forces with the Gaikas?" echoed Mona, horror-stricken at the suggestion. "Why, that would mean that they would cross the very belt of country over which lay Roden's return route."

Grace Suffield was quick to grasp her meaning.

"No, no; not that, dear," she said. "I don't believe myself there is anything to be alarmed at. I believe they are only making a noise; possibly they have a big beer-drinking on, or something. Kaffirs, in their way, are just as fond of jollification as we are, you know; and I think I remember more than once hearing something of the kind before, only as there was no war on, or even dreamt of, we hardly noticed it at the time, I suppose. Yes, I am perfectly certain that is all it means; so now come in, and we'll go to bed. You shall sleep in my room if you like."

Mona suffered herself to be led in, and to be given wine, and generally taken care of: but curiously inconsistent, for all her nervous fears, she preferred to be alone. Then, bidding her relative good-night, she retired to her room, and having fastened the shutters and locked the door, she sat down to think.

Her thoughts flew straight off to one who now was the main object of them. Where was he at that moment? Returning to her, travelling at all speed over a peril-haunted region to return to her, alone perhaps, as he had hinted might be the case; and more than one unspoken prayer went up that it might not be so, or for his safety if it were. Then her recollections went farther back. She recalled many to whom she stood in the same light as she now did to that one—from their point of view, that is—yet none had succeeded in stirring her heart, in causing her pulses to beat quicker, or, if so, for no more than a moment, so to say. She recalled many an impassioned pleading, many a haggard face, grief-stricken, disappointed, down to that of Lambert only the other day, and wondered if they had felt as she would feel were any evil to overtake that one now. How cold, how callous, how inconsiderate she had been to others, she recognised now; and as her thoughts turned to him she felt that, but for the certainty of seeing him again, of all the blissfulness of their reunion, and that in a day or two at the furthest, her life would have been lived—lived and done with for all time.

The house was in dead silence, as in the solitude of her room at last she began to prepare for bed. She had just finished brushing out the thick waves of her hair, when a dull rumble, as of many feet, not far from the window, turned her pale and tottering. Her heart beat like a hammer, and the splendid outlines of her breast, now uncovered, rose and fell with the quick regularity of the roll of surf upon a level beach. Then with the stamping tread there arose a low moaning noise, long-drawn and unspeakably dismal in the dead midnight silence.

"What a despicable coward I am!" she exclaimed, now with a faint smile. Then, with a glance at her magnificent limbs, "I am large framed, and strong, yet the least little thing makes me quake and quiver like a scared child."

She threw open the shutters, and, as she did so, again went up that unearthly, deep-throated moaning, ending in a short shrill bellow. But she knew the sound. The cattle had returned about the homestead, and were collecting at the spot where a sheep or goat was daily slaughtered for the use of the household and the farm hands. In the faint moonlight she could see the beasts bunched together, their noses down to the blood-soaked spot, sniffing and pawing up the ground as they emitted their dismal mutterings; then they would start off, with tail in air and horns lowered, and career a little way across the veldt, and return, as though the fell fascination was greater than the terror which had first appalled them, to resume their weird, hollow groaning as before. The dogs, well accustomed to this performance, forbore to notice it, beyond a low growl or two. Besides, they held the horns of the excited beasts in wholesome respect.

Closing the shutters again, Mona returned into the room. Just as she was about to get into bed, her glance was attracted by something. A great dark object was moving across the floor. Repressing an impulse to shriek aloud, she lowered her candle so as to dispel the shadow in which the thing moved, for it was under the table, and then with a shuddering horror she saw that it was a huge tarantula.

The evil-looking beast was of enormous dimensions. Outspread, it was the size of a man's hand, and its great hairy legs and dull, black, protruding eyes gave it the aspect of a demoniacal looking animal rather than a mere insect, as it came shoggling across the floor; then stopped suddenly, as its instincts warned it of danger.

All in a quiver of loathing and repulsion, she snatched up a large book of bound-up music, and dropped it upon the hideous insect. She left it where it lay, not caring to investigate farther; knowing, too, that the thing would be crushed and flattened out of all life and shape beneath the heavy volume. Where did it come from? Tarantulas were quite rare in that high, open, bracing veldt, though plentiful enough in the lower and hotter bush country. But even there she had never seen one anything like this for size.

The nervous fears which had beset her throughout the evening had brought something like exhaustion in their train. No sooner was the light out, and her head upon her pillow, than she was fast asleep. Yet sound though her slumbers were, a thread of uneasiness ran through them. Outside, in the faint moonlight, the cattle still clustered about the bloodstained spot, and even in her sleep she could still hear the pawing of their hoofs, and the unceasing refrain of their dismal and hollow groanings, half-soothing, half-terrifying in the mesmeric effect which they produced upon the ever-changing waves of her consciousness, that hovering border-line between wakefulness and the dream world. She murmured the name of her absent lover, and again, in her sleeping visions she was soothing him to rest in the still midnight, as he lay in feverish pain, but a few hours after she had drawn him back from death.

Then the great tarantula she had slain seemed to come into her slumbers. She saw the upheaval of the broad book under which it lay crushed, and the hideous thing step slowly forth; and as it did so it spread itself out, black, gigantic, to ten times its original size. It advanced to the side of the bed, and leaped up on to the counterpane and crouched there, glowering at her with its dull black eyes, its great hairy feelers moving, its nippers working threateningly. She felt as one under a demoniacal spell, without even power of movement enough to tremble. Then she feared no longer for herself, for that which the grisly monster threatened seemed to be her absent lover. Now she sees him, sees him faintly and dimly as through darkness; and he, too, is unconscious. It is as though she sees him in a grave, amid the gloomy shadows of the nether world, far down in the dim depths of the black river of Death.

And now it seems that the whole room is full of shadowy, hairy shapes, like that which holds her in its demoniacal spell, that the dim darkness is astir with writhing tentacular legs, and they are closing round something — the pale countenance of a sleeping man. There is the glare of blood in their eager eyes, and oh, Heaven! the face of each crawling horror is a human one, dark, savage, bloodthirsty. And he? — Oh, God! oh, God! The countenance of him who now sleeps there, ready for their blood-drinking fangs, is that of her absent lover! She can almost touch him, yet the terrible spell upon her holds her bound. Horror of horrors! she must snatch him again from this grisly peril or he is lost. Too late! too late! no, not yet too late — one moment will do it! This chain that holds her, can she not break it? If she is powerless to touch him, still can she cry aloud in warning? No, she cannot. The gnome-like fiend crouching there has power over every faculty she possesses. Now these appalling shapes are upon the sleeping man, and now their eyes dart fire as from flaming torches. They seem to burn him, for he moves uneasily. Will he not wake? will he not wake? Too late! Then by some means the spell is broken, and with a wild, ringing, piercing cry, she utters aloud her lover's name in a clarion call of warning, and adjuration, and despair.

" With a wild, ringing, piercing cry, she utters aloud her lover's name
in a clarion call of warning, and adjuration, and despair."

"Mona, what is it? Mona! Mona! What in the world is the matter? Good heavens!"

And Grace Suffield, startled from her bed by the loud ringing cry, stands, candle in hand, within her cousin's room, shaking with apprehension and alarm. And small blame to her.

For Mona is standing at the open window. The shutters are thrown back, and her tall, white-clad form, half shrouded in her streaming hair, is framed against the oblong patch of bright stars. And she is gazing out upon the midnight waste, with eyes dilated in a wild, wistful, anguished look, as though she were striving to pierce the darkness and distance, and would give her life for the power to do so. It was a weird sight, and chilled Grace Suffield with an eerie and awesome creep, for it was evident that, in spite of her erect attitude and open eyes, Mona was not awake.

What was she to do? Mona had never been given to sleep-walking. Some appalling and powerful dream must have disturbed her. To wake her might be dangerous—the shock would be too great. But in this dilemma

Mona turned round suddenly, and her eyes catching the glare of the light, she shut them. Then passing her hand over them two or three times she opened them once more—and beyond a slight start no sign was there that this was other than an ordinary awakening.

"Is that you, Grace!" she said wonderingly. "Why, what's wrong? Any of the children ill?"

"No, dear. But you—I thought I heard you call for something."

Thick and clear the waves of recollection flowed back upon Mona's mind. She started, shuddered, and again that scared look came into her eyes, but she quickly recovered herself.

"It was more than a dream," she said, speaking half to herself. "Yes, it was not a mere dream—it was a warning. Grace, *he* has been in danger, and I have warned him. Yes, I have, and I feel confident now. He is safe. My warning has been heard."

Had it? Had the temporarily released soul, hovering above its slumbering tenement, the power to bridge over such material matter as distance and space? Was it given to the dream-voice, winged by the will-power of the strength and despair of love, to dart forth through the midnight spheres until it should thrill upon the unconscious ears, which a moment later might be beyond hearing aught again in this world? Who can say?

Chapter Twenty One
A Voice through the Night

Having rested himself and his steed, and still farther diminished the contents of his saddle bag, Roden filled and lighted another pipe, and began to think about saddling up.

He sent a last look around, but no sign of life was there, save for a faint column of blue smoke rising in the distance. Attentively he gazed at this. Did it mean another burning house, a smoke signal, or a camp of friend or foe? It was impossible to say; at any rate, it was a long way off, and what was more to the purpose, nowhere near his line of route. Satisfied on this point, and feeling on excellent terms with himself and all the world, he rose and made his way down to where his steed was grazing.

But now some trouble awaited; for he had knee-haltered the animal with too great a length of *reim*, and rather carelessly as to the knot, consequently the latter had slipped, leaving the horse almost as free as though he were loose. So now as he walked quietly up, speaking softly and soothingly, to secure his steed, Roden saw that he would need all his patience.

For the young horse was of a fidgety habit, and, as though aware of his power, no sooner did his rider extend a hand to catch him than, with a loud snort, he swung wildly round, placing his tail where his head should be. Another attempt, more coaxing, only met with a like result. The exasperating brute would allow the hand to approach within halt a yard of the *reim*, then would slew round as before.

This trick is a common enough one in the 'cussedness' of equine economy. It is about as exasperating as anything in this wicked world, and if there exists an average man who, being the victim of it, refrains from using terrible language aloud or *secreto*, why, in the plenitude of our experience we never fell in with him. At any rate, Roden Musgrave was not such a one, though he so far varied upon usual custom by damning, not the horse, but himself, and his own inconceivable carelessness in making such a bungling job of the knee-haltering.

The plan under the circumstances is craftily to manoeuvre the obdurate quadruped against a bush or a fence. Here, of course, there was no fence, and the only bush was that which grew around the stony *kopje* to which we have alluded, and thither, in accordance with the much-belauded equine intelligence—which, by the way, invariably shows itself in the wrong direction—nothing on earth would persuade this fiendish beast to proceed. Anywhere else, but—not there.

Roden tried another plan, that of waiting. He would have given much for a good forty yards of lariat, but 'roping' cattle and horses is a process unknown in South Africa, consequently he was without that highly serviceable Western implement. Then having waited to allow the horse to calm down again, he advanced once more to the attack.

It was not an atom of use. The young horse put his head down with a snort of defiance, and slewed round more wildly than before. He seemed positively to enjoy the fun of the thing, to enter into the joke with a fiendish glee. It was a joke, however, which might prove a grim one for his rider.

And such indeed it did prove. The *reim*, an old one, or containing a flaw, suddenly gave way. His leg now free, and at its normal distance from his chin once more, up went the noble animal's nose into the air, and with a defiant whisk of the tail, which seemed to assert a determination to enjoy his newly gained liberty, away he started at a smart trot, which soon changed to a gallop, heading for all he knew how in the direction of the camp he had left that morning.

Those who prate about the marvellous intelligence of the equine race, are still under the magic of the story-books of their youth. This representative of it no sooner found himself free than he started off—whither? Not, be it observed, for his master's stable, where excellent quarters and plenteousness of mealies and forage awaited, and which in point of distance was the nearer, they having covered more than half of the journey. Oh no; but back to the camp, back to the scene of his recent hard work, patrols, and scantiness of feed beyond that wherewith Nature had covered the veldt. An intelligent beast, in truth! Nor was he a phenomenal specimen of his kind.

Roden Musgrave, watching his steed vanishing in the distance, followed, we fear, the example of the British army in Flanders. He swore terribly. He was human enough to estimate what he would give to be seated across that now departed quadruped for ten minutes or so, armed with a strong new sjambok, and a pair of long-rowelled spurs; and indeed, the provocation was great.

Well, he was in a pretty plight; alone, dismounted, in the middle of the hostile ground, night drawing on, and only a hazy idea of his route. His boast to Darrell that he could easily evade parties of the enemy was well founded enough when he made it, for the Kaffirs possessed but few horses, and those few, thanks to having been ridden almost from foalhood, of weedy and undersized proportions. Now it was different. He could no more distance the fleet-footed savages than they could have overtaken him when mounted. On foot, he was at their mercy.

There was only one thing to be done under the circumstances. Since he could not ride, he must walk. No sooner decided than acted upon. Hiding the saddle and bridle among the bush on the *kopje*, and pocketing what remained of his store of provision, he started. Nearly an hour had been lost in his attempts at capturing his miserable traitor of a steed, and now the sun was already down. Well, so much the better. Travelling would be safer by night than by day.

To one accustomed to ride, nothing is more disconcerting than to find himself unexpectedly dismounted, in wild, little-known, and dangerous country. It is even demoralising, for it engenders a feeling or helplessness. A mere man, the only animal without any speed in his legs, is such an insignificant object amid the wild stretch of nature; his capacity for advance and retreat so limited under such circumstances. And he realises it.

Certainly Roden Musgrave realised it that night as he tramped on wearily beneath the stars. Even finding the way was quite a different matter when afoot to what it had been when mounted. Instead of a few minutes' *détour* to a point whence an observation might be made, now it meant quite a long and toilsome tramp, with the galling consciousness that all that toil carried him no farther on his way. The thin sickle of a new moon hung in the heavens, and for this he felt duly grateful, for without its light, faint though that was, he would have made but sorry progress amid stones and antheaps and thorns and long grass and meerkat holes.

For hours thus he kept on. Once he saw the red glow of a fire not far from his line of route, and his heart leaped. A patrol? No. A moment's thought served to show that no patrol would have its camp-fire alight at so late an hour. It could be nothing less formidable than a Kaffir encampment, and that of a strong force, judging from the fearlessness manifested in the small amount of care taken to conceal the blaze. And a Kaffir encampment meant an enemy's encampment, and that enemy a savage one. So he avoided the vicinity of the light, and held on his way with increased watchfulness.

What weary work it was, mile upon mile over more or less rough ground, every rise surmounted revealing another beyond it, every step covering the possibility of stumbling upon a concealed enemy. Sometimes, too, he would be obliged to deviate a long way from his course, to avoid a deep and bushy kloof, whose vegetation was so dense as to be practically impenetrable. Staggering now with weariness, he was about to sink down to sleep away the remainder of the night, when his gaze lit upon that which banished sleep from him for the moment.

The ground was open there; smooth, and gently undulating. In front, standing in the middle of the flat, was a house.

Was this a delusion? He rubbed his eyes. There, in the faint light of the now setting moon, stood the house, a substantial-looking farm homestead. It was no delusion. Visions of a snug bed, and an inexpressibly welcome sleep, beset the weary wayfarer; of a remount, and a speedy arrival at Doppersdorp—*via* Suffield's farm. Eagerly, joyfully, his step regained its elasticity, as he advanced to knock up the sleeping inmates, who, English or Dutch, would certainly receive him with the customary hospitality.

But as he drew near, again his heart sank like lead. No barking of dogs greeted his footsteps. The kraals were empty and the gates open, the shatters of the windows were up. The house was deserted.

"Of course!" he mattered despondently. "The cursed place is empty. Perhaps there's somebody left in charge, though."

But even as he approached the door he realised that there was that indescribable something about the place which told that no human being was there, a kind of lifelessness that might be felt. He knocked, but only a hollow echo from the empty passage gave mocking and ghostly response.

"Oh, curse the luck of it all!" he growled. "Hang me if I don't break in. They'll have left a shakedown of a sort anyhow, and I'll do a snug snooze; besides, one may chance to stumble upon a bottle of grog stowed away."

He looked around. Close by, a black square mass, indistinct in the waning moon, lay the deserted sheep-kraals. But now he noticed what had escaped him before. Behind the house, perhaps fifty yards distant from it, was an enclosed fruit garden, and the trees seemed weighed down with their luscious loads. Ah! the very thing. In his parched and exhausted condition, what would go down better than a dozen or so of peaches or apricots? So, postponing his exploration of the interior, he directed his steps to the garden, and getting over the low sod wall which encircled it, began with the "know" of a connoisseur to look for the tree which bore the best fruit.

This was soon found. Halting under a peach-tree he gathered the fruit as he wanted it, breaking it open and scrutinising it carefully by what little light the moon afforded; for the South African peach is not to be eaten in the dark, its interior being as often as not a mass of squirming maggots; and of it holds good the same as of some human beings—the more immaculately perfect the exterior, the greater the settled corruption within. However, the light was moderately sufficient for such requisite discrimination, and soon he had made a most luscious and acceptable feed.

This done, he returned to the house and carefully tested all the shutters. They were made of strong slabs, and held firm. But there was one small window at the back which was not shuttered, only protected by a board, fitting to the window-frame. This Roden wrenched away in a trice, and seeing that there was no other way of doing it, proceeded cautiously to break a pane of glass.

Heavens! what a clatter and jingle it made in the stillness of the night— the shower of glass falling upon the stone window-sill, and into the room! Then, carefully inserting his hand, Roden was able to pull back the bolt, and in another moment was in the house.

"Well, this is my first burglary, anyhow," he said grimly to himself, as striking a match he began to survey the surroundings.

Frontier farmhouses are all built pretty much on the same plan, and almost invariably one-storeyed. Roden saw at a glance he was in the kitchen, but it and the living rooms were equally dismantled. The owners of the place, whoever they were, had evidently not trekked in a panic, but in leisurely fashion enough to have taken away with them pretty nearly all that could be taken.

There is always something more or less ghostly about the interior of an empty house at night time. As Roden went from room to room, exploring by the feeble light of a flickering wax vesta, it seemed that in the dark corners lurked the shadows of the former occupants, watching, with resentful and menacing stare, this burglarious intruder. The planks, creaking beneath his footfall, raised loud and unearthly sounds in the hollow silence, and once in the semi-gloom, the swaying of an old blanket, hung overhead on a line, gave him a real start, so strung were his nerves with excitement and fatigue. But the object of his search was a prosaic one enough. He explored every room, every cupboard, the store closet, everything. There were a few old tins of preserved salmon, and a box or two of sardines, half a sack of mildewed flour, and a string of onions. There were utensils of various kinds, all old and worthless, heaped among empty mustard tins and glass bottles of all sorts and sizes. But of what he sought, there was none.

"I'm certain I'd give a sovereign at this moment for a good glass of grog!" he told himself. "However, it isn't to be had, and I was in lack to drop in here in the fruit season. Those peaches were A1. I think I'll go and talk to them again."

But, simultaneously with this determination, a great drowsiness began to come over him. In one of the front rooms, among the heavier furniture which had been left, was a coach, large and massive, and withal comfortable; just the very coach to invite a wearied and exhausted man. So, fixing the shatters so as to admit a crack of air, he flung himself upon the coach, and was sound asleep as soon as he touched it.

Now there came into Roden's slumbers, at first dead and dreamless, a kind of restful consciousness as languorously soothing as at that hoar on the night after his mishap, when Mona had sat at his bed head, charming him off to sleep by the mere touch of her hand upon his forehead, by the soft intonation of her love-thrilled voice at his ear. Surely, her presence was with him now, here in this lonely deserted dwelling in the heart of the hostile country. He had but to reach forth his hand and touch her. Once more the charm availed, and again he sank into the unconsciousness of a peaceful, dreamless slumber.

Soon, he stirred again in his sleep, and muttered uneasily. Her face was before him once more, and on it was imprinted that same expression of love and agony and despair as he had seen there when he hung over that grisly abyss, in weakness and excruciating pain; her hand alone holding him up from the dreadful death. Some mysterious and awful peril seemed to be rolling in upon him now, holding him spellbound and powerless to move. Now, as then, she was striving to drag him into safety, but futilely. He had no power over himself. The weight which oppressed him was terrible. Then her face vanished in a whirl of despairing horror. Once more all was a blank, all was deadness. Only the silence of the lonely house, the regular breathing of the sleeper.

"Roden, wake! My heart's life! my beloved one! Wake, wake!"

The voice thrilled in the sleeper's ear, vibrating through the dense, silent darkness like the notes of a silvery-toned gong. Again there was a flash of a vision of that face again, pale with horror and dread, anguished beyond words—the vision of a white-clad form and long streaming hair.

With a spasmodic start Roden sat bolt upright. What did this mean, what did it portend, this voice of one who was at that moment a long day's journey distant, springing thus out of the darkness? Heavens! had anything happened to her? It was so real, so vivid, that despairing call! What did it mean? what could it mean?

Seated thus upright on the couch, his eyes rested upon the aperture formed by the fixing apart of the shutters. This, hardly distinguishable before, save for a bright star or two beyond it, was now a stave of light. Daylight? That was his first thought; but in a moment he knew that it was not daylight, for it was flickering, changing. The band of light was now a strong, red glare; and together with the sight there came a sound which there was do mistaking.

Roden was wide awake now; as wide awake as ever he had been in his life. Rising noiselessly from the couch, gun in hand, even as he had slept, he made his way, still noiselessly and with great care to avoid knocking against any obstacle, to the window. One wary glance through the aperture, and then he beheld that which came near causing the last shred of hope to die within his heart.

Chapter Twenty Two
Between Blade and Flame

The open space in front of the house was alive with armed Kaffirs. Some were looking at the windows, others were fanning into flame torches which they carried. More and more came crowding up behind, and the subdued hubbub of their bass voices was the sound Roden had heard upon first awakening. They were about as murderous looking a crowd of savages as the eyes of the solitary white man, practically in their power already, could ever have the ill fate to rest on. Most of them were entirely naked, save for a blanket, carried rather than worn, and, smeared from head to foot with red ochre and grease, showed like glistening fiends in the smoky glare of the torches, as their sinuous frames moved to and fro with feline suppleness. A few wore massive ivory rings on one arm, and all were bedecked with some species of fantastic and barbarous adornment; the crest of the mohan, or the long trailing feathers of the blue crane; cows' tails too, and grotesque necklaces of wooden beads made of "charm" wood; also belts of jackals' claws. Nearly all had a firearm of some sort, in addition to a goodly sheaf of dark, snaky assegais. And their intention there could be no mistaking. They were there to fire this deserted farmstead.

Already they were blowing the torches into flame, chattering volubly in their destructive glee, as they told each other what a brave blaze this building was going to make. Already several were dragging up great piles of dry thorns, torn from the fencing of the empty sheep-kraals, amid roars of laughter and joking, as the sharp points would prick the naked carcasses of those who gathered them. This was fun indeed; this was sport. Many of them had worked as farm servants on just such a place as this, one or two perhaps on this very place. Now they were going to enjoy the fun of burning it to the ground, and it would make a merry blaze. And shut up within it was a white man, one of the dominant race who was surely and steadily quelling their futile rising, laying low with its deadly breech-loaders the flower of their youth by thousands. One of that now hated race would figure herein at his own holocaust. But this they did not know.

Roden Musgrave thought for a moment, and thought hard. Not for nothing had the very soul of his absent love thrilled across the mysterious dream-space of the slumber world—to save him. Not for nothing had that anguished voice sounded in his ear amid the darkness of the lonely room, to bid him waken and face the grisly peril which hung over him. A minute more, and it would have sounded too late: was it not, indeed, too late now?

There was one chance and only one—the back window. To it immediately he made his way.

That chance was that the savages had not entirely surrounded the house; and it was a poor one.

He looked swiftly but warily forth. That side seemed clear. Deeming it a deserted dwelling the Kaffirs had not thought of surrounding it. All were now gathered in front watching or aiding in the preparations for a grand blaze. Yet the light of the torches shed a glow even upon that side. Still, to hesitate was death.

He dropped through the window, and as he glided swiftly across the open space, which lay between him and the welcome shade of the fruit garden, every moment he expected the roar which should greet his discovery; the whiz of flying assegais, the crash of bullets. But fortune favoured him, and in a moment he lay crouching in the ditch behind the low sod wall, just as the flame was applied to the piles of brushwood which had been heaped against the front of the house.

His first thought had been to escape while they were busy at their congenial work of destruction. But the house stood upon an open flat, and now as the flames roared upward the whole of the surroundings were lit up as in the light of day. Only the insignificant area covered by the welcome shade of the fruit trees afforded concealment. A rat even, stealing across that illumined space, would instantly be discovered. There was no escape that way.

Peering warily through the tufted grasses which had taken root along the top of the sod wall, Roden's gaze fell upon a scene which was indescribably barbarous and weird. From every side of the house now the flames were bursting forth; windows and doors belching out great red fiery tongues, sometimes with such fury as to drive back helter-skelter a crowd of the savage incendiaries, and in thick, rolling columns the smoke-clouds swept upward, veiling the midnight stars. And forming up in a ring around the burning dwelling the excited barbarians were executing a frenzied war-dance, their red, ochre-smeared frames demon-like as they swung half to one side then to the other, stamping their feet in unison. And above the roar and crackle of the blazing pile the fierce, throaty rhythm of the war-song rose higher and higher, louder and louder, its every note quivering with an insatiate lust for blood. Then, as the frenzy reached its height, leaving their places the savages would ran to and fro, making downward stabs in imitation of slaying those who had been driven out by the flames and were striving to escape. Others again would approach as near as they could, and make believe to be in wait for those who should climb out through the windows — receiving them on their assegais with a deep-throated, bloodthirsty gasp. The pantomime was perfect, and he who crouched there as an involuntary spectator could not forbear a cold shudder, as he witnessed thus vividly represented before him the fate from which he had so narrowly, and by a moment of time, escaped.

But had he escaped it? His present position was one the peril of which it was impossible to exaggerate. Here he lay, imperfectly concealed, within a few yards of at least a hundred barbarians, excited to the most frenzied pitch of ferocity. The fruit garden, which might have covered half an acre, was fenced on the farther side by high, thick quince hedges, through which it would be impossible to make his way noiselessly, if at all; otherwise the idea came to him of attempting flight through the back of the garden while the attention of the Kaffirs was occupied with their barbarous dance. On this side only, that which was bounded by the stone wall, was exit possible, which would mean walking out right into the teeth of his enemies. It was not to be thought of. He was securely trapped — cornered like a snared leopard. Well, he would die like one, fighting to the last. But this resolve afforded not much consolation. We doubt if it ever does.

With an eye to render his precarious position more secure if possible, he gazed warily around. At the end of the sod wall where it joined the quince hedge, he thought the ditch might be deeper, the long grass or other undergrowth thicker. The lay of the ground seemed to point that way. But how to get to it?

Again raising his head to a level with the grass-tufts, he sent a quick, rapid look at the Kaffirs. They were at the very height of their ferocious orgie, and the wild roaring chorus, together with the crash and crackle of the flames, made such a hellish din, that they would have no ears for any sound he might make. So, keeping below the level of the top of the wall, he crept along the ditch.

His hands were lacerated with many thorns, and the pain was excruciating, yet he dared not pause. Any moment the fit might seize upon his enemies to enter the garden. His hopes were to some degree realised. The end of the ditch did afford a greater depression, and its sides were grown with tall grass and brambles. Here, in the corner, he ensconced himself, lying flat to the ground and drawing the undergrowth over him; the while, however, reserving as much freedom for his hands as possible.

Now into Roden's heart, to inspire him with renewed hope, came two considerations. One was the possibility of rescue. Such a conflagration as this would show for a great distance, and would certainly attract attention, and possibly a strong patrol. The other consideration was a superstitious one. That voice—that marvellously clear-sounding voice, which had thrice come into his dreams in miraculous warning, could not be destined to fail in its mission. He had heard it as distinctly as though its owner were standing there visible before him; that he could swear until his dying day. Never could that startling and signal triple warning have been conveyed to him in vain—never, never could it have been sent to rescue him at the moment of one imminent peril, only that he might succumb immediately to another. It was a weird, sweet, irrational ground for hope, but he held on to it firmly for all that.

Then when the frenzy of the war-dance was at its wildest, fiercest pitch, the bright, gushing flames leaped suddenly on high, as, with a roar like thunder, the roof fell in. A volume of dense, reddened smoke shot upward to the heavens, while a vast cataract of whirling sparks fell around in a seething, fiery hail. The uproarious mirth of the savages changed into wild yells of alarm and dismay as they scurried hither and thither to avoid the falling embers; but the panic was only momentary. Grasping at once the harmless nature of this startling change, they quickly crowded up again, making the night ring with their boisterous laughter, as they chaffed each other vociferously over the scare they had undergone.

For a little while they stood staring at the smoking, glowing embers, chattering volubly. Then Roden, crouching half-buried in his ditch, could feel the vibration of the sod wall, could hear the approach of voices now sounding almost in his ear. Ah! They had discovered his presence. With heart beating and teeth locked together he held his revolver ready in his right hand. His hour had come. One short, sharp struggle, the crash of a shot or two, then the searing anguish of the sharp blades buried in his vitals, the sickening gasp for life, and—his being would have ceased.

Again the ground shook above him. In the dim light he could make out numberless shapes swarming over the sod wall. They dropped into the garden, right on, right over the spot where he had at first lain concealed. Well indeed was it that he had changed his position. And now the object of this new move became manifest. No suspicion of his presence had led to it. Another motive was at work, which it was as well he had not till then thought of, else had he risked certain detection in flight, rather than trust to a hiding-place under the circumstances so transparently insecure. They had come after the fruit.

He could see them standing there, drawing down the laden branches and stripping them of their luscious burden; could hear the swishing, gurgling sound of their jaws as they bit into the ripe peaches and apricots, thrusting them whole into their mouths, and throwing the stones at each other in horseplay, like so many British roughs on a Bank holiday. In sheer wantonness they tore off great boughs covered with fruit and heaped them on the ground, till soon every tree was as nearly as possible stripped, and they were gorged almost to repletion. Then others came over to join in the feast, and now Roden's heart was again in his throat, for a bevy of them swarmed over the wall just where he lay, the ankle of one even coming into hard contact with the crown of his head. But the warrior, thinking he had kicked a stone, did not look twice, and that peril was passed. Yet, lying there, liable to be butchered at any moment, slain like a rat in a trap, was appalling, and not far short of an equivalent for dying a hundred deaths.

By this time the first streak of dawn was showing in the eastern horizon, and the Kaffirs, now replete, began to depart. Still, many showed a disposition to linger, gathering up the fruit in their skin tobacco bags and blankets, and the ray of hope which had come with that ray of dawn began to fade again into a darkness that bordered on despair. Would they never go? Every moment the earth was becoming lighter. In a light less than half that of the light of day Roden's hiding-place would afford concealment no more. He would be discovered in an instant.

They had all gone at last, and their receding voices were decreasing in sound and volume; all except one, and this confounded fellow seemed to have a weakness for variety; for now he was coming along the quince hedge, sampling its productions; coming straight upon Roden's hiding-place.

Twenty—ten—five yards—then so close that the latter might have grasped him. Now a particularly fine quince growing just above reach seemed to attract the eye of the Kaffir. He made a spring—seized the fruit, and, missing his footing, stumbled and fell backward bodily on top of the concealed white man.

Roden was up in a moment. With the quickness of a snake he had seized the Kaffir by the throat before the latter could rise, and had pressed the muzzle of his revolver to the man's face.

The shout of dismay and of warning which arose to the lips of the savage died in his throat. The black, murderous shining ring of the muzzle seemed to burn through him even as though already he felt the contents. The countenance of his white adversary was terrific in its fell fury of purpose, for it was the face of a thoroughly desperate man, balancing unsteadily on the brink of that precipice, which is Death.

"One sound," whispered Roden, in Boer Dutch. "Only one sound!" and his look supplied the rest.

Kaffirs are the most practical of mortals. This one was a thick-set and sinewy savage, and were it a hand to hand tussle with his white adversary in which muscular strength alone counted, would have stood every chance. But the first movement would mean the pressure of that deadly trigger, and a head blown to atoms. One shout would have brought his countrymen swarming around him, and the white man would be cut to ribbons in a moment. But that would not result in bringing himself back to life, nor in piecing together again his own head, shattered to a thousand fragments; wherefore he deemed it sound policy to lie still as ordered.

But as he lay there, breathing hard and staring with protruding and amazed eyeballs at the face of the man who threatened him, even the terror of his position could not restrain a smothered gasp; for it was the expression of a mighty astonishment. And his amaze communicated itself to Roden, who by the fast increasing light, now recognised in the countenance of this ferocious-looking and ochre-smeared warrior the honest lineaments of the good-humoured and civil store-boy, Tom.

Yes, it was Tom; each had recognised the other now—Tom, who had come to him like Nicodemus, by night, at the instigation of that unscrupulous rascal Sonnenberg, to endeavour to entrap him into a flagrant violation of the ammunition laws, by inducing him to sell the old gun—Tom who had so deftly turned the tables afterwards upon his scoundrelly employer. Well, he had a gun now, for there it lay beside the assegais, which had escaped from his hand as he fell.

"I know you, Tom," he whispered in Dutch. "I won't harm you if you go away and don't tell the others I'm here."

The Kaffir stared. "*Auf!*" he exclaimed; "let me go, *Baas*. I'll say nothing."

Roden looked into the dark, ochre-smeared face. Even beneath this hideous disguise it had an honest look.

"I trust you, Tom," he said. "Listen, I have not seen you here, you understand, when I return to Doppersdorp, and you—you have not seen me now."

The other nodded violently.

"Go then, Tom. I trust you."

The Kaffir, released, rose to his feet, and seized his weapons. It was a critical moment for Roden. So were those which followed.

For now, footsteps were heard returning, the footsteps of several persons, and voices.

"Hey, Geunkwe!" called out one of the latter, "Have you not had enough yet? Wait, we will come and have some more, too."

"No, no!" cried Tom, *alias* Geunkwe, hurriedly. "I am coming. We had better not linger here. The smoke will attract white men, and the country is too open. Let us hurry on after the others, before it is too late." And springing over the sod wall, he joined those still outside the garden who had returned to look for him; and with inexpressible relief Roden could hear their deep voices receding into distance and silence.

Even then, a misgiving assailed him. Could a savage be trusted, especially in war-time? What if this one, now out of reach of the threatening revolver, should betray him to his countrymen? What if even now the latter were stealing back to surprise and overpower him without loss to themselves? The idea was not an exhilarating one.

But although he understood but little of what had passed, he had been struck by the eagerness with which Tom had striven to prevent his fellow-countrymen from entering, and had succeeded. Even this, however, might be part of the *ruse*. Yet he tried to believe that the Kaffir was trustworthy, as indeed the event proved, for when, after lying concealed for upwards of an hour more, Roden ventured cautiously to peer forth, lo, there was not an enemy in sight.

The sun was now above the horizon, and the bird and insect life of the veldt was starting into glad and joyous being, as Roden, cramped and stiff from his constrained attitude, stepped warily forth to explore. The black ruins of the burnt house still smouldered, sending up jets of blue smoke, and as he stood in the dazzling radiance of the new-born day, contemplating this holocaust of savage hate and vengeance, he thought with a sweet, warm glow around his heart, not unmixed with awe, of how that mysterious voice had called him forth from the slumber which would have ended in the slumber of death.

He turned back to the fruit garden to breakfast on its luscious contents, for his saddlebag had been left within the burning house, and no other food had he. While thus occupied, a sound as of the faint tramping of feet in the distance recalled all his instincts of self-preservation. But he needed to take no second look. Mounted figures crested the sky line—whites—who, to the number of a score and a half, were cantering rapidly towards the still smoking ruins. Then Roden got out and filled his pipe, and having lighted it, sat down on the sod wall and calmly began to blow a cloud.

"Great Scott, Musgrave! is that you or your ghost?" cried Darrell, who was riding at the head of the party. "Why, what on earth has happened to you all this while, man?"

"It's me, I believe, but I'm not quite sure of it even now," answered Roden. "And, Darrell, and you fellows, look there. If you had been spending the night lying bunched up in that corner, while John Kaffir was hooraying around a blazing house fifty yards off, and when he had quit that, jumping right over you, and even on to you, on his way to eat peaches, why, you wouldn't be quite sure of it either."

Then followed explanations, and how the runaway steed had returned straight to camp, and had been at once recognised by more than one citizen of Doppersdorp there under arms; and how Darrell had been able to collect a patrol, and start post-haste in search of so perilously situated a fellow-countryman as one afoot in the middle of the hostile ground. And all stared open-mouthed as Roden narrated all that had befallen him, including his narrow escape from the deserted house. But of the cause which effected that timely flight he said nothing.

"Well, Musgrave, and which way did they go?" said Darrell, when he had done.

"Who?"

"Why, the Kaffirs, of course. We'll go and give 'em hell."

"Darrell, get down into that ditch, there where I was. Tuck your head under your wing, and hold your very breath, and then see how competent you are to form a judgment as to the direction in which any given crowd has retreated."

"Well, we can spoor them."

"I wouldn't. They've got hours of start; besides, they're beastly numerous, and you're not. No, let them alone."

Now the extent of the above start, eke of the numerical strength of the enemy, was an exaggeration, and one of set design. Tom, *alias* Geunkwe, had kept strict faith with him, and Roden Musgrave did not want that honourable savage to be shot or captured, if by a moderate stretch of veracity he could prevent it.

Chapter Twenty Three
A Change

"Well, Musgrave, old boy, I'm glad to see you back again," cried genial Peter Van Stolz, wringing his subordinate's hand, as the latter entered the office just before Court time on the morning following the events last detailed. "There are two or three drunk cases to polish off; they won't take ten minutes, and then I want to hear all your adventures."

So Sannje Pretorius, and Carolus Dirksen, and two or three other worthy specimens of the noble Hottentot, having been fined five or ten shillings apiece, with the alternative of seven days hard, the administrator of Doppersdorp justice lost no time in returning to be put in possession of such more or less stirring facts as the reader is already familiar with. Not altogether, however, for the narrator had a strange repugnance to chronicling his own deeds of slaughter, which, in fact, he so slurred over as to make it appear rather that they had been done by Darrell—a vicarious distinction from which that worthy, at any rate, would in no wise have shrunk. Nor, we hardly need say, did he reveal his meeting with Tom. On that point his lips were sealed, even to his friend. His word, once passed, was inviolable.

It happened that he had come straight into Doppersdorp, abandoning the projected *détour* by Suffield's farm, for a sort of nervous exhaustion, supervening on the strain and hardships of that terrible and trying night, had compelled him to take some hours' rest beneath the first sheltering roof which he came across after his rescue by Darrell and his party, who had escorted him on his road until beyond further risk, returning then to the Main Camp. Hence, reckoning he had been away long enough, he made up his mind to reach Doppersdorp in time for Court. He would ride over to Quaggasfontein in the evening.

Then, at the midday recess, Roden found himself carried off to dine, in order that Mrs Van Stolz might hear his adventures. At that point of his narrative which touched upon the villainous behaviour of the defaulting steed, they all laughed again and again, while recognising that it was no laughing matter at the time.

"What will Miss Ridsdale say when she hears all about it?" said Mrs Van Stolz mischievously. "I suppose you haven't seen her yet, Mr Musgrave?"

Roden answered that he had not, and then a little more sly fun was poked at him. Finally, it became time to return.

"You see, it's post day, Musgrave, old boy," said Mr Van Stolz, as they walked back to the office together, "or I would say, Clear out. I know you are dying to go up to Suffield's. But it may be in early, and there's sure to be nothing of much importance. After it's in, you can clear out as soon as you like. Hark! there's the horn now. The cart's just coming over the neck."

It was. About a mile or so up the road they could make out the rising dust, which should soon resolve itself into a weather-beaten, two-wheeled cart, laden with mail-sacks, and driven by a yellow-skinned Hottentot, tootling on a battered trumpet. Nor was it much longer before a portion of its contents was duly transferred to the public offices.

"Congratulate me, Musgrave!" cried Mr Van Stolz, skipping into his subordinate's room, with an open official letter in his hand. "Congratulate me! I'm promoted!"

But the beaming and joyous expression of his countenance found no reflection in that of Roden, who said—

"As far as you are the better for it, I do most heartily. Speaking selfishly, however, it's the worst news I've heard for many a long day."

The other stared for a moment, then his face softened. No congratulations could have conveyed a more direct tribute to the esteem in which he was held by the speaker.

"Thanks, old fellow," he said, "I know what you mean. We've always got on right well together, I really believe."

"Got on? I should rather think we had. The man who couldn't get on with you could get on with nobody."

Still more did the other stare. This habitually cold, reserved cynic! To hear him now, would be to think the man was full of heart.

"I'm afraid my congratulation is of a rueful order at best," said Roden, with a smile. "And now, where is the transfer to, and what increase does it carry?"

"Barabastadt. It's just such another hole as Doppersdorp—poor old Doppersdorp isn't such a bad little place though. It's away in the Karroo at the foot of the Rooi Ruggensbergen. Good springbok shooting, I believe.

And it means 100 pounds a year more, which is a consideration when a man's hat doesn't cover all his family. Look; there's the letter."

Roden ran his eye down the sheet, which set forth in official rigmarole that His Excellency the Governor, with the advice of the Executive Council, had been pleased to appoint Mr Peter Van Stolz to be Civil Commissioner and Resident Magistrate of Barabastadt, at a salary of so much per annum, in the room of Mr Somebody Else transferred.

"And your successor, what sort of man is he?" he said at length.

"Shaston? Frederick Romsey Shaston. A devil of a name that, Musgrave. Well, he's rather like his name, rather a pompous sort of chap. I remember him four years ago, when he was 'acting' at Maraisburg. He was always getting his judgments reversed. He's not a bad sort of fellow though; not at all a bad sort of fellow at bottom."

This is a species of eulogy which is of the faintly exculpatory order, and from both the words and the tone none knew better than Roden Musgrave that his new chief would be almost certain to prove a direct antithesis to his old one.

"No, he isn't a bad sort of fellow, Musgrave, if you take him the right way. You'll get on all right."

In his heart of hearts the speaker knew as surely as he could know anything that the two would *not* get on all right; however, he was not going to say so.

"It isn't the 'getting on' part of it I'm thinking of, Mr Van Stolz," said Roden. "Can't you credit me with realising that true friends are scarce, and not feeling overjoyed at the prospect of losing a firm specimen of the article?"

"Of course, of course. I understand. But, Musgrave, old boy, you mustn't talk about losing a friend, hope we shall not have seen the last of each other because I have left this. Why, we have had plenty of good times together, and will have plenty more. The wife likes you so much, too. No, no. Of one thing we may be sure. You have always firm friends in us, no matter what happens."

"Thank you. I am sure of it," said Roden, on whom the words struck with something like a presentiment. And the time was coming when he was destined to remember them.

Cantering over the grassy flats in the slant of the golden sun-gleam, Roden's mind dwelt more and more on that mysterious midnight warning which had startled him from a slumber destined otherwise to end in the slumber of death. So signal had been its result, that the anxiety which had at first beset him, lest evil hovered over its utterer, was quite dispelled, giving place to a strange, sweet awe so foreign to his nature that he could hardly recognise his very self. Now, as he drew near Suffield's house, he smiled curiously at his own eagerness, and made believe to check it. There stood the homestead against its background of green willows, away over the flat, then, as the track dipped into a slight depression, he saw it no more.

All the way out, all that day, he had been trying to picture his reception, and very alluring had that occupation proved. He had never, as we have said, been away from Mona before, not away beyond reach, that is. How would she receive him? He thought he knew. Then, as the house again came into view, he strained his eyes for the first glimpse of that supple, exquisitely modelled form, for the first flutter of a dress. Yet no such glimpse rewarded him.

He was in a fanciful vein, and the circumstance of this dejection struck him with a sort of chill. He rode up to the door amid the clamour of the yelling pack, which, ever aggressive, charged him open-mouthed, a demeanour which speedily subsided into much jumping and tail-wagging as his identity became manifest. Then a gleam of light drapery down among the willows caught his eye. Ah, there she was, but not alone; for both Suffield and his wife were there, and the trio seemed to be indulging in the most prosaic of evening strolls. This then was to be that often-dwelt-on first meeting—a conventional hand-shake, a mere platitude of a "How d'you do?" In which especial particular the irony of circumstances manifests itself more often than not.

"Hallo, Musgrave! We were expecting you to-night or to-morrow," sang out Suffield. "Glad it's to-night. Well, how are you? How many Gaikas did you bowl over, and all the rest of it?"

There was no mistaking the cordiality of their greetings, anyway. And the swift glad flash of intense joy in Mona's eyes, and the pressure of her fingers told all that could have been told had their meeting taken place alone.

"Come in and have a glass of grog, Musgrave," went on Suffield, "and tell us the news from the front. Though, by the way, that'll keep till after I've counted in. There's Booi's flock nearly here already, I see. Never mind. We'll have our *sobje* anyhow."

There was something in the situation that reminded Roden of his first visit here; for Suffield soon departed to look after his sheep, and his wife did likewise to see to her lambs—i.e. her nursery; leaving him alone with Mona. How well he remembered it; the same sunset glow, the same attitude, the easy, subtle, sensuous grace of that splendid figure standing there by the open window outlined against the roseate sky. Even now that the moment he had been thirsting for was come, he hesitated to break the witchery of the spell, to disturb the unrivalled beauty of the picture.

She turned from the window and came to him. For an instant they stood gazing into each other's eyes, and then—the promise of the oft-pictured meeting was fulfilled.

"Darling, darling!" she murmured in thrilling tenderness, after that first long sweet embrace, locking her fingers in his with a grip that was almost convulsive. "I hold you now again. I did not believe it was in me to think so much, to suffer so much, on account of any one—any one. Oh, Heaven! how I have suffered! One night—the night before last—I had such a frightful dream. I dreamt you were threatened with the most appalling danger. I could see you, and you were lying asleep in a dim and shadowy place, and I could not warn you, could not raise my voice, could not utter a word. Hideous shapes, horrors untold were creeping up, crowding about you; still I could not speak. Then the spell was broken, and I called aloud, and woke up to find myself at the open window, and Grace standing there in the doorway looking the very picture of scare. For I really did call out."

A strange, eerie sensation crept over her listener. What sort of power was this—of separating soul from body during the mere ordinary unconsciousness produced by slumber?

"And that dream of yours, if it was a dream, was literally the saving of my life, Mona. Listen, now." And then he told exactly how he had lain asleep in the deserted house, and how, thrilled by the startling accents of her anguished voice in the midnight silence, the vision of her troubled countenance, he had awakened barely in time to escape certain death. The hour coincided exactly.

"How was I dressed?" whispered Mona, a strong awe subduing her voice, as she gazed at him with startled eyes, and trembling somewhat.

"The vision was more or less indefinite, all but the face. Yet you were in white, with flowing hair, as on that night when you braved everything to try and make me forget my bruised and battered condition in sleep."

"It is—is rather awful," she whispered, with a shudder. "But in every detail the—the picture corresponds—time, place, appearance, everything. Oh, darling, surely your life is mine, that it has been given me to save twice."

He was thinking the same thing. And then, running like a strand through the entrancement of this first meeting, came the thought of what such a consideration meant. Nothing lasts; love vulgarised by a commonplace legal tie least of all. This was one thing; but love united, with its hundred and one petty, uphill struggles and hardships, its familiarity breeding contempt, its daily friction of temper and will—that was another. He was not young enough to see only the enchantment of the moment, all deliriously sweet as this was. The other side of the picture would obtrude itself—disillusion, life soured. Nothing lasts; nothing which is real, that is. Such moments as this, such transitory blissful moments of a fool's paradise, came as near to happiness as anything this life could afford; yet even they were dashed by the consciousness, the certainty, that they were nothing more. They constituted life no more than the five large beads constitute the whole rosary; happy indeed were it, if the proportionate parallel held good, and that one great joy were allowed for every decade of sorrow, and disillusionment, and deadness and pain.

Greatly concerned was the household on learning the approaching transfer of Mr Van Stolz, of whom Suffield declared that the Lord might have been pleased to create a more thoroughly good sort, but that He hadn't.

"So he's going to Barabastadt, you say, Mr Musgrave?" said Grace. "We may see him again, then. There are some relations of ours living up there, the Rendleshams. We go and stay with them sometimes."

"Up there! Why, they're about sixty miles from the town," said Suffield. "They've got a place called Kameelsfontein, and the springbok shooting is heavenly."

"And the second family is the reverse," said Mona. Then, for Roden's benefit. "There's a second wife and two unutterably detestable step-daughters, and between the three they've managed to oust poor Ida, who is dear old John's only child. She was sent to England to be educated. We were great friends when I was over there last, though I am a good deal older than she is."

To the credit of Doppersdorp be it said, it likewise was greatly concerned over the departure of Mr Van Stolz; and if that genial official had ever felt doubts as to his widespread popularity, no further room for such existed now, if the expressions of regret which met him on all sides counted for anything. And by way of giving public expression to this, a banquet on such a scale was organised at the Barkly Hotel, as to inspire in the commercial mind of Jones regrets that a paternal government did not furnish a perennial supply of highly popular officials to Doppersdorp, providing at the same time for their transfer at least every three months. And how the champagne corks which popped during that historic entertainment constituted a great multitude which no man could number; and how Sonnenberg was of deliberate purpose, and of malice aforethought, set down to carve a roasted sucking-pig; and now he not only cheerfully performed that function, but likewise partook largely of the infantile porker, in direct defiance of his tormentors and of the law of Moses; and how the thunders of applause which greeted the toast of the guest of the evening, caused Jones to tremble lest his property should be engulphed in a fate similar to that which overtook the temple of Dagon; and how Roden Musgrave, responding for The Civil Service, waxed so eloquent upon the virtues of his departing chief, as to draw from the latter the stage-whispered remark, that "butter seemed cheap just then";—are not all these things graven in the annals of Doppersdorp, which is the Centre of the Earth? How, too, many of the assembled worthies, those who ate peas with their knives, and those who did not, finished up the evening by getting gloriously drunk, the anxiety of whom to "chair" home the said guest of the evening being only defeated by those whose regard for that official's valuable existence, even though it should thenceforward be spent elsewhere, was of a practical nature;— this, too, we regret to say, is likewise faithfully recorded among the archives aforesaid. But the enthusiasm of Doppersdorp, if highly demonstrative, not to say uproarious, was, for once in a way, very real.

Chapter Twenty Four
"Who Knew Not Joseph"

Mr Frederick Romsey Shaston, the new Resident Magistrate of Doppersdorp, was in every respect a direct antithesis of the old one.

In aspect he was a square-built, middle-aged man, with grizzled hair, and rather thin, short beard, prominent nose, and cold blue eyes; a man of few words, and those few words, when spoken, conveying distinctly that in the speaker's mind there was but one opinion worth the slightest consideration in all the world—viz., that of Mr Frederick Romsey Shaston.

He was a man to dislike on sight, one whose manner might be termed brusque for the sake of euphemy, but which sometimes and by accident just fell short of being offensive; a man in whom lurked not one spark of geniality or kindly feeling; a cold, flaccid, mental jelly fish.

The flourish of trumpets which had enveloped the departure of his predecessor was an offence to him, possibly as suggesting the certainty of a very different farewell, when his own time should come. In this spirit he went closely into all connected with the office, hoping to discover some pretext for throwing mud at Mr Van Stolz' administration. But he might as well have tried to chip a snowball out of the moon.

To Roden Musgrave he took an intense dislike, which he exhibited in first pointedly wondering at finding a man of his age in that position; an impertinence which its recipient could afford utterly to ignore. From the very first, however, he had made up his mind to bring about a change, partly to secure the berth for a relation of his wife, partly because he only felt comfortable with young subordinates, whom he could treat as he chose; whereas this one, even he realised that he could not treat as he chose.

For he knew that in experience and knowledge of the world, this man was immeasurably his superior; and the better able to hold his own, that he was most thoroughly up to his work. He had mastered all the ins and outs of office and court routine, and had everything at his fingers' ends. He would be an extremely difficult man to oust; yet as we have said, Mr Shasten made up his mind from the very first that ousted he should be.

By the attorneys and law-agents practising in the District Court the new R.M. was most cordially detested. Not one of them but had been snubbed more or less—frequently more—when practising before Mr Van Stolz, but never undeservedly, and this they well knew. So, too, did they know that outside the Court, that sunny-natured official would be the first to crack a joke with them, or lend them his horse, or do them a good turn in any way he could. The present occupant of the Bench, however, was past master in the art of delivering himself of cold, scathing, contemptuous rebukes. The practitioners for once agreed among themselves. They put their heads together and arranged to "go for" him whenever opportunity offered, and now and again it did offer, for Mr Shaston was at times a trifle shaky, alike in his procedure and in his judgments. Then they went for him tooth and nail, Darrell especially, who feared no man living, and between whom find the new official many a passage of arms would occur, of increasing fierceness and frequency.

With the farmers, too, he was unpopular. Mr Van Stolz, himself a Dutchman, had been pre-eminently the right man in the right place. Mr Shaston, however, was utterly devoid of that bluff, open-hearted species of blarney which is the right way to the Boer heart; consequently, by that stolid and wooden-headed race, he was regarded as the most stiff and starched type of the *verdommde Engelschman*. Moreover, rightly or wrongly, he soon acquired a reputation for favouring the native servants, as against their white employers, in such cases as came before him; which reputation once established on the part of a magistrate is a very death knell to his popularity among the Boers, and scarcely less so among their fellow English stock-raisers.

Some among the townspeople he condescended to admit to a certain degree of friendship. Among these was Lambert, the District Surgeon, also Sonnenberg; both of whom toadied him fulsomely, for they began to see in the new R.M. a possible weapon for striking a deadly blow at the object of their respective hate. His dislike of his subordinate was by this time patent, and both worthies now began to chuckle; for they foresaw the not far distant removal of the latter from Doppersdorp. Not that this would satisfy the malice of the vindictive Jew; nothing would, short of the ruin and disgrace of his enemy. Since the gun episode, resulting so signally in the biter being bit, and bit hard, Sonnenberg had cudgelled his crafty and scheming brain to hit upon a plan, but hitherto in vain. As postmaster, the thought had crossed his mind that he might in some way or another strike at his enemy through his correspondence. But then the latter never received or despatched any correspondence; never from month's end till month's end. This in itself was singular, and set the Jew thinking.

Now, if there was one individual whom the change of administration concerned almost more than all the rest of the community put together, that individual was Roden himself. No more was the daily routine lightened by an occasional cheery talk, the ever-present joke, and the sociable pipe, and above all by the most perfect of mutual good feeling. This he was prepared for. But when his new superior began to show his hostility in the most needlessly gratuitous fashion; to find fault, and that too often publicly, where, as a matter of fact, no fault was to be found, his temper, at no time a long-suffering one, began to feel the strain. Still he kept it in hand, observing the most rigid scrupulosity in the discharge of his duties, and giving no handle to the other for putting him in the wrong. He knew that an explosion was only a question of time, and was shrewd enough so to order his doings as to keep on the right side.

But, if in his new official superior he had found an enemy, he had made one in the person of that functionary's wife, though this was perhaps inevitable. Personally Mrs Shaston was a good-looking woman, tall, and of rather striking appearance, who had once been very handsome. But to her husband's brusquerie she added a commanding manner, or, to drop euphemy, a domineering one, which rendered her a trifle more unpopular than himself, if that were possible. She had at first inclined to a modicum of reserved graciousness towards Roden Musgrave, which soon changed to the most bitter and virulent rancour, when she discovered that he had no notion whatever of being turned into a sort of running footman. Her husband's subordinates were her subordinates; such was her creed, and what did a subordinate mean but one who had to do as he was told? So when Roden took the earliest opportunity of differing with her on this point, and that in the most practical way possible, she became his bitter enemy for all time.

Daily his position became more manifestly unpleasant. He had never laid himself out to win anybody's goodwill, and this sin of omission had rendered him as unpopular as those of commission on the part of his chief had brought about a like result concerning the latter. Of two unpopular officials in a place like Doppersdorp, or for the matter of that anywhere, the most powerful would score, and Mr Shaston after all was a power in the community. Moreover, such a community has a special faculty for producing a large litter of curs, wherefore many who had been effusively civil to Roden Musgrave when the latter was hand-in-glove with Mr Van Stolz, now showed their real nature by turning round and barking at *him* unceasingly.

Now, of course such pleasant little amenities as smoking pipes in office hours, or shutting up at all sorts of times when there was nothing particular doing, though tending to render life pleasant, were, after all, irregular, and no one knew this better than Roden; consequently he was quite prepared for all sorts of changes in this direction, and accepted them cheerfully. But his new superior thought he saw a very promising ground of annoyance, which might, if deftly worked, bring about the revolt he desired.

"There is a matter I have been intending to speak to you about, Mr Musgrave," he began one day when Roden had taken some correspondence in to be signed, "and that is your very frequent absences; I don't mean from the office during hours, but from the town. For instance, I find that you are frequently absent from Doppersdorp the whole night, visiting your friends in the country, and not infrequently for two nights."

"But that would be only from Saturday evening to Monday morning early, sir; while off duty."

"A Civil Servant is never off duty, Mr Musgrave, except when he is on leave of absence," was the frigid rejoinder. "Now, I am not aware that the absences to which I refer come under that heading."

With a strong effort Roden mastered his contemptuous indignation, for he saw that his superior had discovered a new form of mean and petty annoyance. He had far too much *savoir vivre* to make any such retort as would have arisen to the lips of nine men but of ten in like position—viz., that Mr Van Stolz had never raised any such objection. So he said:

"Do I understand, sir, that you object to my sleeping the night at a friend's house if outside Doppersdorp, even though I am back punctually for office hours?"

The other felt vicious. The question was unpleasant in its directness, and, while put with perfect respect, its pointedness seemed cutting.

"Er—you see, Mr Musgrave, we are supposed to be resident here—that is, to reside here; the object of which is that we may be found when wanted, and that object is defeated if we are whole nights, or a day and a night, away from the place. It is not a personal matter, not a question of what *I* object to; but supposing any emergency were to arise requiring your presence, and nobody knew where to find you; or at any rate, that you were so far away that it amounted to the same thing!"

"Would you mind, sir, stating for my guidance the precise distance the Service regulations allow an official to ride or walk without having obtained formal leave of absence?"

The other felt very cornered at this persistent attempt to knock his objections to match-wood, and proportionately savage.

A Veldt Official A Novel of Circumstance | 169

"I am surprised, Mr Musgrave," he said, speaking more quickly, "at a man of your age asking such a question. Surely you should know that there is a common-sense medium in all things."

"Still I should prefer to know exactly what restrictions the Service places upon our movements. Do you mean, sir, that we are never to pass the night at the house of a country friend without formal leave of absence?"

"No, no. I don't mean to lay down quite such a hard and fast rule," was the more yielding reply, for this deft plurality imported into the pronoun was disconcerting. "What I would dwell upon, however, is the strong desirability of returning to the town to sleep, unless detained by unforeseen circumstances, such as stress of weather, or anything else which is absolutely unavoidable."

"I shall remember your wishes in the matter, sir," said Roden, in his habitual tone of studied and ceremonious politeness, which was the best commentary on the state of relations existing between himself and his new superior.

But although there was a show of reason in the other's objection, the real ugly motive was manifest—viz., petty annoyance, and the thought of how, at his time of life, his means of existence, or at any rate of that which made existence tolerable, should be dependent on his capacity for eating dirt at the hands of such a mean-minded snob as this Shaston, was bitter and galling to the last degree. The thing was getting past a joke, past all bearing, in fact. Should he endeavour to arrange a transfer? Mr Van Stolz might be able to help him in this. But then he hated to ask anything of anybody: besides, he did not choose to allow himself to be driven out of the place; to yield the ground; to own himself beaten. And then there was Mona.

Mona, the bright beacon star that had arisen upon the grey blankness of his latter-day life. Mona, whose sweet, entrancing spells had woven around the hard granite of his cynical and desolate heart a glittering network of golden sun-rays. Mona, whose secret lore had welled forth warm in its dazzling wares what time he hung helpless over the yawning jaws of death, and the power of whose marvellous love triumphing over the material forces of Nature itself, had again availed to save him. How could he, of his own act, think of leaving her, of going where day after day, week after week, even month after month, nothing would remain of her but a memory? Better endure a little discomfort; better exercise a further stretch of self-control. And then as he thought how sudden had been the change from the former happy circumstances of life, to this wherein his hand was against every man and every man's hand against him, and life was passed in a state of on the defensive, a cold, grey presentiment shot across his heart. What if it were but the precursor of another change? Nothing lasts; least of all, love.

Thus musing, and not looking where he was going, he ran right into somebody. A hearty laugh drowned his apologies. Looking up he found he had collided with Father O'Driscoll.

"You're the very man I wanted to meet," said the old priest, the first greetings over. "See now, Mr Musgrave. D'ye mind stepping round to my place for a moment. I'm in want of a stable-boy, and a fellow has just come to be taken on, but he seems rather lame in one leg. He says you know him, and will recommend him."

"I?" echoed Roden in some astonishment. "Does he know me?"

"He does. And—well, here we are."

A sturdy, thick-set Kaffir was squatting against the gate-post of the priest's house. He rose rather stiffly as they entered, uttering a half-shy and wholly humorous greeting as his eyes met Roden's, his dark face and shining white teeth all ablaze with mirth, which indeed the other fully shared, remembering how and where they had seen each other last. For in the aspirant for stable duty in the ecclesiastical establishment, he recognised no less a personage than Tom, *alias* Geunkwe.

"Hallo, Tom! Where have you dropped from? Damaged leg, eh?"

"Been away to see my father, *Baas*," answered the Kaffir, grinning all over his face. "An ox kicked me on the leg, but it will soon be well."

"An ox kicked you, did it?" said Roden, with a half laugh; for he shrewdly suspected the hoof of that ox to have been of very small size, and made of lead. And the Kaffir laughed again, for he knew that Roden was not deceived.

"You know him? Is he honest now?" said Father O'Driscoll.

"Thoroughly, I believe. What's more, he's a man of his word. I am telling Father O'Driscoll you are a man of your word, Tom," said Roden, translating into Dutch, and speaking with a meaning not lost upon the Kaffir.

"I am your child, chief," replied the native. "*Au*, I would like to serve the old *Baas*. He looks kind."

"Well, Tom, I'll take you on so," said the priest. "Go round now, and see after the horse at once; for faith, it's a long ride the poor beast has just come off. By the way," he added, turning to Roden as the Kaffir departed, "I seem to have seen him somewhere before. Has he been with any one here?"

"He was with that arch-sweep, Sonnenberg, who employed him to do a particularly dirty trick, and got 'had' sweetly in return, as you would be the first to allow if I were to disclose it. There is another thing I might reveal which would convince you that in defining Tom as a man of his word I was speaking no more than the literal truth, only I promised him never to mention it. You have got a right good boy in him, Father O'Driscoll, and if I had any use for a boy I'd employ him myself."

"Oh, I'm quite satisfied, I assure ye, Mr Musgrave. Many thanks for your trouble."

Thus Tom obtained the best place in Doppersdorp, and Roden was able in some slight measure to requite the loyalty and good faith of the *ci-devant* savage warrior, who might, by breaking his word, have delivered him over on that memorable morning to a violent and barbarous death.

Chapter Twenty Five
Lambert makes a Discovery

Lambert's predecessor in the district-surgeoncy of Doppersdorp had an odd hobby—viz., a mania for taking in newspapers representing, not only all parts of the British Empire, but other sections, wild or tame, of the known world. Now, nothing is so cumbersome and space-devouring as files of old newspapers, wherefore those accumulated by Dr Simpson had, by the time of that estimable practitioner's departure, come to take up the whole available space afforded, by two fair-sized rooms.

At this time, however, it occurred to Lambert that he had custodied this bulky collection of bygone journalism about long enough, wherefore, he wrote to his predecessor suggesting its removal. But the answer he received was to the effect that the cost and trouble of such removal would be too great, and that he might consider these musty old files henceforward his own property, the merit of which endowment being somewhat negative, in that it empowered the recipient to destroy the cumbersome gift; and to such destruction Lambert forthwith resolved to proceed, yet by degrees; for it could not be that among all these records he should fail to find other than a great deal of highly interesting and, from time to time, strange and startling matter. So Lambert would frequently lug in some dusty old file, which, having duly shaken and in a measure cleansed, he constituted a companion to his evening pipe. For reading matter was deplorably lacking in Doppersdorp—the contents of the "public library," so called, consisting mainly of ancient and heavy novels, soporific and incomplete, or the biographies of divines, sour of habit and of mind narrow as the "way" they were supposed to indicate.

Lambert had his reward, for these old records reaching back a decade—two decades—judiciously scanned, were interesting, undeniably so. There were representative papers issued in the Australian colonies, in New Zealand, in India and America, and in no end of lands beside. Lambert resolved, before accomplishing his projected wholesale destruction, to scissor out such incidents as were worth preserving, and to set up a scrap book; the main difficulty about this resolve lying in the formidable mass of matter from which he felt called upon to select. But while solving this problem, Lambert was destined to receive a shock, and one of considerable power and magnitude.

He was seated alone one evening, looking through such an old file. The paper was an American one, published in some hardly known Western township. Its contents were racy, outspoken, very; and seemed of the nature to have been written by the left hand of the editor, while the right grasped the butt of the ever-ready "gun." But in turning a sheet of this Lambert suddenly came upon that which made him leap in his chair, and stare as though his eyes were about to drop from his head to the floor. This is what he read:—

> "The Crime of Stillwell's Flat.
> Portrait of the Accused.
> Sordid Affair.
> He Tomahawks his Partner for the sake of Four Hundred Dollars.
> The Man with the Double Scar.
> Clever Arrest."

Such were some of the headings in bold capitals, which, distributed down the column, about summed up the facts of the case, but only cursory attention did Lambert at first pay to these. Not by them had his eye been originally attracted, but by the portrait which headed the column. For this portrait, mere pen-and-ink sketch as it originally had been, was a most vivid and unmistakable likeness of Roden Musgrave.

Yes, there it was, the same clear-cut features, the same carriage of the head—the artist seemed not merely to have caught his expression, but even the characteristics of his very attitude. And—surer, more convincing than all—the same double scar beneath the lower lip. Two men might wear the same marvellous resemblance to each other, but no two men could possibly do so to the extent of both being marked with that peculiar double scar. That, at any rate, rendered the identity complete, and beyond all room for doubt.

"The man with the double scar!" repeated Lambert to himself. "Holy Moses! Am I drunk, or dreaming? No. It's him all right," passing his hand over his eyes in a semi-dazed manner. "No two people could be so extraordinarily alike, and Musgrave's is the sort of face that can't have many 'doubles' in the world. Now to see what they say about it."

Breathlessly he ran his eye down the column. The facts, as reported, fully justified the opening definition of the crime as a sordid one, if proved against the accused; and that there might be no mistake whatever as to the identity of that critically situated personage with the present assistant magistrate of Doppersdorp, he figured in the trial, simply and without disguise, under the name of Roden Musgrave.

With dazed eyes, Lambert read on. Briefly summed up, the heads of the affair were these. Two prospectors established themselves on a claim together at Stillwell's Flat, a lonely spot beneath a northern spur of the Black Hills. Their names were respectively, John Denton and Roden Musgrave, and both were supposed to be Englishmen. One morning Denton was found in the slab hut occupied by the pair, with his head cleft nearly in twain, and beside him a bloodstained axe, and worse still, his throat was cut from ear to ear. The wandering cattlemen, by whom the discovery was made, described the place as like a slaughter-yard. A ferocious and brutal crime, indeed! The motive? Robbery, of course. The dead man, who was something of a gambler, was known to have taken back from the nearest township upwards of four hundred dollars he had won, and of this sum no trace could be found. The perpetrator? Denton's partner, of course, who had disappeared.

Had disappeared to some purpose, too; for a long and vigorous search failed to elicit the slightest clue to his whereabouts, and as the searchers were mostly experienced plainsmen, it was concluded that he was no longer above ground, had probably been killed or captured by the Sioux, who were "bad" about there just at that time.

Then, a couple of months later, when the affair was beginning to fade out of mind, possibly eclipsed by some other and similar tragedy such as from time to time occurs to relieve the monotony of life in the "wild and woolly West," the missing man was unexpectedly arrested on board a Mississippi steamboat—arrested simply and solely on the identification of that double scar, for his description had been so far circulated—arrested and sent back for trial. And lucky indeed for him that a long enough period had elapsed to enable the excitement to die down; for, had he been found during the first days of it, he would probably have had no trial at all. He would almost certainly have been lynched. Not that it could matter in the long ran. The crime was not only a sordid and brutal one, it was also a clumsy one; in fact, about the clumsiest on record. The murderer had knotted the noose round his own neck. No loophole of escape had he, and, this being so, public opinion was, for once, in favour of the law being allowed to vindicate itself. Such vindication there was no need to anticipate in short and summary fashion.

Lambert, his pulses beating, his hands trembling with excitement, rapidly turned over the sheets of the file. What if the report of the trial should be missing? That would be too vexatious. Yet that it had ended favourably to the accused was clear, since here he was. Stay! Had he escaped prior to it being held? Lambert felt that if that were so, why then, he held in his hand not only the prospects and social position of his enemy but the latter's very life. Yet it could not be, since Musgrave had made no attempt at changing his name. And then, for the first time, it occurred to Lambert to glance at the date of the file. The affair had taken place just ten years previously.

Ten years? Why, the portrait might have been taken that day. Ten years? Ah, the accused might have been found guilty on a lesser count, and sentenced to imprisonment only. That indeed would be the best of all, and Lambert fairly thrilled with delight over the prospect of breaking the news to Mona Ridsdale that the man she had preferred to himself was only an ex-gaol bird who had "done time," and who would, of course, now that he was unmasked, be promptly kicked out of the Government Service. Would he never find what he wanted? Ah! There it was.

"The Stillwell's Flat Murder.
Trial of the Accused.
Lawyer Schofield's Eloquent Defence.
Judge McClellar sums up.
Verdict of Acquittal.
The boys talk about Lynching."

Acquittal? Down went poor Lambert's house of cards, crumpled in the dust. His discovery could not damage his enemy now. Still, as he read the final report of the trial and its result, he thought he saw light. For the acquittal, under the circumstances, and obtained as it had been, amounted to a verdict of "not proven" far more than to one of "not guilty."

And the way in which it had been arrived at was ingenious. The evidence against the accused was merely presumptive; indeed, it was no evidence at all. He admitted having quarrelled with the deceased and left him, but totally denied the murder. Moreover, he had satisfactorily explained his movements since. Why had he not returned when wanted? Ah, well now. It was not completely outside knowledge that innocent men had before then been sacrificed at times of popular clamour. But there were two cards which the lawyer for the defence held in his hands, and upon which he mainly relied. The axe-blow which had slain the murdered man had split his head nearly in two, yet his throat had been cut. Now the latter act was quite superfluous, was, in fact, an act of deliberate and cold-blooded barbarity, to which his client, even if he did the killing, would hardly be likely to bring himself. The fact of the dead man's throat being cut pointed to murderers of a very different type. Everybody knew that the tribal mark of the Sioux was cutting the throat, which never failed to distinguish the victims of their barbarity. Well, the Sioux were "bad" around there just then, and Stillwell's Flat was a lonely place; in fact, it was in following the trail of several Indians who had run off some of their steers, that those very cattlemen had happened upon the spot. True, the man was not scalped, but possibly the Indian murderers had been alarmed, and decamped before completing that revolting essential to their barbarous work.

But the trump card of all, and one most skilfully played by the advocate, was this:—His client had served in the recent Indian war, might not the murderers have marked him out as the object of their vengeance, and have mistaken his partner for him? He had been one of that little band of heroes, under the command of General Forsyth, who only the previous year had "stood off" overwhelming forces of the enemy; and who with no other rampart than their own dead horses, and no other food than the putrefying flesh of the animals, had managed to hold their own for seven days against the fiercest and most persistent onslaughts known to Plains history. Moreover, he was one of those who had volunteered to break through at night, braving certain death, and almost certain death by torture, in order to make his way to Fort Wallace, and bring relief to the besieged handful of scouts. Was this the man to commit such a foul and sordid murder for the sake of a few dollars? Was this man, who had fought so bravely to defend their frontier, to be sacrificed to such a preposterous suspicion, to be allowed to suffer for the crime almost certainly committed by representatives of that savage enemy, to withstand whom he had so often and so freely risked his life? With the battle of the Arickaree Fork fresh in their memories, not one who heard him could be of any two minds as to the sort of verdict he would be given.

This clever drawing of a red herring across the trail of the main issue answered. Lawyer Schofield's eloquence had its reward. He obtained his verdict, and his client was acquitted.

But it was not a spontaneous verdict, not a triumphant acquittal. Long and earnestly did the jury debate, and when at last the accused walked forth a free man, he was received with a silence that was ominous. The lawyer, of course, was quite right to do his best for his client, and his strong appeal to sentiment was specious, if successful. But nobody believed overmuch in the theory he had sprung. If the Sioux had killed John Denton, they would have run off all his possessions, probably have fired the slab hut, instead of relieving him of his cash alone. Nor would they have left him his scalp. No. To the frontier community that Indian theory would not wash. Justice had been defeated, and Roden Musgrave had few, if any, friends. But when there sallied forth stealthily that night a band of dissatisfied and justice loving citizens, well-armed, and bearing in its midst an ominous coil of rope, the man who had been acquitted that day was not to be found. Nor, in fact, were they destined ever to set eyes upon him again.

This, set forth in a voluminous report extending over many columns, was the substance of what Lambert read, and, as he grasped all the details, he realised that, although powerless to effect material ruin, there was still that about the equivocal nature of the acquittal which would be sufficient to damage his rival irreparably from a social point of view. Throw mud enough and a great deal of it is sure to stick, is a trite axiom. The crime was an exceptionally brutal one, and the bare suspicion of it still clinging to a man was enough. To do him justice, Lambert himself felt a repulsion towards one who could ever have colourably lain under so horrible a suspicion, which was not altogether the outcome of his hatred of this particular individual. What would Mona think of it? What action would Musgrave's superior take in the matter? Surely no man could continue to hold an official position with such a stigma clinging to him. Musgrave would be called upon to resign, of course. And then an uneasy misgiving assailed the plotter's mind, and there loomed up ugly visions of suits for slander, defamation, what not. The man had stood his trial and had been acquitted. It would be a ticklish matter spreading the story around.

The more he looked at it the less he liked it. Nothing was easier than to start this kind of ball rolling, nothing on earth more difficult than to stop its progress once it was fairly in motion. Lambert wanted to see the end of this thing; to which effect he resolved to sleep upon it.

Having accordingly slept upon it, he decided that two heads were better than one. If anybody in Doppersdorp were competent to carry this affair through, that individual was Sonnenberg.

Not for a moment did it occur to Lambert that he was about to perpetrate a wholly mean and dishonourable act, or if it did, he excused it on the ground that all's fair in love and war. Musgrave had cut him out in a certain quarter; Musgrave had had his day; now he, Lambert, was going to have his. He was not quite fool enough to suppose that he could walk into Mona's heart over, figuratively speaking, the other's dead body; nevertheless he would tumble down their own fair house of cards, would, in fact, separate them; and from this purpose he never swerved.

Sonnenberg, when put in possession of this new weapon against their common enemy, fairly howled with delight; when he saw the portrait, and read the report of the case, his exultation knew no bounds.

"We have him! we have him, by God!" he yelled. "Ha, ha! I shall get the value of my fifteen pounds now. This is worth fifty of the gun-selling trap."

"But, wait now. Let's be careful," urged Lambert. "It's an awkward thing, you know, spreading about a story of this kind. Might get ourselves into trouble, eh?"

"Trouble? Trouble be damned! By to-night, or to-morrow at latest, it shall be all over the district. Even if we did render ourselves liable to any action by passing it on—which we don't—there's a better way of doing it."

"What is it?"

"Why, filter it through Chandler. It won't take long to run through him."

"By Jove, the very thing!" cried Lambert.

Chapter Twenty Six
A Sword—Long Rusted

Every small community, permanent or temporary, comprises at least one old woman of the male sex, frequently more than one.

It is difficult to particularise whence this product springs. The average club perhaps is pre-eminently its forcing house, for there you shall find the growth both multifold and luxuriant. Likewise on board passenger ships it thrives and flourishes; indeed, so well known is the type as not to need defining here. In up-country townships, too, its roots strike most congenial soil, and in such surroundings its ramblings not unfrequently tend to bestir the monotony of life, even if they should occasionally meet with rough and violent usage.

Now Doppersdorp was no exception to the universal rule, for that historic place owned a really prize specimen of the male "old woman." This was a brisk, elderly, dapper individual, the primary article of whose creed was that what he didn't know was not worth knowing. In aspect he was somewhat Hebraic, with the predatory eye and prominent "beak" of a certain phase of "the tribes." He was shortish of stature, and wore his curly grey hair brushed up aggressively over his ears and neck, eke a beard of the same hue and texture. By profession he described himself as an "agent," a nondescript term which might mean anything or nothing, and how he procured the requisite equivalent for the necessaries of life was ever a dark mystery. But that the highest heaven and a fairly sordid section of the lower depths of earth might meet in his individuality, he rejoiced in the name of Michael Chandler.

In saying he knew everything we are short of his merit, for he knew a great deal more than everything. He knew very much more than really existed or had ever happened. You could not mention a name or a place but forthwith would stream copious anecdote either relating to individual or locality, delivered in a darkly mysterious tone. Certain it was that no event concerning anybody could be mentioned in his hearing, but that event became common property throughout Doppersdorp within the space of half a day at the furthest.

He had a spiritual side, too, as befitted one thus named from the angelic spheres. He would deliver himself of highly moral and consoling precepts for the improvement of those who sat daily at Jones' not too well-appointed board; eke would he invent anecdotes whose first narration had, according to him, moved the most hardened to tears. He was full up with unction, too, and would frequently "expound" from the pulpit of a certain chapel of the "omnium gatherum" persuasion, whence was dispensed Sabbath nourishment to the bulk of English-speaking Doppersdorp. And he loved not Roden Musgrave.

Now the said Michael Chandler, commonly known among the irreverent as "Old Buzfuz," held the office of librarian of the Doppersdorp public library; wherefore Lambert's proposal to endow that useful institution with some of the files of newspapers bequeathed him by his predecessor, was hailed with genuine elation. The idea was an excellent one. There was plenty of room, and old records were always most interesting. Perhaps though—er—he suggested, turning on some unction, perhaps—er—Dr Lambert would not mind him looking over some of the files he so very kindly wished to present, just to make sure there was nothing objectionable in them. All sorts of people used the library; all ages and sexes, he explained, with another unctuous gulp.

Lambert could have yelled with laughter. Why, this was the very thing they had intended. So with many protestations to the effect that the other's scruples did him the greatest credit, and so forth, he loaded up "Old Buzfuz" with three or four previously assorted files, deftly contriving that that of the *Bryonville Sentinel* should occupy the most prominent place among them, and thus engage attention first.

All was going magnificently. This time the plot could not miscarry. Sonnenberg was half beside himself with vindictive elation. He had got his enemy in the hollow of his hand, and would crush him utterly.

Now, towards evening there came a knock at Lambert's door, which opened to admit Chandler, looking very solemn and mysterious indeed. Would the doctor kindly step round with him to his rooms? Lambert, affecting the greatest surprise and mystification, was not slow to acquiesce. Then, when Chandler, having carefully locked the door, proceeded to draw forth and spread upon the table the sheet containing the very portrait which had so dumfounded himself the previous night, he was ready to choke with stifled mirth. The long and unctuous rigmarole wherein the other set forth the painful—the extremely painful—discovery he had so unexpectedly made, was all thrown away. Lambert was struggling hard to preserve his gravity and keep up the assumed mystification; and it was a struggle.

"By Jove!" he cried, "I never was more astounded in my life. Why, you might knock me down with a feather. But, hang it, the thing can't be genuine. It's only an extraordinary coincidence—a likeness. A devilish good one, but still a mere likeness."

"It's more than that, unless the name is a coincidence too. Look at the name!"

"By Jove!" cried Lambert again, staring with admirably feigned amazement at the paper handed to him.

"When people are so very reserved about themselves it usually means that their past has not been a creditable one—ahem!" ejaculated Old Buzfuz, piously shaking his head. "But this is awful—awful. A murderer, too. A murderer!"

"But, what's to be done? We'd better destroy the papers and keep it to ourselves—eh?" said Lambert. "You see, the thing ends in an acquittal of a sort. How about actions for libel? I don't want to risk anything of that kind."

This was putting matters uncomfortably. "Old Buzfuz" cleared his throat.

"There is no question of anything of that kind," he said. "You see, Dr Lambert, you offered to present these files of papers to the Doppersdorp public library. Now, besides looking through them myself, it will be my duty to submit them to Mr Shaston, who, as chairman of the institution, has a considerable voice in admitting or excluding its contents."

"Eh, what?" cried Lambert, in pretended alarm. "Why, it may get Musgrave into trouble. He might get the sack."

"Any action which Mr Shaston may take rests with himself, not with us. Meanwhile, my duty is plain, and I propose to discharge it unswervingly."

And "Old Buzfuz" pulled a very long face, heaved a very deep sigh, and looked the other straight in the eyes. These two humbugs thoroughly understood each other now.

A couple of mornings later, Roden Musgrave, emerging from his quarters, was surprised to behold two or three groups scattered on the footway and on the other side of the road, intently but furtively watching his house. He noticed, too, that those composing them turned away as he came forth, as though to disguise their intent. And simultaneously with the quick flash of vision in which he took in all this, his eye was attracted to something on his front door, and if his nerves were momentarily shaken it is little to be wondered at. For right across his door, boldly drawn in charcoal, its head daubed with splotches of red, was a great axe; and underneath this, in red lettering, were inscribed the words,

"Stillwell's Flat."

The suddenness of the bolt might well have staggered him—the utter unexpectedness of it. How had this grim skeleton been thus dug up from its far-away and long-covered grave, and dangled here before him? Who had done it? And, as his gaze wandered over the groups, it met that of Sonnenberg, and on the evil countenance of the Jew was a smirk of vindictive triumph. *He* did not avert his glance.

The sight, however, was of all things the best that could possibly have happened. It acted as a tonic. His nerves completely braced now, Roden turned and deliberately examined the daub, looking it up and down from top to bottom. Those furtive groups began to peer anxiously, eager to see what he was going to do next. They expected to see him blanch, grow agitated, perhaps turn faint; instead of which he stood examining the hideous practical joke, with the ghost of a satirical grin drooping the corners of his mouth. He had not turned a hair.

Then he called a native who was limping along on the other side of the street.

"Tom."

It was indeed the *ci-devant* warrior, now the priest's stable-boy. He trotted across, grinning, and saluted.

"Where are you off to now, Tom?"

The Kaffir explained that he was going nowhere in particular. His master was absent, and times were easy.

"Very well. Go inside and get a bucket and brush, and clean that beautiful drawing off my door, while I'm at breakfast," said Roden, chucking the boy a sixpence, and strolling leisurely down the street in the direction of the Barkly.

Cool though he was, however, the incident had disturbed him not a little. How had this thing come about? Who there could know anything of his past? He saw in this the beginning of the end.

Was it with design, too, that throughout breakfast Chandler should so persistently keep dragging round the conversation to the year 1868? It looked like it. Nor was there any mistaking, either, the constraint in the manner of others. Well, if they intended that sort of annoyance they should learn that they might just as well spare themselves the trouble.

Thus musing he went down to the office. A few Court cases had to be disposed of, during which from his seat in front of the bench he could see Tasker, the agent, who bore him no goodwill either, ostentatiously sketching a gallows on his blotting pad. Darrell was absent, having returned to the Main Camp.

"Would you mind stepping this way, Mr Musgrave?" said Mr Shaston, when the court had risen, leading the way into his private office. "Sit down, please. There is a matter of very serious moment on which I should like a little conversation with you. Perhaps it will save a great deal of explanation, and beating around the bush, if we come to the point at once. In a word, *this* has come under my notice—no matter how—and if you have any explanation to offer I shall be glad to hear it."

"This" being the file of the *Bryonville Sentinel* open at the report of the Stillwell's Flat case. Roden took it, and looked at it hard and earnestly—his own portrait, lifelike at the present day, the sensational headlines, the equivocal verdict, the acquittal.

This, then, was how the matter had been unearthed; for as he glanced at the paper he recalled old Dr Simpson's hobby. That kindly-natured old man would not have stirred a finger to harm him. It was Lambert who had unearthed this, Lambert whom he had to thank. Ten long years ago! and now here, in another hemisphere thousands and thousands of miles away, this blood-spectre sprang up once more, hideous and blighting.

"Well?" said Shaston, as he handed it back.

"I have no explanation to offer."

"Do I understand then that you admit your identity with the—er—the person, whose trial is here reported?"

"You will please understand that I admit nothing. I do not feel in the least called upon to make either admissions or explanations. I will, however, just add this remark. The person, whoever he may be, whose trial is there reported, appears to have been acquitted. That means, I take it, that he has been cleared of the charge."

"All very well as a legal fiction, Mr Musgrave," was the icy rejoinder; "but you and I know perfectly that the manner of a person's acquittal makes all the difference in the world."

"Then, if a man is once under suspicion, he is always under it, no matter how completely or publicly he may have been cleared? Is that your deliberate opinion, Mr Shaston?"

The other turned white with rage as he glared blankly and furiously at his imperturbable subordinate, whose countenance betrayed no sign of purpose underlying his rejoinder. Yet the latter contained about as hard a hit as could have been dealt, for rumour darkly hinted that Shaston in his younger days had been badly mixed up in some defaulting transaction; and although exonerated, on inquiry, from anything more culpable than gross negligence, the circumstance had placed a black mark against his record, materially retarding his advancement in the Service. As a matter of fact, however, the shaft was an accidental one, Roden being entirely unaware of such an occurrence.

"That may be why I afforded you the opportunity of making an explanation," said Shaston as soon as he had recovered himself; "for I have considered the matter very carefully, and deem it my duty to bring it to the notice of the Government; unless, of course, you would prefer to resign of your own accord, and thus avoid unnecessary scandal and publicity. In that case I shall be willing to stretch a point."

"I shall certainly do nothing of the kind, Mr Shaston. And allow me, with great respect, to recommend you to consider the matter yet more carefully; for any step you may take in it as regards myself will be taken at your own serious risk. The same holds good concerning others."

"As you refuse explanation, I may tell you, sir, that I have no doubt whatever as to your identity with the Roden Musgrave mentioned here. Moreover, I am informed that the inhabitants of this place are preparing a strong memorial on the subject. I have even reason to fear that you may become the object of a most unpleasant popular demonstration. All this means scandal to the Service, and serious detriment to the efficiency and smooth working of my establishment. Wherefore you must see, I am sure, that in bringing the matter officially under notice, I am discharging a most necessary though painful duty."

"We are alone, I believe, Mr Shaston," answered Roden, and there was a look in his face which the other had never seen there before and did not half like now. "That being so, we may as well talk with a little more plainness. I would ask you, therefore, to glance at that report; and granting, for the sake of argument, that your theory as to my identity is correct, to say whether you think it likely that the man whose record is there given is the man to be bullied into anything, let alone cowed by such a threat as that of a 'popular demonstration,' on the part of the runaway swindlers and fraudulent bankrupts and forgers and ex-convicts who form such an important element in the population of this highly moral village? Do you really share such an opinion?"

The other stared. He simply did not know what answer to make. Roden continued —

"It might be as well, if I may respectfully say so, before undertaking the grave responsibility of branding me or anybody else as a murderer on the strength of a report in so authoritative an organ as the *Bryonville Sentinel*, to ascertain first, that there is such a place as Stillwell's Flat; secondly, that a murder actually was committed there; and, lastly, that I ever was there in my life. And now, have I your permission to return to my work, sir?"

"You have, sir. It's only fair to tell you that my opinion and the course of action I have decided upon in consequence of this — er — of this revelation, remains unchanged."

But, after his subordinate had withdrawn, Shaston felt horribly uncomfortable. That last bolt had gone right home. What if the whole thing should turn out a fiasco after all?

Chapter Twenty Seven
"Thou shouldst have known me true"

In hinting that a public demonstration, hostile to his subordinate, was preparing, Mr Shaston was so far right in that it was no fault of Sonnenberg, and one or two others of like kidney, that something of the sort did not come off. Even then the tender conscience of collective Doppersdorp, whose main ingredients Roden Musgrave had not inaccurately defined, was wounded to the extent of expressing its feelings in a series of petty manifestations of spite and malice. Thus the disfigurement of his front door was repeated, with the difference that this time a gallows, with a man hanging on it, was substituted for the axe. Or, if he passed a knot of youthful loots loafing at a street corner, his ears could not fail to catch some deft allusion followed by a yahoo bray of laughter. And although once or twice reference would be made to tar-and-feathers, still no act of overt hostility was attempted. It might have been, indeed, that upon this virtuous crowd was forced home the same consideration which Roden himself had suggested to his official superior—that, granting the identity, a man with his fighting record was not one to be roughly handled with impunity; especially as during that brief expedition into the Gaika location, he had given substantial guarantee that the record might be a true one. And if in any way this consideration influenced the virtuous public of Doppersdorp, why, it only showed that, among that agglomeration of mischievous turnip-heads, there lingered even yet a stray grain or so of wisdom.

Still his position was an unpleasant one, and grew daily more so. Here and there would be somebody not ill-disposed towards him, but, beyond a feebly apologetic defence when he was out of hearing, they did not care to say so, let alone to parade their sympathy, fearing public opinion or their own women-kind, who in turn feared Mrs Shaston; for of such are the wheels which revolve within each other in the small community.

Now the tongue of Mrs Shaston wagged oft and freely enough to have laid her open to any number of distinct actions for slander. But although Roden had asserted his intention to "take it fighting," he was growing more and more sick of the whole position every day. This wretched poky little hole-and-corner village, where people grovelled away their lives by the score of years at a time; what was it to him? What was this handful of shopkeepers and pettifogging practitioners, whose main ambition was to squeeze a few extra shillings out of the unwary native, or the wooden-headed Boer, on some pretence just falling short of legally fraudulent, and not always that? Why, nothing, of course—less than nothing. A month after leaving it he would have forgotten that such a place ever existed, have forgotten it utterly and entirely.

All but for one consideration; and that he owned to himself, both in sorrow and in wonder, would never suffer him to forget this passage in his life as long as that life should last. In sorrow, because unaccountably he had a chill presentiment that even that stay would fail him in the hour of need. In wonder, because it seemed little short of miraculous that, having left the cream of life behind him with the capacity for faith and warm trust, he should have been required to take up that life again almost, as it were, from the very beginning—should be called upon to suffer the ordeal of trust and feeling, even after losing all belief in the genuineness and durability of any such transitory illusions.

Since the bursting of the bomb he had not seen Mona, nor bad he heard either from or of her. The same held good of Suffield's household in general. It almost looked as if they pointedly refrained from coming into the town. Had they heard about it? Why, of course. How should they not have? When a community such as Doppersdorp fastens on to a scandal of that magnitude, why, it worries it for all it is worth.

Now, Charles Suffield, though an excellent fellow under the ordinary circumstances of life, was not the man to stand by a friend at a pinch, if the said pinch should chance to be of abnormal tightness. He was one of those good, commonplace souls to whom a public scandal is a thing of terror; wherefore it is not surprising that, when he came to learn that the friend with whom he and his had been upon such intimate terms, had stood his trial for murder of a peculiarly brutal and sordid nature, narrowly escaping conviction, and that only on the cleverness and eloquence of his counsel rather than on the merits of the case, it is not surprising, we repeat, that he should have been, to use his own definition, knocked end ways. He remembered that friend's studied reticence, instances of which were continually cropping up, and how they had all frequently laughed at and over such; now these all stood accounted for. The whole thing was hideous, hideous beyond words; less the actual murder than the motive—the pitiful, paltry robbery which had prompted it. And to think that the man should have been mixing with them all this while upon intimate terms. And Mona—oh, great Heavens! what amount of mischief might not be done there?

Suffield's mind, being largely diluted with commonplace, floundered about in a panic, landing its owner in rather a contemptible hole. For in his horror of scandal, and disgust for the reputed crime, he was quite ready to condemn his former friend right out of hand. His reasoning was of the feminine order, "Everybody says so, therefore it must be true." Curiously enough it was from a feminine mind that a little wholesome common sense was brought to bear upon the question—the mind of his wife, to wit.

"I won't believe it, even now," said Grace sturdily; perhaps with a vivid recollection of that awful post-cart journey, the flooded river, and the broken cord. "There may be some explanation, but anyhow it seems rather unfair to put a man on his trial again after he has been acquitted."

"Where there's smoke there must be fire," rejoined Suffield, with proud originality. "And here I'm afraid there must be a great deal more fire than smoke."

"Still I won't believe it. Looking at only one side of the question is supposed to be a feminine characteristic. It strikes me that our sex has been libelled."

"That's all very well, Grace, but we've got to be practical. What about Mona? They are engaged."

"Not actually."

"Well, as good as. It amounts to the same thing."

"I don't know," was the reply, more thoughtfully given. "Speak to her yourself about it."

Mona received the news as though semi-dazed with its ominous magnitude, and by some curious and subtle instinct believed it. Yet not quite—not quite the whole of it, that is. The motive was too horrible. In that she would not believe, unless he assured her to the contrary. Still, the other was bad enough, whichever way you looked at it. It was appalling. A gulf, a chasm, seemed to open under her feet, paralysing her faculties, deadening everything.

Such was the state of the family councils when Roden, resolved to know the worst, saddled up his horse and started for Quaggasfontein. It was Sunday morning, so he would have the whole day at his disposal, and as he cantered out along the familiar track—how many times had he been over it before?—it was with a very sure foreboding that he was travelling it now for the last time. And as he journeyed he called to his aid all the iron hardness of his now schooled nature; a hardness which he had suffered to be penetrated, though never dispelled, but which events of late had riveted once more in armour layers. Not upon any softening reminiscence would he allow his mind to dwell now, and the very first glance at Mona's face would justify his resolve; justify it for all time, or—

He was prepared for the constraint with which the Suffields greeted him—so different to his former welcome—the more marked perhaps because of a certain laboured effusiveness in order to render it equally cordial; for even Grace, her first spirited defence of him notwithstanding, could not quite free her manner from the effect of the distilling canker-drop of suspicion. He was prepared for this, and at the moment thought but little of it as he entered with them.

It was a lovely, cloudless morning, and the scent of flowers with the hum of bees and the chirrup of the cicada wafted in at the open windows of the cool, half-darkened sitting-room. By one of these Mona was standing. She turned, as with an effort, jerkily, constrainedly, and her eyes met his.

All was over.

What her countenance expressed it would have been difficult to define. What it did not express was that loving, eager sympathy, that proud, fearless trust, which should range itself beside him in defiance of the whole world, such as he had scarcely expected, yet still owned a deep-down hope that he might find there.

All was over.

While this trial and verdict, swift as a lightning flash, was going on, Suffield had been bustling about the room with the blundering, ostentatious tactlessness of a not very clever man under awkward circumstances, who has more than half lost his head; under cover of which bustle Mona slipped away and was gone, but ere vanishing she left behind a whisper:

"Soon. At the willows."

"Hallo, Musgrave! I thought Grace was here," cried Suffield, turning. "Have a glass of grog after your ride, eh?"

"No thanks."

"What? Did you say you wouldn't? By the way, you haven't off-saddled," glimpsing through the open door the other's horse still standing in front of the *stoep*.

"I'm not going to off-saddle," said Roden. "I don't think I can stay very long."

Suffield hardly knew what to answer, so he fired off volleys of commonplaces, which, treading on each other's heels, soon merged into the most drivelling of incoherences. Roden, watching him, felt moved to pity and contempt: pity for the man who could make so gratuitous an ass of himself, contempt for one whose "friendship" thus collapsed at the first knock, and that knock an outside one.

"If you don't mind, Suffield, I rather want to have a word or two with Miss Ridsdale," he said at last. "I think I saw her strolling in the direction of the willows."

"Certainly, certainly; you're sure to find her there," assented Suffield effusively. "When you come back you'll perhaps change your mind about not off-saddling."

Roden did not hurry as he took his way along that well-known path. His gait to the superficial observer was that of a bored lounger, strolling to kill time; and as he caught the glimpse of a white dress beneath the leafy canopy in front, so far from quickening his pace, he deliberately halted, and affected to pick up and examine a leaf or a pebble which lay in the path. And as he did so he began softly to hum to himself, and the words which he found himself humming were:

"'Twas here we last parted, 'twas here we first met."

Chapter Twenty Eight
"Dead Separate Souls"

She turned as he overtook her. For a moment they thus stood face to face. Then he spoke.

"I have come to say good-bye."

"To say—good-bye?" echoed Mona, dully, staring at him as though she were walking in her sleep.

"Yes. There is a gulf between us now such as can never be bridged, never. It is not good that you should even so much as speak with a murderer. A murderer, I repeat."

The faces of both were white as death. The frames of both were rigid and motionless, as they stood confronting each other beneath the willows— there, where they had first met, there, where those passionate words of undying love had been interchanged, there, where those long, long kisses had stamped their seal upon that love. And here they had met again—to part.

"Roden, say it was not true!" she gasped at last. "You were acquitted at the trial. It is not true; it cannot be true! Say it is not; say it is not!"

"But, what if it is?"

The words forced themselves out with something of a snarl. His lips seemed drawn back, and his eyes glowed like those of a cornered wild beast, as he watched her troubled face.

"But it is not! No, you could never have done such a thing—you! You could never have been a cold-blooded midnight murderer, and robber. No, Roden, I will not believe it!"

" Form your own opinion and hold it. . . We disappear out of each
other's lives for ever. "

"But you do believe it. You believed it from the first, because that half-start away from me when our eyes first met this morning meant nothing short of belief. That little act of shrinking fixed my mind irrevocably—reft a gulf between us never to be passed in this life. A cold-blooded midnight murderer—and robber—*and* robber!" he repeated; and now indeed the expression of his face was more than ever like that of a dangerous animal at bay. "And you believe that!"

"But say it is not true! Oh, Roden, say it! Your bare word will be sufficient to restore me, to restore us both, to the blissful heaven we were in before!" she adjured, her voice quivering with anguish.

"Nothing on earth will ever restore that. You killed the possibility that little lightning-like moment when you half turned away from me, looked at me with doubting horror. Now I will say nothing—nothing, you understand. Form your own opinion and hold it, for henceforth it can be nothing to me. We disappear out of each other's lives for ever."

Mona made no reply; her face half averted, her lips compressed, her beautiful form erect and rigid. Why was he so terribly strong, with a strength of purpose that was almost appalling, demoniacal, scarcely human in its unparalleled inflexibility? Why did he give no sign of softness, of yielding? She had, as he said, involuntarily, though half-unconsciously, shrunk from him. That was enough. Never again would she see those eyes gladden to the light of hers, never again hear the love tone of that voice. And yet, amid the awful agony of her loss and its realisation, there was still room for that same feeling of shrinking as from the perpetrator of a hideous and sordid crime; and like the mocking whoop of demons in her ears came that cutting, stinging, gibing refrain—the echo of his words, spoken there:—

"Nothing lasts! Nothing lasts!"

She had reached that point where mental anguish becomes physical pain, without in any way losing itself therein. Her brain seemed bursting, her heart refusing to beat. The climax came. She sank down in swooning unconsciousness.

Even then that human being turned to iron repressed the step which he had made towards her—repressed it with a shiver, but still repressed it. Not his the right to touch her—he from whom she had shrunk as from a murderer and midnight robber. Then another thought struck him.

"Yes, it is better so," he muttered, stepping to the side of the unconscious form, its nobly moulded lines as beautiful as ever in insensibility. "It is better so. Looked at thus for the last time, I can think of her ever as though I had looked upon her in death."

Then he struggled with himself, fought to restrain the overmastering impulse, for the last time to bend down and press his lips long and hard to her unconscious ones—fought, and conquered, and refrained.

"It would be a murderer's kiss," he muttered, between his teeth. Then turning, he lifted up his voice and sent forth a long, loud call.

"Miss Ridsdale has fainted, Suffield," he said, as the latter came running up. "You had better get her taken to the house. Good-bye, Suffield!"

"Stop, Musgrave, stop!" cried Suffield, who was now supporting Mona's head. "Don't go away like that, man. Hang it! after all this time, you know."

"I won't shake hands with you, Suffield," answered Roden without pausing, as he was walking rapidly away to where he had left his horse, still saddled. "You don't want to take the hand of a murderer—*and* thief, especially the thief. Good-bye, Suffield."

He rode away in the broad glare of noontide, the shimmer of heat from the scorching plains rising mirage-like in the distance. The screech of cricket vibrated shrilly upon the burning, glowing atmosphere, to cease abruptly in a silence that was well-nigh as oppressive; then bursting forth again with a strident suddenness which brought back the nerve-racking din tenfold. In the cloudless blue of the heavens, high overhead above the brink of the rock-embattled crest of the mountain range, something black was wheeling and soaring. He looked up, drawn by the distant and raucous cry of the huge bird. It was a *dasje-vanger* of noble size, like that which he had shot on the eventful day whereon the secret of this new love had been opened to him, and now, in his fierce and hard despair, it seemed that the great eagle was the sprite of the one which he had slain, shrieking forth its hate and exultation.

This then was love! A thing that could take sides with the spiteful clamour of the mob against its object. This then was the Ever Endurable! The first adverse blast had scattered it to the winds. "Mine for ever, throughout all the years," had been the declaration of that love, yet the course of but a few months had sifted the passionate vow, and had left—a few husks of chaff!

He had gained the "neck" where the waggon road crossed it, and beneath lay the unprepossessing little township. There not a friendly hand would be extended to him, not a friendly voice be lifted in greeting. Those who looked on him would turn their backs, any group he approached would quickly melt away. Yet, for such as these what cared he? Hugging themselves in the security of their sordid daily swindles, in whose very pettiness lay their safety, they would thank God devoutly they were not as he, not as one who had struck down life, sacred life! No, not for the good word, the good fellowship of such as these, cared he. But his mind, seared beyond all further capacity for feeling, reverted to that one heart which was shut towards him, to the pallid death-like face upon whose lips he had refrained from pressing that last kiss, upon those eyes into whose depths he had looked his last upon earth, as surely as though the dull echo of the clods was sounding above a coffin. Yet now—now, while realising the ever-impassable gulf which lay between, he loved her as he had never loved. Yet now he would have given all the world for the one consoling memory of that last kiss, which he had refrained from, had refused. The sterility of those long pent-up springs of love had lent tenfold force to the effort by which at last they should burst their rock-prison—only to end thus. Yet towards the eternal ruling of things it was that all bitterness of feeling was due, not towards her, for had not his uttered premonition from the very first been, "Nothing lasts, nothing lasts?"

That afternoon he sought out his official superior. The latter looked coldly surprised, also a little uncomfortable.

"I desire to say, Mr Shaston, that I have changed my mind. I am prepared to resign my position in the public service, and I have no doubt it will save you a good deal of trouble. If I adopt this course, however, it is subject to one stipulation. I wish to leave at once."

"When do you desire to leave, Mr Musgrave?" said the other, unbending somewhat, for he was overjoyed. He could get his wife's relation into the berth now, and would be rid of a subordinate whom he thoroughly hated and at times feared.

"To-morrow at midday, if it can be managed. I shall be prepared to submit everything to your inspection, and formally hand over the keys."

Shaston readily assented, hardly able to conceal his misgivings lest Roden might think better of it in the interim. He began, however, a pompous commendation of the very proper wisdom displayed in deciding upon such a course, which at once put an end to a very unpleasant state of affairs, and so forth, but found himself ruthlessly but very politely "shut up." He had got his way, however.

The next day, accordingly, having formally handed in his resignation "on the ground of very urgent private affairs," and delivered over all that had to be delivered over, Roden prepared for his start. He placed his effects in the hands of an auctioneer, except such few as he cared to remove, and these could follow him at leisure. His intention was to leave the country which had brought him nothing better than an irremovable curse, the curse of a mind roused to feeling again after many years of cold, philosophical quiescence.

In his desolation, his hardly acknowledged longing for one friendly word, the lonely and shunned man thought of Peter Van Stolz. Would he too have turned against him—he with his open, generous nature? Alas, and alas! When love failed, what was friendship? The voice whose quivering whisper had entranced his ear, had irradiated his heart, had been lifted against him in cold condemnation. The head which had lain upon his breast was averted in repulsion. The lips which had kissed his were hardened in scorn. Where then was there room for friendship? Nothing lasts!

Leaving his private quarters, he rode over to the Barkly Hotel, to settle up his score at that sumptuous caravanserai. A group of men were on the *stoep*, smoking their after-dinner pipe in noisy discussion. His arrival was the signal for a sodden silence. Of this he took no notice—standing in the doorway, with his back to the street, while Jones went inside to receipt the bill.

"And how are ye, Mr Musgrave? It's a long time since I've seen ye, anyway, and me only just back."

Roden turned quickly. The jolly voice with its touch of brogue, the rusty black coat and stove-pipe hat, the kind face and thick white hair, could belong to no other than Father O'Driscoll. And—he was advancing with outstretched hand. Roden stared, first at that very substantial member, then at its owner. But he did not respond, beyond a stiff bow.

"Ah, an' is it like ye, to wish to cut an old friend?" said the old man, his hand still held forth, and a look in his eyes that there was no mistaking. For it said, as plain as words, "I know all—all. But understand, *I* am not called upon to judge you, however some here may reckon themselves to be, God forgive them!"

Roden's hand closed upon that of the old priest in a warm grasp.

"An old friend, did you say, Father? I am proud of the word as coming from you; of the thing as existing between us."

"Ah, and what'll I do now without all our talks about the ould counthry and the fishing? Sure they've brought back the chimes of Shandon bells, and the days when I was a bit of a gorsoon a whippin' the trout out of the Shournagh, wid a long shtick and a crooked pin, faster than the garrison officers could get at 'em with their grand new rods. See now, I've only just got back, and the moment I heard ye were leavin' us I hurried off to find ye. Now come and have a bit of dinner with me before ye leave, and a parting tumbler of punch."

This in the face of all Doppersdorp, for the benefit of those who had condemned and shunned him. No one was more capable than Roden of keenly appreciating the manner in which his old friend had come forward to stand by him, combining as it did a rare delicacy with the maximum of effectiveness. But this last invitation he could not but decline. To delay his departure even for an hour could serve no good purpose, and he shrank from laying bare so much as a corner of his heart, even to the sweet-natured old Irishman.

The latter, quick to read thoughts, saw through his motive, and did not press him.

"Well, if you've got to go I won't be detaining you. Good-bye, Mr Musgrave," shaking his hand heartily. "We don't profess the same creed; but it'll do ye no harm to know that wherever you go, and wherever you are, there's an old man's blessing following you. Good-bye now!"

Such was the end. And as the great spur of the mountain, glowing green and gold in the afternoon sunlight, shut out the last of Doppersdorp behind him for ever, Roden Musgrave was conscious of a feeling of starting forth once more into the world, destitute and alone. Since the day which witnessed his entry into that sordid little township, he had gained that which he had never thought to win again—a restored faith in that marvellous mystery, which, while it lasts, avails to make a very paradise of the heart in which it takes up its most inexplicable abode. Was it a gain? Well, he had lost it now. Never, never could it be restored. Had he done wrong in refusing to speak that word which should exculpate himself? No. Whatever others might think, however circumstances might point most conclusively to the truth, Mona ought to have stood firm. Not for a moment could he admit that he ought to have conceded: Rightly or wrongly that one falling away was enough. Even had he yielded, that would have stood between them for ever.

Now he began to feel strangely aged as he went forth once more into that most dreary of exiles to the man who is no longer young, and whose means are too scanty even for his barest needs—to face the world afresh, that is. In the braced-up strength, and freshness of mind, and elasticity of spirits, of youth, such a prospect is not one to shrink from; on the contrary, it is one which is welcomed with many a buoyant laugh. But later, when strength is waning, and all things pall, and hopes and illusions are laid to rest for ever, buried in a grave of corroding corruption and bitter ashes;—ah! then it is a dark and craggy desert prospect indeed. And as these thoughts started up spectre-like in Roden's mind, he began to think of death.

Not of the suicide's death. Oh no. Putting it on the lowest grounds, such an act would be a feebleness, an imbecility, such as found no part within his nature; for it would be a concession to the unutterably contemptible tenet that there existed such a reality as love. Not in him was it to afford such a triumph as that to his enemies, let alone to her who, when tried, had been found so pitiably wanting. No, it was death in its natural order that now filled his mind. Would all things be at rest then? or would it be indeed, as the jarring tongues of striving sects and hair-splitting 'ologies all agreed—the one point on which they did agree—that that death, not so very formidable in itself, was only to open the gate of woe, endless, unutterable, to those who had eaten their full share of the bread of affliction in life—namely, the vast bulk of human kind?

He passed his hand over his eyes. Had it all been a dream? No, no! and yet in a way it had; but a dream from which he had now thoroughly awakened. Nevertheless, as he paced his horse steadily on, mile after mile over the glowing, sunlit landscape, the torment which seethed the soul of this outwardly cool and imperturbable wayfarer might have moved the pity of angels and men. For strive and reason as he would, the love which burnt within his heart flamed more strongly than it had ever done—yet now he had renounced it—and its object he would never again behold in life.

Chapter Twenty Nine
"O Love, Thy Day sets Darkling"

The same proud, fearless strength of nature which had allowed Mona to give herself up so unreservedly to this wonderful, all-absorbing love, once she were sure of it, now enabled her to suffer and make no sign. She was not one to wear the willow ostentatiously. Suffield, indeed, was lost in amazement over what he had termed her cool way of taking it. His wife, however, who could see below the surface, knew what a smouldering volcano this "coolness" covered. Sadly, too, she recalled her own words, "Wait until it comes, Mona, and then tell me how enjoyable you find it." Well, "it" had come, and could anything be a more disastrous, more complete wreck? She would watch her relative with a kind of awed wonder; for Mona never made direct allusion to anything that had gone before. A trifle graver, more reserved perhaps; otherwise as serene, as imperturbable as before. Yet deep down in her heart the wound bled, ached, and throbbed—and that almost unbearably. For she could not move a step without being reminded of the times that were past—if she needed reminding. No way could she turn her eyes without being so reminded. Every object, every feature in the surroundings was fraught with such associations.

Then she would force herself to look things in the face—to take to herself a kind of reckless, *bizarre* comfort. She had youth, and the glow of healthful beauty throbbed warm and strong within her. The world was great. Life was all before her. And she had pride. She could face the whole world with such an armoury.

There was one thing which, so far as the outside world was concerned, rendered her position easier. There had been no regular engagement. Nothing formal or binding had so much as been hinted at between them. They had been content to live on, penetrating deeper and deeper into the golden mazes of love; no thought for the end, no thought of a barred gate across their way, beyond which should lie a smooth, dead-level road, unending in its placid monotony. Nothing therefore had been "broken off," nothing claiming explanations, and, more hateful than all, laying her open to condolences.

But the fact that there had been nothing definite between them had its drawbacks. She could not shut herself up; and at times, when visiting among their acquaintances, she would be forced to listen to remarks which cleft her heart, but which she must bear and show no sign; to strictures on the absent one which made her blood surge and boil with suppressed wrath. One such occasion befell about a month after his departure, the time and place being an afternoon call, and the offender Mrs Shaston, who, she suspected, was talking not without design, expatiating to a roomful of people upon what a snake in the grass had been so providentially hunted out of their midst. The hot, passionate blood coursed madly in Mona's veins, and her eyes began to flash. Suddenly they met those of Father O'Driscoll, who, with his hands crossed on the head of his stick, was seated on the other side of the room as though not hearing what went on. Suddenly the old man leaned across towards the speaker.

"Is it Mr Musgrave ye're talking about, Mrs Shaston?" he said in his gentle Irish tone.

"Yes. He was once a great friend of yours, Father O'Driscoll, if I remember rightly," and there was a scarcely veiled sneer underlying the remark.

"Was once a great friend of mine?" repeated the old priest quietly, but in a tone clear enough to be audible to all in the room. "But he is still a great friend of mine, Mrs Shaston, though I doubt if we shall ever meet again, I'm sorry to say."

It was like flinging a bomb into that côterie of scandalmongers. The lady stared, wrathful—then smiled sweetly. The magistrate's wife was not an easy person to "put down."

"As a clergyman you would of course take a charitable view of things, Father O'Driscoll," she answered, "and I'm sure it's quite nice to hear you. But we poor every-day people—"

"See here, Mrs Shaston," broke in the old man, in his most genial tone. "I remember in the old days in Cork springing a riddle on some of the fellows; there was a lot of talk going on at the time, I forget what it was all about, something political most likely. This was it: Why is Shandon steeple like every question? D'ye think they could answer it? They couldn't at all. The answer was 'Because there are two sides to it; a dark one and a light one.'"

The application of this was pretty obvious, and gave rise to a constrained sort of silence. Pausing just long enough to lend effect to this, the old man went on, in his frank, merry way. "And the best of the joke is, that some of the fellows, although they'd been born and raised in old Cork, didn't know that Shandon steeple had two sides at all. I give ye my word they didn't. They thought it was all dark or all light all round."

And then, turning to a fellow-compatriot of his, Father O'Driscoll asked whether that particular curiosity of their native city had escaped her notice too, and having launched forth, manoeuvred from one droll anecdote to another, of course leading the conversation farther and farther from the topic of Roden Musgrave; whither indeed it did not return upon that occasion.

By accident or design, Grace Suffield and her cousin took their leave at the same time as the old priest.

"Why do you never come out and see us, Father O'Driscoll?" said Mona, as they gained the street. Her eyes were eloquent with thanks, with unbounded appreciation of the tactful, yet unequivocal manner in which he had championed the absent. "We have not the claim upon your time which your own people have, still you might ride out and see us now and then."

"Ah, don't be putting it that way, Miss Ridsdale. Sure, we're always very good friends in spite of our differences, are we not, Mrs Suffield?"

"I can't answer that, Father O'Driscoll, until you positively promise to come out and dine with us at the very earliest opportunity," replied Grace. "My husband will drive in and fetch you and take you back again, if you will only fix the day. If you don't, why, then I sha'n't believe you mean what you say."

"Our *friends* do come and see us, Father O'Driscoll," added Mona with meaning; and her eyes again were eloquent, for they said, "*You* at least were his friend. *You* at least lifted up one voice on his behalf, and that with no uncertain sound, when all tongues clamoured against him. I want to say more about it, and—perhaps about *him*" And it is probable that their meaning was read aright, for the required promise was readily given, and as, having bidden the ladies good-bye, Father O'Driscoll took his way down the street, he shook his head sadly to himself as he thought over what had happened; for the heart of this sweet-natured old man was very full of the pain and trouble and separation which had come upon these two.

Beyond the successful working out of it, Lambert had not taken much by his vindictive scheme. In fact, he had taken rather less than nothing; for if he expected to find the road now clear, or at any rate rapidly becoming so, into Mona's good graces, why, then he never made a greater mistake in his life. She would hardly speak to him, and then only to snub him pitilessly, and with a cold and haughty politeness which left him no road open for a colourably dignified retreat. His revenge must be its own reward. Well, at all events, he had that.

So had Sonnenberg, but he, at any rate, fell into evil case. For he was a good bit of a Lothario of a kind, was this vindictive and plotting child of Israel, and somehow it happened that during the height of his exultation over the utter discomfiture of his enemy, a great and mighty fall awaited himself; for in the very thick of an intrigue whose central figure was a native damsel, "black but comely," he was surprised by a party of Kaffirs, and most soundly and unmercifully thrashed. Now prominent among the thrashers was the thrashee's former store-boy, Tom; wherefore the rumour failed not to creep around, that Roden Musgrave had bequeathed a debt of vengeance and a largess to that sometime warrior; and, in short, that Sonnenberg had walked blindly into what was nothing less than a cunningly devised and successfully baited trap. Whether this was so or not, we are uncertain. But the evil Jew, though his bruised bones smarted for many a long day from the whack of the Kaffir kerries, dared make no public stir, by reason of the very circumstances of the case, towards securing the punishment of his assailants; wherefore these went unpunished, and laughed openly.

So time went on, and weeks grew into months, and even the strange affair of Roden Musgrave became ancient history in Doppersdorp, and discussion thereof began to pall, except upon "old Buzfuz," who was never tired of publicly thanking Heaven for having chosen him as its instrument in unmasking and driving from their midst a most wicked and dangerous impostor; and Roden's successor, a good-hearted sort of youth of the very ordinary type, fell desperately in love with Mona, but at a distance; and Grace Suffield thought regretfully over that terrible night in the post-cart, and wondered uncomfortably if they had not given their support to a very great act of injustice; and her husband ceased to think any more about it; and things jogged along in Doppersdorp pretty much as they had always done. And some wag, of malice aforethought, turned loose the whole of Emerson's "Chamber of Horrors," the ingredients composing which spread themselves over the township, and took a week to collect, save such as incontinently retreated to their native wilds, and two snakes which got into the bank-house and bit Emerson's native boy, involving much treatment from Lambert, for which their owner had to pay, swearing terribly.

Thus several months went by.

Chapter Thirty
The Portal of the Shadow

The R.M.S. *Scythian*, homeward-bound, was steaming through the smooth and fast darkening waters of Table Bay.

She had hauled out but two or three hours since, and now, as the flashing light of Robben Island was dwindling astern, the second dinner bell rang forth its welcome summons; welcome this evening, at any rate, for, as we have said, the water was smooth, and it would take a very determined sea-sick person indeed to remain away from table. So the passengers, of which there was a full complement, trooped in, to a man and to a woman, and there was much arranging of seats, and a little of discontent with the result of such arrangement.

"This is your seat, sir. And the captain sends his compliments, and hopes to be down before dinner is over."

Roden Musgrave took the seat indicated by the steward. It was the end chair of one of the three long tables, which ran the length of the saloon. That at the head of the table was the captain's chair, at present empty. Unoccupied, too, was the seat on the captain's right. The others were all filled.

He cast a careless glance over the brilliantly lighted saloon, with its sparkle of plate and glass and coloured fruit, and vari-hued dinner-dresses. There were a great many passengers of the usual type. Some might prove good company. Those in his own immediate neighbourhood did not look interesting.

In silence he began his dinner, for he felt depressed. It seemed but yesterday that he was seated exactly as he was now, yet more than a year had gone by since then. A year is nothing of a time, but this had been *such* a year—for it had comprised a great experience. And now he was leaving this land, whither he had come to try his latter-day fortune; leaving it for ever; himself in far worse case than when he had first sighted it. A hand dropped on his shoulder, and his musings were dispelled.

"Well, Musgrave, I'm glad we're to have the voyage home together, and it has come about sooner than either of us expected." And Captain Cheyne, resplendent in gold lace and shining buttons, slid into his seat at the head of the table. They had met already on board and exchanged a hurried greeting in the bustle of hauling out, but had had no time for more than a word.

"Yes, I arranged it so, when I saw that you had got this ship. I say, though," looking around. "She's a cut above the old *Siberian*, both in size and fittings, eh?"

"She is. Well, and how have you been getting on? Been at that place—er—er—I forgot the name—that none of us knew where to find, ever since?"

"No. I've just come off Pilgrim's Rest gold-fields, so called, presumably, because the 'pilgrims' leave there the *rest* of whatever they took with them."

Two or three in the neighbourhood laughed at this, and the conversation became general. But Roden dropped out of it. Mechanically, he took up the wine-list, and began studying it. While thus engaged he heard the rustle of skirts. The occupant of the empty chair was seating herself. Even then, so utterly without interest in her identity was he, that he did not immediately look up.

"Shockingly late, I'm afraid, Captain Cheyne. But I was doing a lot of unpacking, and time ran on."

Then he did look up, and that sharply. The whole room seemed to go round, yet outwardly he was as composed and imperturbable of feature as ever he had been in his life. But even to him that moment brought a powerful shock. For, in the occupant of the hitherto vacant chair, he found himself, thus suddenly, unexpectedly, marvellously, face to face with Mona Ridsdale.

Her apologetic remark, laughingly made, ended with a little catch of the voice, as she caught sight of him. She, too, was undergoing her share of surprise, marvel, agitation, but was bravely self-possessed. The quickened heave of the full, beautiful bosom, as revealed by the low-cut dinner-dress, and the wide, appealing dilation of the clear, hazel eyes, were read in all their significance by one; but to the rest they might be due to a not unnatural flurry, consequent on her late appearance. Then both heard, as a far-away, misty-sounding hum, the voice of the captain, introducing them to each other.

This was a happy solution. In their present state of mind, any admission or sign that they were previously acquainted, could not fail to afford some indication of the nature of that acquaintance; and more especially did this hold good of Mona. At any rate, it would draw attention to them both; which in the agitation evoked by this startling surprise was the very last thing they desired. But luckily, the conversation, once it had become general, did not drop; the more so, that a voluble lady, two seats off, began asking the captain question after question of the usual type, varying between the mildly idiotic, and the hopelessly, frantically insane, such as whether he had ever seen so many passengers not sea-sick before; or, if they would reach Plymouth at night or in the daytime—Plymouth then being three weeks distant—or whether a ship like the *Scythian* would sink at once, if rammed by a sword-fish, or would allow them sufficient time to take to the boats. All of which caused the captain to nudge Roden under the table, while his bronzed and handsome visage wore a comical look of resigned, hopeless patience.

"Remember our last glass together, Musgrave?" he said, as soon as he could conversationally break away. "We'll do a first one again now," as the steward deftly popped the cork of a champagne bottle. "What do you think, Miss Ridsdale? When we dropped anchor in the bay he found himself appointed to some place up-country. He bet me a bottle of this stuff I couldn't tell him where it was, and he won, for, by George, I couldn't. The best of the joke was, *we* could hardly find any one who did know. What was the name of the place, Musgrave?"

"Doppersdorp."

"Doppersdorp. Of course it was. We passed the word, 'Where's Doppersdorp?' and hanged if any one knew. Well, I suppose you found it at last?"

"Oh yes."

"Did you go to the gold-fields from there?"

"No, I put in about a month at a place called Barabastadt, with my old friends the Van Stolzes. He's R.M. up there now."

"Van Stolz? I know him," said the captain. "He used to be in the Customs, or something, at Port Elizabeth years ago. He was only there a little while though. A thick-set, brisk, jolly little man, isn't he?"

"Yes. That's him."

"I remember him. Good sort of chap, although he's a Dutchman."

"Good sort of chap!" echoed Roden. "I should rather say he was. He's a rare specimen in this world, I can tell you. One who once a man's friend remains so for life."

Mona bent down over her plate to hide the sudden rush which welled to her eyes. He was too cruel. The tone—light, easy, cynical—conveyed no special meaning to the other listener. But to her—ah! she felt the full force of its lash. During the foregoing, the other passengers had fallen into their own conversation, leaving this to the trio who are our special acquaintances. But if Roden edged his words with a bitter sting, discernible only to the ears of the one who knew what lay behind them, it was that he felt bitter at that moment—cruelly, remorselessly bitter. Why had she thus risen up before him to revive the sweet and witching mockery of that utterly hollow past? There she sat, in all the bewildering beauty of her splendid form, all grace and seductiveness; she who had so passionately, so fervidly vowed herself his—his for ever in life and in death. There she sat, only the width of the narrow table between them, yet as far removed as though an impassable gulf a thousand miles in breadth divided them. For she had fallen away from him in the hour of trial, and his faith in her was killed. 'For ever in life and in death!' had been the hollow ringing vow. 'In death?' Ah! that might be; in life, never. And then a strange, weird, ghostly presentiment came upon him, like the black edge of a shadow, as he sat there satiating his eyes with this vision of a most entrancing embodiment of deception, the while mechanically sustaining his share or the conversation.

The saloon was brilliant with light and life, cheerful with voices, for the crowded diners had now found their tongues, presumably about halfway down the gradually decreasing bottles. Laughter?—Oh yes, plenty of that— airy feminine laughter—with the explosive male guffaw. Knives and forks clattered, corks popped. Oh, plenty of light and life here; but without—the dark waters, deep and wide, the dim expanse of unfathomable ocean lying black beneath the stars. "For ever—in life and in death."

"And how many big nuggets did you pick up on the gold-fields, Musgrave?" said the captain presently.

"Nuggets? Fever's more plentiful around there than nuggets, and dust than gold-dust," answered Roden wearily. "The place is a fraud."

His *vis-à-vis* was watching him now. Yet the feeling which she had so valiantly repressed came near overpowering her once more, as she noted the change which had crept over his appearance. He seemed to have aged, to have grown leaner and browner, as though he had gone through a hard, hard struggle, bodily and mental, of late. And from the bronzed complexion, wind-swept, sun-tanned by months of open-air life, of toil and exposure, the strange double scar seemed thrown out more prominent, more livid than ever. It was marvellous, well-nigh miraculous, that they should have met again thus.

She too showed traces of the struggle. There was a tired, wistful look about the eyes, the suspicion of a melancholy droop at the corners of the mouth, which imparted to her face a very different expression to that of the self-loving, self-indulgent, and rather heartless Mona whom he had first beheld reclining easily, sensuously, in her hammock under the green willows at Quaggasfontein, now more than a year ago. Had she too suffered? Why then had she been found so lamentably wanting when put to the ordeal? Surely a nature which had proved so weak could have no great capacity for suffering, at any rate, for any length of time. No, it was all a most miserable mistake, all too late. This wonderfully unexpected meeting had shaken him more than he cared to allow. The wound, barely skinned over during these six months or so, now broke open again and bled afresh—bled copiously. More careless, more terse became the tone of his conversation, and beneath it lurked a biting cynical sting, as of the lash of a whip.—Not altogether could his glance refrain from that royally moulded form opposite him, and meeting the tender, wistful appeal of those clear hazel eyes, there shot from his own a flash as of contempt too deep even for resentment. Thus did he arm, fence himself against his own weakness.

The dinner was over at last, and several of the ladies were already leaving the saloon. Mona rose.

"I think I will go on deck for a little," she said. "Is this delicious smooth weather going to continue, Captain Cheyne? I am a most wretched sailor."

The captain responded gallantly that he devoutly trusted it would, and she left them. And now that her presence was withdrawn, it seemed to Roden that a blank had fallen. Yet he had but to ascend the companion stairs. It seemed to him that her very announcement embodied an invitation. Still he remained as firmly fixed in his seat as though nailed there. And nailed there he was—by the long, jagged, rusty, and passingly strong iron of an unbending pride. She had turned from him once; was he to go begging to her feet now? No—no. A thousand times, no.

"Nice girl, isn't she?" said Cheyne, reseating himself and refilling Roden's glass. "Fine-looking girl, too."

"She seems alone. Is she under your charge?"

"Not exactly that. She came on board at Port Elizabeth, and I made them put her place next me here at the table. When I got your letter saying you were going to join us at Cape Town, I moved those other people a place up. At any rate, we'll have a snug corner for the voyage, eh?"

Another surprise was in store for Roden. A group of male passengers who had occupied places at the far end of the saloon was passing them on the way out. Before he could reply his glance was attracted by the face of one of these. It was that of Lambert.

Their glances met. Far less under the control of his feelings than the other the young surgeon gave a violent start, and a half-uttered exclamation escaped him as he met the indifferent, contemptuous gaze of the man whom he had injured. But quickly recovering himself, he passed out with the others.

Lambert, of all people in the world! What on earth was the fellow doing here on board? Oh, the reason was not far to seek, he thought, in derisive pity for his own weakness, with which during the last hour he had been so exhaustively battling. And yet things didn't seem to fit in, for here was Mona sitting alone at the captain's table, while Lambert was right away at the other end of the saloon. That was not the explanation. It might be a coincidence that the two were on board together, just as his own presence there was. As before at Doppersdorp, so now, Lambert did not count for anything in the affair.

"Seems to me, Cheyne, you've got all Doppersdorp on board," he said. "First Miss Ridsdale, then that cotton-headed chap who just went out. Now trot out a few more of them."

The captain stared—then laughed.

"So you knew each other before, did you? Deep dog, Musgrave, deep dog!"

"Oh yes, considering I was there the best part of a year," he replied, offhandedly. "But that fellow you saw just now making faces at me is a good bit of a sweep. I don't care about having much to do with him."

Lambert's presence on board did away with the expediency, or indeed the advisability of reticence, and it was as well to tell his own story first. So they sat there a little longer, and he gave Cheyne a sort of outline of a good deal—though not all—that had befallen him since they said good-bye to each other last.

"Come round to my cabin for a smoke before turning in, Musgrave," said Cheyne, as he rose from the table. "I must go on the bridge a bit now, but I'll send and let you know when I come down."

Quite a goodly number of passengers were sitting about, or walking the deck, as Roden emerged from the companion. It was a lovely night, and great masses of stars hung in the zenith, their reflections mirrored forth on the smooth surface of the sea, rivalling the phosphorescent flashes glancing like will-o'-the-wisps rising and falling in the dark depths. The loom of the coastline was hardly discernible, for the captain chose to keep plenty of sea room along that dangerous and rock-fringed shore; but the moist, dewy atmosphere, fresh with the salt breaths of the great deep, was delicious;

and ever with the voices and laughter of the passengers mingled the steady clanging of the engines, and the mighty churning throb of the propeller, and the soft, soughing wash of the scintillating, blade-like wave curving away on each side of the cut-water of the great vessel.

Roden, moving leisurely in the gloom, tried to persuade himself he was glad, for his eyes rested not upon that well-known form; and in all good faith he did not feel certain whether he was or not, so over-powering had been the shock of the surprise. Then, leaning over the bulwarks, he gazed meditatively forth across the starlit waste of black waters to where the uncertain loom of the land was fading on their starboard quarter, and as he did so all the morbid side of his character came to the fore. Was ever a more utterly forlorn, aimless, God-forsaken wanderer afloat on life's sea? Here he was returning, with what object he knew not, poorer in pocket, a good ten years chipped out of his life—at least it seemed so—and nothing to look forward to on this side the rave. And by a strange coincidence, separated from him only by the few inches of iron and planking immediately beneath his feet, stood one other gazing forth through the open scuttle at the same starlit scene of sky and sea. With a weariful sigh Mona turned away from the window; then, opening her dressing bag, she took out a small bottle and held it to the light. Yes, she would do it. Only a few drops. Sleep was what she wanted—sleep, sleep—blessed—oblivious sleep, sweet, illusion-bringing sleep.

Chapter Thirty One
"Dark Roll the Deepening Days"

In the very circumscribed limits of shipboard it is difficult enough for any two people who want to avoid each other to do so. Given, however, two who are, even in spite of themselves, animated by no such wish, the thing is well-nigh impossible.

Thus it proved to these two. Roden Musgrave, for all his steel-plated armour of pride, for all his strength of purpose, was conscious of a weak place, of a joint in his harness. Deep down in his heart was a great craving, even for a little while, for the old time as it had been. Again he reviewed all that had gone before; again he began to find excuses for her. She had been startled, shocked, horrified. She had been "got at" by Suffield, who, he feared, was at heart a bit of a sneak. Moreover, he himself had hustled, had scurried her too impetuously. A little further time for reflection, for accustoming herself to the—it must be owned rather startling—idea, and she would have acted very differently. He had expected too much—had unconsciously fallen back into the old, old blunder of his salad days, expecting to find something of the nature of an angel; discovering, of course, only a woman.

Not all at once did he come round to this change of opinion. He could not forget that she had believed the charge against him in its entirety—believed that he had treacherously slain a comrade for the sake of robbery; and a very paltry robbery at that. That she should believe him guilty of the homicide was nothing; but of theft! No, that he could never forgive.

Yet as they sat at table three times a day—sat facing each other—her demeanour was hardly that of one who believed him capable of anything so despicable; and soon, all unconsciously, the cynical ring faded from his tone; the drift of his remarks became no more than normally biting. And often, as though, by some strange, sweet magnetism, it would seem to those two that they were making conversation for themselves alone, talking to each other with a kind of subtle understanding imperceptible to the rest, even when the talk was general.

The captain was right in congratulating himself upon having a snug corner for the voyage. This is just what it was, notwithstanding the vicinity of a bore or so, providentially not quite near enough to put idiotic questions very often. And to two, at any rate, the sound of the bell was a welcome one, though for a widely different reason to that which caused the residue to hail its distracting clamour. For it brought them together for a space.

Only for a space! They might have been together all day and every day had they so wished it. Yet they were never seen together alone. Other couples in plenty, philandering in cane chairs during the torrid heat of the day, pacing the deck by starlight, or leaning against the taffrail rather close together when the moon rose over the sheeny, liquid plain; but these two, never. They would converse, but always in the presence of that third person which in such instances is jocularly supposed to constitute "a crowd." Sometimes, indeed, the good-natured third person, actuated by the best intentions, would drop out of it, not ostentatiously either. But then it was not long before Roden found some excuse for transferring his presence elsewhere.

Now as the days went by Mona began to grow bitter and reckless. To her, too, the appearance of this man on board the *Scythian* had come with the shock of a mighty surprise. Her voyage to England was being undertaken indirectly through his agency, for such a depression and lowness of spirits had been the result of her high-strung efforts at unconcern as seriously to undermine her health; and, as a last resource, she had resolved upon that change which to the Colonial-born woman is the most welcome of all—a trip to the Old Country. And here on board this ship, under circumstances which would bring them together daily for at least three weeks, she had found him again, and—he would have none of her.

Had she not shown him how bitterly she repented her demeanour on that day; shown him by word, by look, by every subtle tenderness which she knew so well how to import into both? But of telling him so in plain language he seemed determined to afford her no opportunity. There were moments when she thought of punishing him by arousing his jealousy, if he had got one spark of that evil combustible within him. It was easily done; there was no lack of material to hand. But, fortunately, she recollected that he had not—except in the form of unmitigated contempt—and that however such a plan might answer with some men, with this one its only result could be to fix the gulf between them more irrevocably wide than ever. For the first time in her life Mona found herself unpopular with the opposite sex; for not by any representative of it as there gathered together could she be induced to indulge in moonlight walks, or protracted sitting out when dancing was forward, or, in short, in the barest suspicion of any approach to a flirtation whatsoever.

Towards Lambert she made no attempt to conceal her dislike, her detestation; and this she was able to indulge on the pretext of being well aware why he had selected this ship for his own trip home. So, seeing that she would have nothing to say to him, he desisted, and retired in snarling exasperation. But he consoled himself by watching her and Roden Musgrave on every available opportunity. The latter, in his surprise, he had at first greeted with a stiff, jerky nod, which had not been returned. Looking him straight in the eye Roden had cut him dead. Furious with jealous hatred and impotent spite, Lambert vowed an easy revenge. The murder story. It would be just as effective here as at Doppersdorp. Yet—would it? And Lambert remembered uneasily that his own word was all he had to go upon here. Never expecting to see Roden again he had left the papers with Mr Shaston. On the whole, he decided to let that story alone for the present. But whatever Lambert might or might not think fit to do mattered not twopence to Roden Musgrave.

The latter seemed to get through his time without an effort. He read a good deal and chatted a little, took a passive part in anything that was got up, whether as appreciative audience at charade or theatrical, or contributing his quotum to the sweepstake upon the daily run, diligently organised by Israel and Judah. He passed many an evening in Captain Cheyne's cabin, where these two cynics would sharpen their sardonic wit upon the grindstone of their species. In short, he seemed to be laying himself out for a good time generally, and to have it. But all the while the iron was in his soul; for the days were going by with flying rapidity, and each day brought the parting nearer.

The parting? Why, they had not yet met, not in reality, at least. Well, it was better so, he told himself. He had to face the world afresh. He was in worse plight than a year ago, infinitely worse. What prospect did life hold out? A straggle, and a profitless one. Faith in all things shattered and dead—what remained?

"Would you like to hear the circumstances under which I killed John Denton?"

Mona started from the taffrail over which she had been leaning, and turned—her heart thumping. She was alone, and it was night. She had not heard his approach. Her first intimation of it was the voice—low, even, and clear.

"You—you did kill him, then?" she faltered, her eyes dilating in the starlight.

"But I did not rob him."

"Oh, could you not see? could you not see? I never believed that, never really. Have I not shown you that much; here, since we meet again? Tell me, tell me—did you ever love me, really love me? You are too strong, too self-contained, too unbelieving. You do not know what it is to love, to love really!"

She had caught both his hands, and was wringing them to and fro in a vice-like grip, as she sobbed forth those wild, rapid sentences in a tone that was indescribably passionate and despairing. It seemed as though she were afraid of losing him if she relaxed her hold for a moment. This, the first time for all these days, the first time they had been alone together—if anybody can be said ever to be alone in so limited a space as that afforded by a ship—she was in an agony of dread lest the opportunity should slip away from her, never to recur. The stem of one of the ship's boats, swung in upon chocks, made, with the taffrail, quite a snap little corner. The decks were nearly deserted, for there had been heavy tropical showers throughout the day, rendering the planking steamy and damp.

"To love, did you say? What *is* love?" he rejoined coldly, scarcely even bitterly. But beneath the now fast yielding crust the molten fires were raging. "Too strong, too self-contained did you say? Well for me that I am. But if you would care to hear that episode I will tell it you—now."

She made no answer beyond a bend of the head. Why did he torture her thus? He was exacting to the last fraction a truly terrible revenge. For were he murderer, midnight robber, twenty times over, it made no difference to her now. She loved him, as that six months of separation, final as she thought it, had taught her how she could love. And he, triumphing in his strength, in his ultra-human, well-nigh demoniacal capacity for self-control, he was tearing her very heart strings. It was a refinement of cruelty. Yet her only fear was lest this meeting—they two, alone together at last—should be shortened by a single moment. Still she kept tight hold of his hands, half-mechanically now.

The vessel was gliding smoothly through the oily waters of the tropical sea: the clang of the engines, the throb of the propeller, the soft wash of the wave from her stem, the only sounds. The surface was flooded with patches of phosphorescent light, and here and there in the dim offing hung a dark and heavy rain-cloud.

"The facts are very ordinary and soon told," he began. "Denton was a distant relative of mine, and we had grown up close friends from boyhood. Then we became rivals—in love, you understand—and I was the favoured one, for I was well off in those days. I believed in people then—a little— consequently the last thing I dreamt of was to suspect Denton of being the thief and liar he afterwards turned out. He had the management of all my affairs, for he was a little older than I, and shrewd and clever; and, as he afterwards told me, in pursuance of a set purpose of revenge he started to ruin me. He succeeded, too, and that very soon, and so completely as to divert pretty nearly all that had belonged to me into his own pocket; so craftily too, that the law was powerless to touch him. For I was something bad in the way of a fool in those days, and trusted everybody. Well, I stood ruined; a very ordinary and every-day occurrence.

"Then I began to find out the real meaning of the word, love—the real worth of tenderness and passion and inexhaustible vows. I have found out since on more than one occasion, but it did me no harm, because then I knew what the upshot would be, and merely stood by watching into which hole the solitaire marble would find its end, and laughed. That first time though, it hurt. It was badly done, too; badly and heartlessly, and after a while John Denton stepped into my shoes. All this, of course, took some little time; but it is commonplace enough, so I pass over, it quickly.

"Well, I had learned a thing or two by then, so I made no sign that I even felt I had been wronged. I took a leaf out of their book, and professed great friendliness still. You know—the frank and can't-be-helped sort of article. I meant to lie low and wait, but I meant to be even with master John one of these days. So I went to America, and led a strange, hard, knock-about life for some time. I was in the thick of it through '66 and '67, when all the Plains tribes were out on the war-path; and it was in one of those ructions that I came by that queer double scar, for it was chipped out by an Indian arrow whose tip had become curiously split.

"Well, I was watching my opportunity, and it came at last; came earlier than I expected. Denton soon got into difficulties, for he was an awful gambler, and lost pretty nearly all he was worth; all that should have been mine. What easier than to induce him to come out West? There were always openings there. For, mind you, I had remained on outwardly friendly terms with him.

"He came, and from the moment he did so, I determined to kill him, not as I eventually did, that was more than three parts accident, but in fair stand-up fight. The worst of me is I am of the most vindictive temperament in the world, I cannot forgive—still less could I then. We went into all sorts of things together, but all the time I hated him—all the time I was only watching my opportunity.

"I meant that he should meet me in fair fight, that we should stand an even chance. But that night at Stillwell's Flat, when he came back after a successful gamble, more self-sufficient, more overbearing than ever, I could hold back no longer. I proposed to him that we should fight it out—a duel *à outrance*. But he came at me unawares, swearing I wanted to plunder him of his winnings; came at me with an axe. We had a desperate struggle, an awful struggle. It was touch and go with either of us, and then all the devils in me were let loose as I thought of what he had done. I killed him—killed him without mercy.

"I will spare you a repetition of the detail, which to you would be horrible; and it was horrible. Yet, even then I did not regret it, nor have I ever done so since. But the instinct of self-preservation arose at once. Had he fallen in an open and daylight quarrel, sympathy would have been with me, or at any rate I should have been held harmless. But there was a dark and murderous look about a secret and midnight deed, which would in all probability mean swift and unreasoning retribution. So by way of obscuring the trail I hid away the money, thinking, like the fool I was, that that would divert suspicion from myself, that no one would suspect *me* of killing a man for the sake of a few hundred dollars. Another idea occurred to me. The Sioux were 'bad' around there just then. By putting their mark upon the body—the throat cutting—I might throw the suspicion on to them. Then I departed, intending to return shortly and affect unbounded surprise. But I fell in with a war-party, and was clean cut off from the settlements; and the running I had to make for nearly two weeks right through the Indian country simply bristles with marvels. Well, the affair was after all a very commonplace instance of vendetta, with no sordid motive underlying it. There the dollars are still; I could put my hand upon them at any moment, unless, that is to say, somebody else has already done so, which isn't probable. Now you have the whole story, and can hardly be surprised that I had learned caution, and was not one to give away all my life's history to the latest comer."

Mona made no reply; she could not at first. The wild ecstasy of joy with which she listened to this revelation was too great—for she believed every word of it, only wondering how she could ever have believed anything to the contrary. It resolved itself into a mere accidental affair, a tussle—a fight for life. Moreover, she could hardly realise it. The thing had happened so far away, so long ago, that the recital of it seemed more like a book narrative, a story at second hand, than the confession of a terrible deed of blood at the lips of him who had perpetrated it. There were a few moments of silence as they stood gazing at each other's faces in the darkness. Then came a startling interruption. A whirring rush through the air, and something fell—plashed down upon them where they stood. One of the heavy showers hanging about in pillar-like clouds was overhead, and now it fell. To the shrill whistle of the boatswain's pipe a squad of sailors came tumbling aft, springing like monkeys on to the taffrail, casting loose the lashings of the awning. Down it came with a rush, the roaring, hissing, tropical rain, each spout as it struck the dark, oily surface of the sea throwing up rings and globes of phosphorescent light till it seemed that the whole expanse was one mass of wreathing, glimmering tongues of flame—a scene of weird and marvellous beauty.

Even in the moment it took these two to reach the shelter of the companion, so vehement was the downpour that they were not a little wet. They had the deck to themselves, however, for in anticipation of something of the kind, most of the passengers preferred the dry comfort of the smoking-room or saloon. From the latter came up now snatches of talk and laughter, but it was late, and most were already for turning in. Still these two lingered, looking forth upon the sea hissing into flame with the discharge of the cloud-torrent.

How would that interview have ended but for this inopportune interruption? Were the very heavens fighting against them? thought Mona, with a sick pain at her heart. But still the fountains of the skies roared down, streaming over the decks, carried in seething torrents along the scuppers. Not again could they venture forth to-night. Long before the state of the deck would allow of it, even if the rain cleared off, it would be too late.

"I must go below," she said at last. "They are putting out the lights already. Good-night. I shall see you again in the morning."

This was obviously a superfluous statement; yet there was a meaning in the words as she uttered them—a volume of meaning—gratulation that such was the case, that the ice was broken, that the past was healed, or nearly so—ah! a world of meaning. Then they clasped hands; the first time since they had met on board. Was there a lingering, clinging pressure in that grasp—on the part of one—on the part of both? It may have been so.

Mona went down to her cabin, of which, the crowded state of the ship notwithstanding, she by favour enjoyed sole possession. There, alone, her mind went over all that had passed between them during that all too short interview. Why had that miserable interruption been allowed? It was too bad, it was heart-breaking, she thought resentfully, as she dried the wet, curly rings in her hair where that first detestable rain-splash had left them. Then a strange, eerie sense of apprehension came upon her, just such a feeling as had tormented her that night at Quaggasfontein, a heavy foreboding of evil, combined with present and personal fear. Then it had proved a true one—but now? Her nerves were all unstrung. Her reflection as she saw it in the glass was haggard and heavy-eyed. There was a weird ghostliness about the phosphorescent water lapping so softly without, and stifling as the tropical heat was, she felt almost tempted to close the scuttle, as her fancy pictured nameless horrors—cold, slimy tentacles entering through the aperture, feeling their way around the cabin in the darkness. And throughout all these nerve-tormenting apprehensions mingled the dull, aching sense of loss.

To such a pitch was she wrought up, that there was left but one way of ensuring the sleep she needed. Out came that phial again.—No hesitation this time; the process had acquired a certain familiarity. Holding the bottle to the light, she measured out the drops, adding somewhat to the usual portion. The effect was well-nigh instantaneous. A sudden drowsiness came over her. Still wrapped in her dressing-gown, she sank down, already half-unconscious, upon the outside of the bed, and slept—slept hard and dreamlessly.

Chapter Thirty Two
Within the Shadow

By some strange, mysterious influence, Mona's forebodings were shared by her late companion. After the latter had parted with her, the rain having ceased, he betook himself to the silent decks to think, and then it was, in the weird gloom lighted only by the twinkle of the binnacle light and the corpse-candle ghastliness of the phosphorescent surface, that the presentiment came upon him. So strong was it indeed, as to move him to do a strange thing. He went down to his cabin, of which he, too, was the sole tenant. Arrived there he produced from his baggage a large pewter flask which would contain perhaps something over a pint. Into this he carefully measured a modicum of brandy, filling up the whole with water. This done, he took a few hard biscuits from a case, and two or three skins of concentrated soup, each about three inches long by an inch and a half in diameter. These he enveloped tightly in a very thin, light, waterproof substance, placing the whole just inside his portmanteau again. He did not even laugh at himself for taking this strange and somewhat ominous precaution. He had been in far too unexpected and particularly "tight" places to laugh at any precaution. The only thing that did cause him the ghost of a smile was, in imagination, the faces of his fellow-passengers could they only have seen what he was doing.

This done, he took his way to the captain's cabin. It was only his shaken nerves, he told himself, as he picked his way across the wet and slippery decks. He had put a pretty stiff strain upon them of late, and now they were paying him out. That was all. Still he did not laugh at himself on account of the precautions he had been taking, nor would he do so even in the safe and cheerful light of to-morrow morning.

"Hallo, Musgrave," cried Cheyne, "I had about given you up for to-night. Thought you had turned in. However, roll up, man. Better late than never." And diving into a locker, he produced a bottle from his private store, for the bar was long since closed for the night. "Turton was up here just now, but had to go down and settle some row that had broken out among his lambs. Those are passengers I don't care about."

This was in allusion to a number of soldiers who had been sent on board the *Scythian* at the last moment, in charge of a captain and subaltern; and a mutinous, unruly crowd they were.

"Those time-expired men are the devil of a nuisance, Musgrave," went on Cheyne. "Why on earth can't they send them home in a troopship, or charter a vessel on purpose, instead of saddling them on to us? Crowded up, too, with ordinary passengers as we are."

"But they're not all time-expired men, eh?"

"Not much. About a third of 'em are lunatics or prisoners under sentence, or bad hats generally."

"Been up to anything fresh then?" said Roden, blowing out a cloud.

"Nothing in particular; but they are always more or less unruly. The last people I want to see on board ship are a lot of soldiers, especially time-expired ones."

"How many of them are there, skipper? Couple of hundred, eh?"

"Less five. If that lunatic, who jumped overboard yesterday morning at bath parade, had gone down it would have made yet another less. We were delayed about twenty minutes or more, and when the boat came up with him the beggar tried all he knew to swim away from it. I was watching him through the glass, expecting every minute to see him risen by a shark, but no. If he'd been a sane man and a useful member of society, something of the kind would have happened; but being of no earthly good to himself or anybody else, it didn't."

"Quite so. Two hundred, less five, I think you said. Crowded up too, fore and aft, with passengers. What would happen if we came to sudden and unexpected smash? In the matter of the boats I mean."

"What sort of croaking vein are you in, Musgrave? Well, in such a case it would be a mortal tight fit, I don't mind telling *you*. We fulfil all the requirements of the Board of Trade in the matter of boat carrying, but if we have a couple of hundred damned soldiers crammed on board at the last moment, what are we to do? Why, just drive ahead and trust to luck; and that's what brings us through far oftener than you landsmen ever dream."

The talk veered round to other topics, and presently one of the quartermasters came in to report that the weather was thickening into a regular fogbank.

"I'll go up on the bridge a bit, Musgrave," said the captain. "It isn't often we get fogs so near the Line. But the weather has been beastly this voyage, as hot and steamy as I've ever known it; and there are a lot of waterspouts about too."

They bade each other good-night, and already as Roden left the cabin, the more measured throb of the propeller told that the vessel had slowed down to half-speed. Then the hoarse, rasping screech of the foghorn rent the night as the ship drove slowly through the smother, whose steamy folds blotted out the stars. Again and again the voice of the foghorn was lifted, uttering its hideous, vibrating whoop—causing the sleeping passengers below to start up wide awake in confused doubt as to whether the end of the world had come, and a hazy uncertainty as to whether they themselves were just arriving at Waterloo station or at the Judgment Seat. There was one, however, whom the unendurably distracting sound did not awaken; who slept on—heavily, tranquilly, dreamlessly.

Roden, though intending to go below, still remained on deck, held by a kind of fascination, as the ship glided slowly through the silent fleecy smother. Then again the jarring blast of the foghorn rolled out, and—on Heaven! Was it an echo—louder, more appalling than the sound itself? For, as he gazed, there leaped forth something out of the mist. In that rapidly flashing moment of time was photographed upon his brain a massive hull, the loom of a huge funnel, a towering cut-water—a human figure, wild with horror, upon the extremity of the latter. Then came a shock which flung him, bruised, partly stunned, to the deck.

Keeping his presence of mind amid the awful and appalling crash, he managed to save his head from injury; then, before he could rise, came another shock more jarring, more shivering than the first, and with it the blasting screech of escaping steam. He saw a heavy body, flung from the bridge, fall head downwards. He heard the grinding, crunching sound of that cut-water shearing through strong iron plates; the frantic shrieks and yells now arising beneath, which even the deafening demoniacal blast from the steampipe could not drown. Then, his confused senses whirling round, he saw the great hull—the towering cut-water which had crashed into them right amidships, recede and vanish into the mist. The *Scythian* floated once more alone upon the fog-enshrouded waters, and it needed no abnormal instinct of prescience to tell that very soon she would float no longer.

And now there followed the most indescribable scene of terror and confusion ever witnessed in the annals of ocean tragedy. The saloon passengers, already alarmed and uneasy by the repeated blasts of the foghorn, came pouring up the companion; crowding, crushing past each other in their furious panic. The second-class passengers, too, from the tore part of the ship, tore aft, crying that the water was already flooding their cabins. Each fed the other's fears; till the decks were alive with what seemed nothing less than a surging crowd of shrieking, fighting maniacs. And then, to complete the chaotic unwieldy horror of the situation, the time-expired men made a rush for the boats, and casting two of them loose before they could be prevented, poured over the side into them with the result of capsizing both.

Not all behaved thus. There were several cool heads among them, but in such a minority as to be utterly powerless to sway that screeching, frantic mob. And when it was discovered that the captain was lying atone dead, having been hurled to the deck by the shock when about to descend from the bridge, and the chief officer so injured as to be unconscious and beyond recovery, why then, all hope of quelling the panic was over. In vain the remaining ship's officers strove to guard the boats with revolvers. The weapons were knocked from their grasp, and themselves trampled under foot or hustled overboard. The stalwart quartermasters were dragged from their footing and the seamen so separated among the dense, impenetrable crowd, that cohesion was impossible; under such circumstances, even to some of the ship's company a little of the demoralisation communicated itself. In like manner the two officers in charge of the troops were helpless, and the efforts of all were further impeded by the masses of screaming, praying, fainting women, dashing themselves about the decks in the frenzy of their panic.

Not many minutes had gone by since the first crash, not many minutes of this shocking scene, and already the beat of the propeller had ceased. The great gasping hole which was letting out the ship's life was letting in her deadly enemy, the sea. The fires in the engine-room were already out. There was a horrible stillness now as of the fabric settling more and more beneath their feet.

Throughout the indescribable horror of this hideous panic Roden Musgrave kept his head. It was nothing to him that the whole of this shrieking, demoralised horde should perish, provided he could save one life. One life! but where was the owner of that life? Himself jammed against the bulwarks by the swaying frantic crowd, it required his utmost efforts to prevent the breath from being crushed out of him; but while thus occupied, never for a moment did he lose sight of the ruling idea. His eyes scanned the scared faces and wildly rushing forms, but that which he sought was not there. He heard the furious tumult of oaths and curses and beast-like yells, where men, brutalised in the face of death, yielding to the unbridled selfishness and cowardice of their real nature, fought wildly for the boats, trampling down and hurling aside women and children indiscriminately, and, in short, all weaker than themselves. The great crowded passenger ship had become a floating hell of all the evil sides of human nature. All this and more did he hear; and still with a wild despair at his heart, he strained his eyes through the smother, now so thick that they could hardly see the width of the ship. But she for whom he sought was not there.

"Oh, Mr Musgrave, for Christ's sake get us a place in one of the boats!" gasped an imploring voice. He turned, and beheld a lady with whom he had been on fairly friendly terms. Her two little ones, pretty, engaging children, were clinging to her hands.

"Where is Miss Ridsdale?" he asked, stone deaf to her appeal. "Her cabin is next to yours."

"She's in yonder boat. I saw her lowered into it. Quick, quick! Take me there. She is there, I tell you."

"Are you sure?"

"Quite, quite. Oh, lose no time!" wringing her hands piteously.

"Come, then!"

With a deft rapidity that was marvellous under the circumstances, he forced a way through the swaying crowd, now very much thinned out. The boat she had pointed to was worked by some of the ship's company, who, cool-headed, had left the panic to take care of itself, and were devoting their efforts to rescuing such of the women and children as they could. The boat was lying by, already loaded down to the water's edge.

"Here's another passenger for you, Smithers," sang out Roden, recognising one of the quartermasters. "Now, Mrs Mainwaring, down you go! I'll hand down the little ones."

But she refused, until the children were first taken off. Then she followed.

"Is Miss Ridsdale there, Smithers?" he cried.

"Very sorry, sir, but we can't take you off. No more room for any males."

"I didn't ask you to take me off. Is Miss Ridsdale with you?" And just then, a recumbent figure in the after-part of the boat caught his eye in the misty gloom. Yes, that was Mona. He was satisfied.

"Stay, stay!" shrieked Mrs Mainwaring, the lady whom he had just rescued. "Take him with you, if you are men. There is room for one more. All the women are safe in the other boats—I saw them! We were nearly the last. Come, Mr Musgrave!"

The old quartermaster looked doubtful, then yielded.

"Jump, sir, jump! We haven't a moment to lose. That's it. Give way, my lads."

The heavily laden boat laboured ponderously from the side of the big ship. The sound of hoarse shouting through the misty smother, the shrieks of hysterical women, the splash of the oars, the raucous, suffocating cry of a drowning wretch, sinking back exhausted here and there, made a weird and appalling situation, such as those now in it would remember their lives long—if their lives were spared them. And, settling down more and more, black, and hardly distinguishable in outline, lay the huge, helpless hull of what a few minutes back was a mighty steamship, and any moment might witness the final plunge. Already most of the boats were out of sight of each other, almost out of hail, having made all the offing they could from the foundering ship. But of the great steamer which had crashed into them there was visible no sign, no, nor even audible. Had she left them to perish, or had she herself foundered instantaneously? Surely this awful hubbub was audible for miles. Surely if she were above water, her people could not leave them thus to die. Still—of her no sign.

"Put back, Smithers," said Roden. "Miss Ridsdale is not in the boat."

A storm of murmurs arose.

"She is in some other boat, then. It's too late to put back."

"She is not. She's still on board the ship. Would you leave a woman to drown? Put back."

The storm of discontent redoubled. Here were many women and children. If the boat got back, she would certainly be drawn down in the vortex of the sinking ship. It was better that one should perish than many. Besides, how did anybody know that that one was still on board?

Well, one did know, but how he knew was another matter. For, as sure as though he had heard her voice crying to his ears, did Roden Musgrave then know that Mona was still on board the doomed hull, left to die alone.

"Very well. Do as you like!" he answered; "I am going back." And before any could prevent him, he had flung himself into the sea, and was striking out, with long, easy, vigorous strokes, for the ill-fated *Scythian*.

"We'll stand by for you," sang out old Smithers. "But be quick, sir."

Roden seized the rope-ladder by which the boat's load had been lowered, and soon regained the now silent and deserted deck. But, as he did so, a panic shout went up from those in the boat. The hull, now very low down in the water, was seen to lurch, and to heave. The cry went up that the ship was already sinking, and all hands, straining with a will at the oars, thought of nothing for the next few minutes but to poll as far as possible outside that dangerous and fatal vortex.

And, thus abandoned, Roden Musgrave stood upon the deck of the doomed ship—alone.

Chapter Thirty Three
Alone on a Wide, Wide Sea

There was something inexpressibly weird and spectral in the aspect of the deserted saloon as Roden made his way through it. The few lamps left burning for night purposes flared in the gloom, the rolled-up carpeting, the round-backed table-chairs, the bottles and glasses in swinging racks, each had a ghastly and eloquent expression of its own, each seemed to show something of dumb protest against being left to its fate by man, whom it had served so faithfully, to sink down and rot among the far and slimy depths of the black night of waters. And upon the dead silence of the deserted ship came, ever and anon, rushings and gurgles, and ghostly cavernous boomings, as the water rose higher and higher within the doomed hull.

Roden's heart sprang to his throat as he felt a sudden and sickening tremor in the planking beneath his feet. Was the vessel already heaving up for her final plunge? Still cool-headed, his nerve as steady as iron, he would not suffer himself to be flurried out of one single precaution. He went straight to his own cabin, and, unlocking his portmanteau, took out the slender stores which by such marvellous prescience he had put up ready the evening before. If they were picked up by one of the boats, he intended to keep this secretly for Mona's use, should the worst befall. The boats were provisioned to a certain extent, but provision might run short. Others might starve—perish; she should not. Then he reached for the cork lifebelt usually stowed above his bunk. It was gone. All the lifebelts in the cabin had been removed.

Not many seconds had these precautions taken, nor did it take many more to reach Mona's cabin. Standing on no ceremony he turned the handle. The door was locked.

"Mona! Mona! Are you there? In God's name open! Open—quick!" he cried, shaking the handle furiously in his despair. But there came no reply.

"Mona—open! It is I! There is danger! Open—quick!" he almost screamed, at the same time raining a succession of blows upon the door. This time he heard a confused murmur and a sound of movement. Then the bolt of the door was shot back.

She stood before him in some clinging white garment. Even at that awful and critical moment he recognised it as the dressing-gown she had worn that night at Quaggasfontein, when she had come in to soothe him in his pain. In the faint and feeble light from the saloon lamps he could see that her eyes were unnaturally large as she confronted him, but dull and heavy. The drug had left its mark upon them.

"What is the matter? Where are we?" she said in a drowsy murmur, staring in amazement at him and his wet and dripping condition. Without a word he stepped past her into the cabin, and snatching the cork lifebelt stowed above her bed buckled it around her.

"Come," he said. "No—just as you are!" noting a movement to turn back. "We have not a moment to lose. Quick—trust yourself to me."

As they passed through the saloon, she with his arm around her, still drowsy and half stupefied, which perhaps was the best state she could have been in in such an appalling emergency, the quivering tremor of the deck had increased, and louder sounded the hollow booming of the water. There was a list which nearly threw them off their feet. A wash of water swept the scuttles, then the ship lurched slowly over to starboard, and again the scuttles were under the brine. Surely they were going—going. It would be awful, shut up there to drown like rats in a hole, awful—awful; the same death up on deck in the free open air seemed easy, pleasant, by comparison. Yet as he held her closely to him, supporting her with his right arm while with his left he groped and steadied his way—both their ways—ascending the companion stairs, Roden Musgrave was conscious that even death in this fashion held no bitterness for him. No, there was a strange, fierce, delirious sweetness in the situation, which he would not have exchanged at that moment for life and safety. When her absence was overlooked, when she had been left to die, he alone had thrown away safety, life; he alone had returned to die with her. And he had his reward. Were they entering paradise together? It seemed like it at that moment, when they were about to die together, she in his arms. In such lightning flashes of thought did his mind whirl in the brief minute which had elapsed since the opening of her cabin door.

In close, dank, airless folds, the heavy mist still lay around—dark, impenetrable as a curtain. The night air, however, and the weird eloquence of the utter solitude, the disordered deck, the great towering funnel, the ruined deckhouses, the serpentine lapping of the water, roused Mona from her semi-lethargy.

"Where are they all?" she said, a start of terror shaking her frame as she looked around and began to realise her position.

"Gone! I only am left; and I am going to save you, if I can: if not, to die with you; and death will be sweet."

Something of all that had been passing through his mind passed through Mona's now. She pressed her lips to his, clasping him convulsively.

"You came back to die with me? Oh, my love! my love!"

She was quite calm as the whole truth struck upon her. Love seemed utterly to dispel all terrors of death. But Roden did not intend that it should come to that if he could help it. Keenly and carefully he had been looking around. Every life-buoy had disappeared, snatched off by the panic-stricken crowd. The deck cabins, though yawning and seamed, were so firmly stanchioned that he could not drag out so much as a plank. The skylights were unloosed. There was nothing. Again the deck beneath them gave that convulsive, shivering lurch.

"Mona, darling," he whispered, "act now with that splendid courage you showed before. I will not leave go of you, but don't clutch me or struggle. We shall go down, but we shall come up again. Now—come."

But before he could gain the side of the ship with her there was an angry, seething swirl—and there leaped out of the gloom and mist in front huge wreaths, white and spectral, and hissing like snakes. Then with this appalling spectacle their footing gave way, and it seemed as if they were being whirled up into the very heavens. The after-part of the great hull reared itself aloft, and with a roaring, thunderous plunge, the *Scythian* disappeared from mortal sight for ever.

Down, down, into the farther depths—down, down, ever down, with a vibrating and jarring and crashing as of the destruction of ten million worlds. The weight of ten million worlds seemed upon these two, as, socked down in the vortex of the foundering ship, the swiftly flashing brain realised the terrific, the soul-curdling barrier that lay between them and the upper air. Down, down—ever down—down through those roaring, jarring realms of space and of darkness, of black and rayless night.

Never for the fraction of an instant did Roden relax his grasp; never in that swift, sickening engulfment, while dragged down and down to the black depths of creation; never, as the starry fires of suffocation dared and scintillated before his strained and bursting eyeballs. Never would he; for even the last awful struggle of dissolution should but rivet the embrace tighter. Then the engulfment, the suction, seemed to slacken. A vigorous effort, and he felt himself rising; yes, distinctly rising. Ha! air! light! yet not light. With a rush as of a bird through the air, he—they—soared up from that vast ocean depth, gaining the upper air once more.

Then in nameless fear he put his ear to her lips. Was she still living— or had she succumbed to that long suffocating immersion? A faint sigh escaped her breast; but that little sound caused his heart to leap with a wild and thrilling ecstasy. She lived—lived still. And then, drawing her closer to him as they floated, he kissed those lips, cold with semi-unconsciousness, wet with the salt brine of ocean; and it seemed to him that the kiss was returned. Did ever the world see stranger love passage,—these two alone, floating in the night mist; alone on the vast expanse of a silent ocean, nothing between them and death but the cork lifebelt of the one, and the far from inexhaustible swimming powers of the other?

Would any of the boats be hanging about the scene of the wreck? Not likely. Those which had escaped the havoc wrought by the first rush were crowded to the water's edge. The panic-stricken castaways would sheer off as far as possible, eager to pat all the distance they could between themselves and the vortex of the foundering ship. Yet there was just the chance, and to this end, as soon as he had recovered breath Roden sent up a long, loud, penetrating call. His voice rang eerily out, rendering the slimy stillness more dead, more oppressive than before. But—no answer.

This he had expected. The hopelessness of their position was with him throughout. It was useless exhausting his forces in swimming hither or thither; wherefore he employed just enough movement to enable him to keep himself, and Mona, comfortably afloat. Again he raised his voice in a louder, clearer call.

Stay! What was that? Echo? Echo from the vastness of the liquid solitude? No. It was not an echo.

There floated out through the mist a fainter, shriller cry. Roden's pulses beat like a hammer, and a rush of blood surged to his head. The boats had waited around, then? They would be picked up, saved—for the present. Again he shouted, long and loudly.

And now a strange, awesome, wonderful thing befell. Through the enshrouding mist there darted a nebulous expanding ray, as from the disc of some mighty lantern, and upon the curtain of vapour was silhouetted, black and gigantic, the horizontal form of a coffin; and rising from it and falling back again, the head and shoulders of a man, of huge proportions, black as night. Heavens! what appalling shade of darkness was this, haunting the drear, horrible, inky surface of that slimy sea?

The Thing bore down upon them, was almost over them. Roden, convinced that this new horror was a mere illusion begotten of the mist and his own exhausted state, closed his eyes for a moment. When he opened them again it had vanished.

But in its place was something else. Brighter and brighter shone the nebulous ray, and now, parting the mist folds a half-moon looked down; looked down on these two heads, mere tiny specks upon the vast ocean surface—down, too, upon that other thing. And seeing what it was, the revulsion of hope which shot through their two hearts was terrible.

There floated what looked like a plank. No, stay! Was it a plank? It seemed more solid; it was oblong; and upon it, stretched out and clinging wildly to its sides, was the figure of a man. This, then, grotesquely exaggerated and distorted by the mist, was what had constituted the coffin apparition.

In the shock of this blank and bitter disappointment Mona had well-nigh lost consciousness. But upon her companion and protector the sight produced a strangely reinvigorating effect. A gleam as of a set, fell purpose shone from his eyes, as, beneath the sickly, moist light of the fog-veiled moon, he watched the plank and the clinging man draw nearer and nearer, while he guided himself and his charge silently, imperceptibly towards it; and the meaning of the lurid, predatory look was this:—

He meant to have that plank.

But the man who was already on it?

Well, he must get off it. Whatever the support was it certainly would not uphold two, let alone three. Mona must have it—must take the place of its present occupant. He himself could continue to swim, to float as he was doing, just aiding himself by the support of a hand upon its edge. The man who was on it now must yield it up.

Faint and shrill again came the cry which they had at first heard, and it had in it the quaver of exhaustion, of terror, of despair. This time no reply was made. But keeping behind and out of sight of the floating waif, Roden, with a few noiseless but vigorous strokes, brought his now unconscious charge and himself to within grasping distance of the concern. And as he did so he could hardly control his joy. The thing was a solid hatch, and was fitted with two strong ring-bolts, one at each diagonal corner.

Just then, alarmed by the faint splash, the man turned. His teeth were chattering with cold and fright, and his limbs shaking as he clung convulsively to his support. The moon, falling for an instant upon his anguished features, revealed the face of Lambert.

"What—who are you?" he quavered. "There's no room—no room here. The thing won't carry more than one. Oh—Musgrave, by God!"

"Yes. Musgrave, by God!" answered Roden, a kind of snarling triumph underlying his sneer. "You're right. The thing won't carry more than one, and that one is going to be Miss Ridsdale. So off you get, Lambert."

"But I can't swim another stroke. I'm done up," stammered the other.

"Don't care. You can go to the bottom then. Get off, will you?"

"No, I won't," yelled the unfortunate man in the fury of despair. "My life's as good as other people's. I'm here first, and here I mean to stick."

"Oh, do you?" And dragging down the side of the impromptu raft which was nearest him Roden suddenly released it. Up it went with a jerk, flinging its occupant to the other side, where, losing his hold of the ring-bolt, he rolled off into the sea. By the time he could recover himself and think about striking out, the hatch was quite a number of yards away.

"Musgrave, Musgrave!" shrieked the despairing man, "for God's sake don't leave me! Let me just rest a hand on the thing to support myself; I won't try and get on it. I swear I won't."

The only answer was a laugh—a blood-curdling laugh, a demoniacal laugh, sounding, as it did, from the very jaws of death upon that dark and horrible waste of waters.

"I wouldn't believe the oath of such a crawling sneak as you, Lambert, if taken on your deathbed; and that's about where it is taken now. Remember the valuable discovery you made at Doppersdorp. Well, you thought to ruin me, but you only twisted the rope to hang yourself with, for if your discovery hadn't driven me from the country I shouldn't be here to-day to take your last plank from you. Now we are quits; for I tell you, if this thing would carry fifty people, *you* shouldn't get upon it."

While Roden was thus speaking Lambert had been drawing gradually nearer. Now making a sudden last despairing effort, with a sort of spring out of the water, he succeeded in seizing the edge of the hatch, upon which Mona had already been lifted, and was lying unconscious. It began to slant perilously.

"Let go, will you!" spake Roden, between his teeth, in a voice like the growl of a wild beast. "What? You won't!" And with all his force he struck out, aiming a blow between the other's eyes. But Lambert saw it coming, and dodged it.

It was a strange and soul-curdling scene, that upon which the ghastly moon looked down, these two men, both within the very portals of death, striving, battling alone in the black oiliness of the midnight sea, fighting for that small slab of wood—fighting, the one for his life, the other for a life that was far more precious to him than his own. And of all the horrific and heart-sickening acts which that pale orb has witnessed, it can seldom have looked upon one more appalling.

Now Lambert made a frantic clutch at his adversary, hoping in his frenzy of despair to drag the latter down with him. But abandoning his hold of the raft for a moment Roden dived, then rising seized Lambert by the neck from behind, battering his head against the hard wood. The unfortunate surgeon, more than half stunned, relaxed his hold, and fell back into the sea.

"Good-bye, Lambert," cried the other, with a glee that was hellish in its ferocity. "Pity I haven't got Sonnenberg here to send after you. Well, you and I are quits now, at any rate. Good-bye, Lambert!"

For reply came a frightful noise, a gurgling, gasping, inarticulate yell. Then the struggles of the despairing wretch ceased. A boil of bubbles came glittering up to the surface of the now moonlit water, then they too ceased. Roden Musgrave and his unconscious charge were alone together once more—alone on the dark, silent, midnight sea.

Chapter Thirty Four
"Air, Light, and Wave Seemed Full of Burning Rest"

Morning dawned. The sun shot up from his liquid bed, a ball of fiery splendour, purpling the vast immensity of a sailless ocean, shining down with rapidly increasing and merciless heat upon the speck formed by the impromptu raft amid the utter boundlessness of that blue-green, slimy, and now most horrible expanse. Not another object was visible far or near, not even so much as a stick of wreckage which might have come to the surface. Had they drifted with some current far from the scene of the night's awful disaster?

Roden Musgrave, supporting himself by resting a light grasp upon the hatch, had been swimming mechanically all these hours, and well indeed was it that the water in those semi-tropical seas was more than ordinarily buoyant, for this and his coolness of brain had enabled him to spare all superfluous waste of energy. He had managed to secure his unconscious companion to the ring-bolts with a piece of cord which he had thrust into his pocket in view of some such emergency, and this timely precaution saved much expenditure of valuable strength in holding her in her otherwise precarious position. Yet now, upon himself, the night's exhaustion and horror were beginning to tell; and he was, as we have said, swimming mechanically and as one half-asleep.

Now a hand stole forth and rested softly and caressingly upon his head.

"Love, why did you not leave me to my fate?" The voice, low and dreamy in its sweetness, resumed: "It would have been all over by now. Yet you threw away safety to come back and give your life for mine."

The voice, the touch, awakened him, roused him to consciousness as wide as it ever had been.

"I would not be in such safety now if I had the opportunity," came the reply, from the swimming head. "Our chances are desperate, yet I am happier at this moment than I have been at any time since—that day."

"My darling, how selfish I am, resting at ease here while you have been struggling all these hours in the water," she said. "Come up here and rest beside me, sweetheart. The thing will carry us both. Then we can talk nearer—closer to each other."

"No. It will hardly carry you dry and comfortable. Besides, I might capsize it, and what then?"

For answer she began deliberately to untie the knots of the lashings that secured her.

"What—what are you doing?"

"I am going to take your place. Then you will be able to rest."

"Mona! Mona I don't be foolish. You can't swim a stroke."

"But the lifebelt will keep me up, and I can get the same amount of support you are having."

"No, no, I tell you. Don't loosen the knots. I might not be able to lash them again so easily. Stay. I will try if the thing will hold us both, if only for a little while."

By the most careful and wary manoeuvring, and alert to lower himself if the hatch listed dangerously, he managed to worm himself upon it. Even then, lying beside her, the additional weight submerged the impromptu raft by nearly a foot. Still, by avoiding any violent or sudden movement, the position was comparatively a safe one. Then, for the first time for many hours, the first time since rising to the surface after being drawn down in the vortex of the foundering ship, they kissed, and there, crouching on their few feet of planking, it the only frail support between them and the vast green depths of that awful ocean abyss, themselves not even entirely above the surface, with all the terrors of their indescribably appalling position vividly brought home to them by the oozy, lifeless silence of the deserted sea, and the fierce, darting rays of the ascending sun, these two alone together were happy—strangely, mysteriously, awesomely, but most unequivocally, happy.

"We are not altogether without supplies," said Roden, almost light-heartedly, as he produced the water-tight cartridge bag and began to extract some of its contents, using the utmost care lest a drop of sea water should by any chance be splashed upon the latter. "But we must be as sparing of them as we know how, for Heaven only can tell how long our cruise is likely to last. If any of the boats of the *Scythian* are picked up we shall be searched for."

"And if not?"

"We must take our chance. We cannot be out of the track of the mail lines."

His hopeful tone was full of comfort to Mona, who quite overlooked the vastness of ocean, and the comparatively small area commanded from the bridge of a mail steamer, also the well-nigh invisibility of so small an object as the hatch of a ship, which, presenting a flat surface, would hardly attract attention even at a very short distance. She ate a morsel of the biscuit and concentrated soup, and sipped a little of the weak spirit and water out of the pewter flask, then declared that she felt able to go for a long time without more.

"But what are you doing, dearest?" she cried, as having satisfied himself that she was in earnest, he had deliberately shut up and replaced the supplies. "No, no, I won't allow that. You shall not starve yourself."

"I don't want anything; not yet, at any rate. The rest has set me up more than food would do."

But to that sort of pleading Mona would not for a moment listen. Not another morsel would she touch until he had taken his share, she vowed. Besides, putting the matter on the very lowest and most selfish grounds, if he starved himself, how would he keep up his strength to watch over her?

This told. He yielded, or pretended to, at any rate, to the extent of a slight moisten from the flask.

"I don't want any food; I couldn't eat, even if we had enough to last us a year."

This was simply the truth. The man's high-strung nerves, with the excitement and peril, and consciousness of the success with which single-handed he had met and so far overcome the latter, had thrown him into a state of strange exaltation which lifted him above mere bodily cravings. There was something too of a sensuous witchery, a fascination, in floating there in the warm lapping heave of the tropical waters, rising all smoothly in imperceptible undulations. It was as though they two were in a kind of intermediate state, between earth and Heaven, the world far away, floating in a Nirvana dream of stirless and peaceful rest.

Not a word had escaped Mona as to that ghastly midnight struggle. The discovery of Lambert, and his fate seemed to leave not the faintest trace in her mind. If not wholly unconscious at the time, the incident must have seemed to her as nothing but an illusive dream. She did not even speculate as to how she had been placed upon this bit of wreckage which was supporting her, supporting them both, thus providentially.

So the day went by—the long, glaring, blinding day—and floating there these two waifs lay and talked—talked of strange things unseen, of the Present and of love; and in the midst of the vast immeasurable solitude heart opened to heart with well-nigh the unearthly voicing of the spirit-land. Again the sun dipped his red run to the lip of the liquid world, and plunged out of sight in a bathing flood of glory.

"I have never known what happiness meant until this day. I tell you, my Mona, although there is nothing but a plank or two between ourselves and death, speaking selfishly, I have no wish to be rescued, no wish for further life. I have done with life and its illusions. For your sake I trust that help may come, for my own it is the last thing I desire."

"Darling, I don't want to live without you. But think—think what life will mean to us together. Do not say, then, that you have no wish for rescue."

"I have thought—and a presentiment has been upon me for some time. Hope and trust in me are dead. I said it was with life and its illusions I had done, for the two are convertible terms. I have had a strange foreshadowing of what has happened, and that it would be for the best. Love—my love—so strangely, so miraculously recovered, when I looked upon you for the last time on that day it was with the flash of a sure and certain conviction that I should behold you again—how and where I knew not; only that it would be at the hour of death, in some sort of magnetic extra-natural way as that in which I beheld you before in my dream, there in the burning house."

Solemnly, unimpassionedly the words were uttered, and the voice was that of a man who has done with life, and is glad that it should be so. A sob shook Mona's frame, and her tears rained down, mingling with the oily smoothness of the tropical sea. She clasped him wildly to her in a warm, passionate embrace, and their lips, wet with the salt brine, again met and clung.

"Love, love!" she whispered. "What a sweet word that is, since it can turn to sweetness and light such an awful position as that in which we now are. For I know the peril of our position—know it and realise it to the full.

Coward that I was to let you go as I did. No wonder you turned from me with scorn and loathing, you who alone taught me what love really was. But I will not let you go again. We will live together or die together. We will not be separated again. We will not—we will not!"

In truth the scene was a passing strange one, a marvel. Her voice warmed and quivered with tenderness, and the smile which curved her lips and threw a melting lustre into her eyes was radiant, as though those words were uttered in peaceful security with a lifetime of happiness opening out before her—before them both. Yet, half submerged, upborne by the frailest of supports, they two were floating out upon the stupendous expanse of dusking waters—drear, solemn, silent—horrible in their awesome loneliness as in the far back ages of the world's birth, while yet darkness brooded over the face of the deep.

Thus closed the first day.

Then, as the blackness of night fell, a faint breeze stirred the water, and there came a change, one of weird and unearthly splendour. In their countless myriads the stars sprang forth, and great constellations gushed redly through the spheres, throwing a revolving ray athwart the lesser luminaries in the transcendent brilliance and beauty of a tropical sky. Roseate meteors, too, falling in streaks, and lo, the whole surface of the sea blazed with phosphoric incandescence.

And the effect was wondrous, for bathed from head to foot in the phosphorescent flame, clothed, as it were, in shining clusters of stars, Mona's splendid form was as that of some inexpressibly beautiful goddess of the sea; the oblong of the planking whereon it rested framing her as with a golden glory. And stirred by the cool night breeze, the gentle lapping of the ripples rose and fell in strange musical cadence as of the far-away sighings of a spirit world, varied ever and anon by the gasping snort of some mysterious monster of the deep.

Dawn rose at last—the dawn of the second day. Of how many more days would they behold the dawn, these two, cut off from the world, from all human help? How many more days before languor, weakness, exhaustion, should overtake them, before their scanty stock of provisions should fail? Yet no lingering, maddening agonies of hunger or thirst should attend their dissolution. Death would be easy and swift, and, above all, would involve no separation. Both spoke truly in denying the grim King his terrors.

The sun hung like a ball of fire in the unclouded blue of the heavens; the sea was of that translucent green so inseparable from the tropics. Mona, who had been intermittently sleeping, awoke to find herself alone. An affrighted cry escaped her; and but that she was secured to the ring-bolt she would have fallen into the sea.

"Love! love! where are you?"

"Here. Don't be alarmed, my dearest," was the soothing reply. "I have been swimming a little, as before. I thought you had been under water long enough."

For the raft, relieved of his weight, was now floating level with the surface. The dews of the tropical night, as well as the soaking effect of her long immersion, had given way to the potent rays of the sun, and Mona felt quite warm and dry. Still, with it she felt a shivering feeling which was ominous, together with a languor and depression such as she had not hitherto shown. The lustre, too, had gone out of her eyes, leaving them dull and heavy. Was it the beginning of the end, of failing vitality, of final exhaustion?

Upon her companion and protector, too, the strain was beginning to tell, nay, as he recognised to himself, was much more than beginning. Pale, and hollow-eyed, he seemed to be putting forth a good deal of effort, swimming as before, with one hand upon the hatch. With the weakening of their bodily state a reaction had set in, dispelling the exaltation of the day before. Both seemed to recognise the imminence of a grim alternative—an early rescue, or a speedy end.

And now, as he swam thus, Roden's glance lit upon an object the sight of which caused his blood to tingle in a curdling, creepy thrill, a small object, dark, wet and glistening; and a great horror came upon him, for he knew that object well. *It was the triangular dorsal fin of a shark.*

Here was a new and truly appalling peril. Strange that up till then this form of it had hardly occurred to him. Infested as the tropical seas are with these horrible creatures, yet from the swiftly moving steamer none had hitherto been sighted. In all the excitement of getting clear of the sinking ship, in the hour of effort and of action, his whole mind had been centred on the means of keeping themselves afloat, and once afloat, of the wherewithal to sustain life as long as possible. Now the imminence of this hideous peril was forcibly thrust upon him. He momentarily expected to feel the sudden crunch of one of these voracious monsters "rising" him from the depths beneath.

He looked at the wet, gliding fin. It was moving *away* from their frail floating refuge, *increasing* the space between. This conveyed but small comfort. He had known sharks swim round and round a ship for hours, ever keeping at a respectful distance, ever appearing to be moving in the contrary direction; yet somehow there they were ever about the same distance ahead. This one was not going to leave them: no such luck. Besides, where there was one there were more.

"Mona, dear. I think I will get up on the hatch again, and rest a little," he said, wishing to spare her the alarm, the consternation, of his terrible discovery.

She reached out a hand to him with a murmur of welcome. He climbed to his former position, for he, too, was growing very weak, and he wanted to rest and think. And as he did so, his eyes fell upon another glistening fin, seeming to appear on the very spot where he had seen the first. Great Heaven! there were two of them.

And the result of his thinking was that Roden Musgrave, himself no stranger to peril, came to the conclusion that if ever living mortal had found himself in a situation of more unique and ghastly horror, why, then he had never heard of it. The raft, submerged by their double weight, might afford a sufficient depth of water for the sharks, growing bold, to snatch them from it, or possibly to capsize it. On the other hand, were he to resume his swimming he might be seized at any moment, and certainly would be sooner or later.

Suddenly he became conscious of a shock, a slight momentary jarring, as though their precarious support had bumped, had touched a sunken reef; yet not, for there was a most distinct feeling that the impact was that of something living. Quickly, but carefully he looked forth, just in time to catch a glimpse of a long, hideous, ill-defined shape changing from white to dull ugly green, as it turned over with serpentine writhe and sank out of sight in the opal depths.

Mona saw it too, and a low cry of horror escaped her. She started up, shivering with fear, her eyes wild and dilated. The hatch listed dangerously on its balance. Then in a tone of unutterable terror which curdled her listener's blood, she cried,

"Look! look! It is coming again!"

It was. Emboldened by their apparent helplessness, the tiger of the sea was bent upon making another attempt to obtain his prey. The grisly snout, the cruel eye, the white belly, the long glutinous tail, every detail of the sea-demon stood clear, as it rushed straight through the water with an unswerving velocity, which should throw it right upon the hatch. But, with lightning swiftness, it sank, and, as it passed underneath, again that shock was felt, this time with increased violence. Then, as they looked forth, behold several of those gliding, glistening, triangular fins, cleaving without effort in their stealthy, creeping way through the mirror-like surface. Here, indeed, with only a few square feet of submerged planking between them and destruction in the most hideous and horrible of forms, they realised their utter helplessness. The ravening monsters closed in nearer and nearer.

And now as the very lowest depths of despair seemed reached, hope dawned once more, faintly enkindled, but still, hope. Low down upon the far horizon hung a dark vaporous cloud. It grew, waxing larger and larger. The smoke of a steamship.

Both had seen it, both with their heads on a level with the surface of the sea. Then came another jarring shock, followed immediately by another, and a rushing swirl as the tigers of the deep, now growing bold in their impatience, as though divining that their prey would soon be snatched from them, darted to and fro, striving to capsize the cranky support.

"We are saved! But—will they see us? Will they see us?" gasped Mona, in agony, straining her eyes upon the now rapidly advancing object. The latter became plainer and plainer every moment, and resolved itself into the masts and yards, then the funnel and hull, of a large steamship. And the course she was steering could not fail to bring her very near.

But the heads of two people do not constitute a very prominent object of attention on the surface of the wide sea, even at a short distance. The vessel drew nearer and nearer, till she was almost abeam. But not nearly so close as they had at first expected.

By now they were in the midst of a perfect shoal of the ravenous monsters; black fins glistening above the surface; dull, tumbling, snaky shapes, writhing, turning over beneath it; the glint of a ravening eye; the gap of a frightful month, armed with its bristling rows of pointed teeth. The sea boiled and babbled with the rush of the hideous beasts. Scarcely a minute went by without bringing with it the shock of their onslaught. And the ship was passing — passing.

Then both these castaways, lifting up their voices, sent up a long, loud ringing shout. But what avail was that in the great immensity of space? Why, the clanging of the engines, even the chatter of the passengers on board the passing vessel, would be enough to drown it.

But the cry on Mona's part ended in a wild, quavering shriek of terror. There was a shock greater than any that had hitherto occurred, and a most horrible crunch of something. The hatch rocked terribly, trembling upon the very verge of capsizal. A huge shark had risen, and turning over had seized a portion of Mona's robe which trailed out beyond the edge, at the same time crunching splinters out of the hard wood; and it was the lash of his tail as he discovered the empty nature of his find, and sounded again into the depths, which had come so near capsizing the hatch. Well indeed might Mona scream and nearly lose her mind with horror, as she realised what would have happened but for her being secured to the ring-bolt. Nature would bear no more. She was half fainting.

Her companion saw it all too; realised what had happened as thoroughly as she did; more, he realised what would happen, failing one alternative. With the rapidity of mind which was characteristic of him, that alternative had already presented itself, and it was a ghastly one. This was it. *One of they two must abandon the hatch, abandon it altogether.*

The quiet, easy death of the deep waters, the death by drowning, he would have welcomed, did they but share it together. But now? The picture of her, rent limb from limb by these tigers of the sea! Horror! That put another face on the affair. The ship was already passing. With two on the hatch, the latter was submerged, and their heads presented no point of attraction. But with only one upon it, it would float flush with the surface, and its dark, oblong shape would stand a far greater chance of being sighted from the passing steamer. Further, it would be almost secure from capsizing.

"Kiss me, Mona! Mine in death!"

They lay close together on the hatch. Shuddering, shrinking still with the horror of that last terrible fright, she clung to him, and thus — their lips washed by the phosphorescent brine of the tropical ocean, in the extreme moment of their peril — they kissed. Gently, but forcibly, parting her grasp,

Roden raised his head, and sent forth over the waste of waters a long, piercing, pealing shout. Then, sliding from the raft, he sank.

The hatch, relieved of his weight, rose immediately, floating square upon the surface, the dark wood framing its white burden in its midst. But the moments vent by, and still no hideous stain rose to empurple the green translucent plain of liquid light. Had the dauntless resolution of his sacrifice carried him down into immeasurable depths, whither even the ravening sea-tigers did not penetrate? It seemed so. "Love! love! where are you?" whispered Mona, her exhausted voice wild with alarm. And then such a curdling, piercing shriek rang out over the immensity of space as even to surpass that call for help uttered with the last breath of a dying man. "Love! love! you have given your life for mine! O God! O God! take mine, for it is worthless to me now!"

Chapter Thirty Five
Conclusion

"We therefore commit her body to the deep..."

The voice of the captain of the *Launceston Castle* takes on more than the ordinary solemnity which almost invariably comes into the voice of the nonprofessional reader of that most solemn office, the Burial of the Dead at Sea. The demeanour, too, of his audience—officers, crew, passengers alike—is more than ordinarily solemn, while many of the female portion of it are sobbing aloud. There is something so pathetic, so heart-rending in this last stage of a terrible drama of the sea—the only survivor of a terrible tragedy being thus cast up in their midst: this royally beautiful form, a noble embodiment of youth and health and grace, found floating, lashed to the ring-bolts of a ship's hatch; alone in the immensity of ocean; rescued from the deep, only to return immediately to the deep again. For Mona is dead. Her overwhelming agony of grief, combined with her recent terrors and exhaustion, had done its work; and no sooner had they safely lifted her to the deck of the *Launceston Castle* than the spirit fled, leaving a name trembling upon the lips of its forsaken tenement, and that name they who stood by could hear.

Yet it was a name which, coupled with many a passionate adjuration, had been heard already and many times by some. When the hatch, lightened of its double weight, rose above the surface, its dark oblong at once attracted the eyes of the look-out on board the *Launceston Castle*, outward bound. At the same time the wild, pealing cry of agony and despair came faintly yet distinctly to horror-stricken ears.

The officer in charge of the boat which took off the frenzied, delirious castaway from her frail support, was able to glean, amid those most awesome revelations of a wandering mind, not only the heart-rending outlines of a life's drama and a deliberate and exalted act of self-sacrifice, but a very fair inkling of the nature and magnitude of the hideous catastrophe which had befallen; and as a direct result the ship was enabled, within a day or so, to pick up two boatloads of the survivors of the ill-fated *Scythian*.

And now the flag drooping at half-mast, the propeller of the *Launceston Castle*, slowed down almost to stopping point, beating drearily in the depths as though in sombre and measured dirge, amid the sobs of women and the husky and suspicious clearing of male throats, the grizzled captain, his book trembling in his bronzed, knotted grasp, pronounces the commendatory words:

"'We therefore commit her body to the deep—to be turned into corruption—looking for the resurrection of the body—when the Sea shall give up her dead...'"

There is a hollow, splashless plunge. All is over.

Far down into the dim, waveless, rayless depths, Mona has gone. And there, where he who gave his life for her, and gave it in vain, has already gone, she will rest—they both will rest—until the Sea shall give up her dead.